MIDAIR

MIDAIR

CRAIG K. COLLINS

Foreword by Charles T. Kamps
US Air Force Air Command & Staff College

Guilford, Connecticut

An imprint of Rowman & Littlefield

Distributed by NATIONAL BOOK NETWORK

British Library Cataloguing in Publication Information Available

Library of Congress Cataloging-in-Publication Data
Name: Collins, Craig K., 1960– author
Title: Midair / Craig K. Collins.
Description: Guilford, Connecticut : Lyons Press, 2016. | © 2016
Identifiers: LCCN 2016007522 (print) | LCCN 2016008023 (ebook) | ISBN 9781493018635
    (hardcover : alk. paper) | ISBN 9781493026838 (electronic)
Subjects: LCSH: Vietnam War, 1961–1975—Aerial operations, American. | Aircraft accidents—
    South China Sea. | Air pilots, Military—United States—Biography.
Classification: LCC DS558.8 .C65 2016 (print) | LCC DS558.8 (ebook) | DDC 959.704/348—
    dc23
LC record available at http://lccn.loc.gov/2016007522

♾™ The paper used in this publication meets the minimum requirements of American National Standard for Information Sciences—Permanence of Paper for Printed Library Materials, ANSI/NISO Z39.48-1992.

Contents

FOREWORD BY CHARLES T. KAMPS VII

CHAPTER ONE. 1

CHAPTER TWO 4

CHAPTER THREE. 11

CHAPTER FOUR 19

CHAPTER FIVE. 23

CHAPTER SIX 27

CHAPTER SEVEN. 29

CHAPTER EIGHT. 33

CHAPTER NINE 37

CHAPTER TEN 44

CHAPTER ELEVEN 46

CHAPTER TWELVE 52

CHAPTER THIRTEEN 54

CHAPTER FOURTEEN. 61

CHAPTER FIFTEEN. 66

CHAPTER SIXTEEN. 70

CHAPTER SEVENTEEN 73

CHAPTER EIGHTEEN. 75

CHAPTER NINETEEN. 80

CHAPTER TWENTY. 88

CHAPTER TWENTY-ONE. 91

CHAPTER TWENTY-TWO 95

CHAPTER TWENTY-THREE. 99

CHAPTER TWENTY-FOUR 105

CHAPTER TWENTY-FIVE. 117

Contents

Chapter Twenty-Six 122
Chapter Twenty-Seven 131
Chapter Twenty-Eight 151
Chapter Twenty-Nine 167
Chapter Thirty 177
Chapter Thirty-One 181
Chapter Thirty-Two 185
Chapter Thirty-Three 190
Chapter Thirty-Four 203
Chapter Thirty-Five 214

Foreword

Don Harten's name is not common knowledge in America, even within the service to which he dedicated his adult life. This, to be sure, has something to do with the fact that Don's war—Vietnam—is not normally revered in heroic terms in US military history. But, just as surely, his name is what the term "unsung hero" is all about.

Above all, Don was a warrior who could be mistaken for someone who would feel more comfortable in the age of medieval knights except for one thing: flying jets. His driving ambition was to be the very best at his profession. While his comrades-in-arms received accolades for shooting down enemy MiGs or, less fortunately, for showing great leadership among fellow POWs at the Hanoi Hilton, Don's goal was to be the absolute best at precisely delivering high explosive ordnance on enemy targets and bringing his flight mates home to talk about it.

With great determination he pursued that goal through multiple combat tours in three different aircraft types that were as different as night and day: the B-52, the F-105, and the F-111. This itself was an achievement that set him apart from his contemporaries. Becoming an expert in these diverse platforms, he not only successfully took them into the jaws of death but dedicated himself to improving their capabilities and tactics.

The B-52, of course, is the centerpiece aircraft of this story. One can only imagine the horror of two massive jet bombers heading right for each other at high speed over the middle of the South China Sea and, oh yes, at night during a typhoon. Don's survival story is harrowing indeed. The near disasters, the near rescues, the sea conditions, and last but not least, the sea creatures, keep you on the edge of your seat with a quiet "I'm glad that wasn't me" going through your head.

When I was asked to write this foreword, I expected to be treated to a standard military biography, but that's only half the story. Interspersed among the narratives of Don Harten in Vietnam are vignettes of the extended tribe that produced a man like him. These passages are captivating as one identifies family traits that show up in Don. To be sure, there is a good bit of dysfunction here, and a lot of recurring behavior that, in normal individuals, would be considered character flaws, but in a combat pilot are positive attributes. The result is a well-rounded picture.

Although combat pilots have occasionally been maligned with having reputations as hard-drinking womanizers who like fast cars, they seldom fit such a one-dimensional mold. In more than two decades of working with them at the Air Command & Staff College in Montgomery, Alabama, I've found them, as a whole, to be dedicated professionals with a high degree of analytical skill outside of their own areas of expertise. The Vietnam generation of pilots was no different. Popular history likes to brand the Vietnam-era pilot as someone with a cowboy mentality and a "stabbed-in-the-back-at-home" complex, who shouldn't be taken seriously when it comes to analyzing the war.

Serious history, however, comes down on the side of the pilots and the generals. In studying the documents and interviews dealing with critical decisions of the war, both sides agree that massive bombing in 1965 would have severely crippled North Vietnam's ability to wage war. For example, Assistant Secretary of State for East Asian and Pacific Affairs William Bundy and Assistant Secretary of Defense John McNaughton, the two architects of President Lyndon Johnson's eventual "incremental" bombing campaign, admitted in their draft cover memorandum that the Joint Chiefs' "Option B" for a heavy dose of air power was more likely to produce results than the other options on the table. On the other side of the hill, since it is always good to ask the people who won, Sr. Col. Bùi Tín of the North Vietnamese General Staff remarked in an interview: "If all the bombing had been concentrated at one time, it would have hurt our efforts. But the bombing was expanded in slow stages under Johnson and it didn't worry us. We had plenty of time to prepare alternative routes and facilities." Don Harten believed that at the time, and has held that position ever since.

Just what was it that Harten and the Air Force were expecting to do when his wing deployed from Mather AFB, California, to Andersen

AFB, Guam, in February 1965? The plan, which was developed but never executed, was as follows:

First Night: Strike by thirty B-52s from Guam against the jet fighter base at Phúc Yên, north of Hanoi, followed the next morning by sixty-eight fighter-bomber sorties striking the Gia Lam air base in Hanoi and the Cat Bi air base in Haiphong, as well as revisiting Phúc Yên.

Phase I (3 weeks' duration): Continuous attacks on lines of communications and military installations south of the 20th parallel in North Vietnam.

Phase II (6 weeks' duration): Isolation of North Vietnam by destroying rail links to China.

Phase III (2 weeks' duration): Isolation of North Vietnam by mining port approaches and destroying port facilities; destruction of supply and ammunition storage in the Hanoi-Haiphong area.

Phase IV (2 weeks' duration): Destruction of all remaining targets on the Joint Chiefs of Staff 94-Target List and re-attack of other targets not completely put out of action by initial attacks.

At that time such a program was undoubtedly achievable as North Vietnam had weak air defenses with only thirty-four fighters, no surface-to-air missiles, and comparatively few anti-aircraft guns. Unfortunately, we waited years to finally launch a serious air offensive that would ultimately bring the enemy to the negotiating table. The shame is that we didn't do it sooner, avoiding the investment in blood and treasure that followed the "gradualism" policy.

As our famous North Vietnamese opponent, Gen. Vo Nguyen Giap, observed in an interview with PBS in 1983, "There is only one rule in war: one must win." Don Harten never forgot that, but our policy makers did.

Charles T. Kamps
Assistant Professor of Joint Warfare Studies
US Air Force Air Command & Staff College
Maxwell AFB
Montgomery, AL

MIDAIR

CHAPTER ONE

THE B-52 IS A GREAT BEAST OF A PLANE. IT WAS DESIGNED BY MEN with the end of the world on their minds—conceived amid the fallout of Alamogordo, Hiroshima, and Nagasaki. It was built for destruction—a destroyer of nations packed with a nuclear arsenal—always aloft, always alert. It lumbered to life in the fifties, ascended to the skies, and flew headlong into the dark maw of the Cold War.

Roughly the size of a 747 with twice the number of engines, the B-52 has a slender fuselage and long wings with tips that droop nearly to the tarmac when the plane is loaded with weapons and fuel. It has an angular shark fin of a tail that rises four stories and slices ominously through the air. Within its fuselage and wings are vast reservoirs holding the equivalent of three residential swimming pools of jet fuel. It accommodates a flight crew of six, plus an entire backup team, who can fly in shifts. It can be refueled in midair. Should the end of the world be nigh, the plane and its crew can circle the skies continuously for days, weeks, or even months.

My first encounter with a B-52 came at Mather Air Force Base near Sacramento. I was five years old in the summer of 1966, riding on the back of my uncle Don Harten's Honda 500 motorcycle. We roared across the black tarmac that was already sending up shimmering waves of heat beneath the early morning sun. I clutched my uncle's shirt, and the engine rumbled beneath me. I leaned to the right and blinked with watering eyes into the hot wind that blew tears back across the sides of my face.

In the distance was an entire fleet of B-52s, parked wingtip to wingtip, nose to tail—football fields full of weapons of war, bristling beneath a scorching California sun.

With a twist of his wrist, my uncle gave the motorcycle one last full throttle as we approached his plane. We then coasted before racing past the B-52's nose, banking hard left and circling counterclockwise around the jet. My uncle rolled to a stop under the shade of the plane's wings, turned off the engine, stomped the kickstand into place, and dismounted. He lifted me beneath the armpits and swung me to the ground. Though the motorcycle's engine no longer roared, it sat smoldering and hissing inches from my arm. I walked in awe, staring upward at the plane, which stood some ten feet above me, as though I were looking at the ceiling of some soaring cathedral.

My uncle was a top-gun pilot before there were top-gun pilots. He was Tom Cruise before there was a Tom Cruise. In addition to his motorcycle, he drove a red MG convertible with silver-spoked wheels. I recall him on leave, roaring up to our house in the MG with his dark, wavy hair and aviator sunglasses. The entire neighborhood would step onto their porches and walk to their lawns to catch a glimpse. He was Hollywood handsome and a magnet for beautiful women. At five feet nine, he was the perfect size for a plane jockey. His vision was 20-15. He had the strength of a wrestler, the reflexes of an athlete, and the timing of a musician. His ego was as large as the planes he flew. He once told me, years hence, with matter-of-fact sincerity that he was the best fighter pilot in the world. I reflexively laughed. His eyes seethed. I then thought about it. Maybe there was some Russian MiG pilot who was better. Maybe another hotshot American. Maybe not. Regardless, there was a time when my uncle could make an authentic claim to be king of the sky.

We walked toward the front of the plane. I pounded my fist into the rubber wheel that looked small from a distance but was taller than I was. My uncle pointed out bomb bay doors and the two Hound Dog missiles attached beneath the wing on either side of the fuselage. The front third of the plane was emblazoned with ten-foot-high block lettering that spelled U.S. AIR FORCE, beneath which was the number "034" and the insignia "PARKER'S PRIDE," for one Col. Van Parker, Commander of the Strategic Air Command's 320th Bombardment Wing, for which my uncle flew. Bomb silhouettes were painted beneath the official markings, signifying the number of missions the plane and its crew had completed over North Vietnam. My uncle explained that in addition to its missiles, the plane could carry a full capacity of twenty-four bombs on its wings and twenty-seven in its bomb bay.

As a child, I had always possessed an intense interest in large machines. Every time I saw a locomotive chugging across the Nevada desert pulling a one-mile length of freight cars, I would yell and point with glee. But to see and touch an actual leviathan of the sky and to really know someone who had commanded it in flight—well, that was an almost mythical experience.

After about fifteen minutes of inspecting the plane from just about every angle, my uncle led me back to his motorcycle and lifted me onto the rear of the seat. He straddled the bike in front of me, checked to see that I was holding his shirt tight, and accelerated with a roar across the tarmac. We rumbled across the wide-open blacktop, slowed to salute the checkpoint guard, swerved onto a nearby residential street, and then sped north, racing beneath a cool canopy of elm trees.

Chapter Two

The Milky Way stretched in a glimmering band against the black-ink darkness that pressed against Don's cockpit window at forty-five thousand feet above the South China Sea. Above, a waning moon, nearly full, gleamed icy white. Below, Super Typhoon Dinah, a category 5 storm with winds of 185 mph, spun in a massive counterclockwise spiral, denuding tropical islands and churning mountainous waves. Its thunderheads pulsed ominously with flashes of light.

From his copilot's seat, Don scanned the night sky and marveled at what he could see of the great storm below. Though the view was otherworldly, Don found that flying B-52s for long distances was an exercise in boredom. He may as well have been driving a bus. Nothing ever happened for hours on end.

The flight from Andersen Air Force Base in Guam to the squadron's target in the jungles northwest of Saigon was about 2,500 miles. The mission called for radio silence, midair refueling, and nonstop flying. It would be like flying from New York to Los Angeles, circling once, and then flying back.

In front of Don were two sets of white knobs. Each knob was connected to throttles that controlled each of the plane's eight engines. The only times Don actually touched the knobs and flew the plane were during takeoff and landing. Once cruising altitude and speed were set, the plane essentially flew itself. The only thing left to do was monitor fuel levels and engine performance, which were displayed on a large panel of forty round, glass-enclosed dials—five dials per engine. But even that was a mind-numbing redundancy. In its nearly decade of service and millions of hours of flight time, there had been only a handful of times that a B-52 had lost power to an engine.

And so the plane droned on toward its target.

"Gunner," Don said flatly over the intercom. "Copilot. Oxygen check."

Another of Don's duties was to make verbal contact with the gunner in the rear of the plane to ensure that oxygen was properly circulating and that the gunner wasn't slumped over from hypoxia.

Don waited. Nothing.

"Ah, gunner," Don repeated. "Copilot. Oxygen check."

He waited again. Nothing.

Don wasn't alarmed in the least. Crew members routinely took turns sleeping on long runs. The gunner had probably nodded off.

Nevertheless, the gunner was Don's responsibility. No one was dying of oxygen deprivation on his watch.

"Gunner. Copilot. Oxygen check."

Still nothing.

Don gave the rudder controls two hard taps that made the back of the plane waggle sharply.

Then he waited.

After about five seconds, Don's intercom roared to life.

"Goddamn it, copilot," yelled the gunner. "I just pissed all over my leg. Jesus."

Don glanced left at Maj. Jim Gehrig. They laughed.

"Speaking of piss," Don said as he unbuckled his harness.

"Take a leak for me, too," Jim said, nodding.

The major lowered the plane to thirty thousand feet as it approached its refueling rendezvous. On his way back to the cockpit, Don stopped to talk with the navigators, who were usually either drowsy or asleep. This time, however, they were busy with calculations, chattering numbers back and forth and cursing the mission's meteorologist, who had forgotten to include the impact of Typhoon Dinah on the squadron's airspeed. As a result, their plane would be arriving nine minutes early to the aerial refueling center southwest of the Philippines' Luzon Peninsula. The navigators were trying to figure out how best to lose nine minutes in a behemoth jet loaded with fifty thousand pounds of bombs at thirty thousand feet.

Don quickened his pace, clambered upstairs, and hopped back into his copilot seat. Fastidious about standard procedure, he cinched his parachute straps, clicked his seat harness, and checked that his ejection pins had been removed.

But Jim was irate. He threw off his harness and scrambled down-stairs. The major was an old hand with thousands of hours of combat flight time. He'd flown fighter jets in Korea, KC-135s during the Cold War, and now B-52s in whatever conflict they were now heading toward. If Jim was alert and antsy, Don thought he should be, too.

"Gunner," Don said over the intercom. "Copilot. Oxygen check."

"Roger," the gunner replied.

"And, gunner," Don continued, "we're about to begin refueling."

"Roger," the gunner replied, and then went back to sleep.

The B-52s traveled in cells of three. When cruising, they were staged a mile behind and five hundred feet above one another. It was June 18, 1965. Don's wing of thirty bombers was on a top-secret mission that would thrust the B-52 into combat for the first time and place America squarely, firmly, and irrevocably into what would become the Vietnam War. Instead of circling the Arctic with nuclear weapons, the planes had been retrofitted to carry dozens of conventional bombs each. They'd been repurposed for something for which they had not been designed. No B-52 had ever dropped a bomb in combat. The crews and the mission planners had all been trained in the art of nuclear deterrence. And for that reason, Maj. Jim Gehrig was uncomfortable and on edge.

Don peered into the blackness, no longer bored. He studied the bea-con lights from the two planes in his cell that were ahead of him. The first plane banked hard left. The second rolled left with him.

"Hey, radar," Don called over the intercom. "What are they doing up ahead? A 360?"

"Rog," answered radar technician Terry Lowry. "Where have you been?"

"Just got back to my seat," said Don.

The maneuver didn't feel right to him. It just wasn't something that was typically done prior to refueling. Though irritated, he rolled the auto-pilot knob into a thirty-degree bank and followed the cell leader.

Don began doing calculations in his head. Each cell was flying four minutes apart. Don's plane was locked into a twenty-five-mile-diameter circle that would take eight minutes to complete. At the four-minute mark, they would be flying in the exact opposite direction before continuing their bank that would bring them, full circle, back to their current location.

"Radar," Don called out to Terry. "You do realize that if there's another cell four minutes behind and on the south track, there's a good chance that we'll pass by them head-on?"

"Rog," replied Terry. "Keep your eyes open."

Don liked this maneuver less and less as each second ticked by. It was outside the scope of standard procedure and disturbed his fastidiousness.

Jim jumped back into his seat, angry.

"What the hell are they doing?" he bellowed. "A 360?"

Don nodded. He then recinched his parachute straps, rechecked his seat harness, and reinspected his ejection pins.

He leaned over to Jim and pointed to the major's seat harness. Jim had a habit of regularly walking around the plane and checking in with his crew. Don had chided him on previous occasions for not buckling his safety harness immediately after returning to his seat. But Jim was clearly upset, and his attention was elsewhere. He was the ranking officer, so Don shrugged, tried to ignore Jim's unbuckled harness, and didn't press the issue.

The intercom then blasted to life, flooding the cockpit with the sound of high-decibel fear.

"We've got beacons at four miles and closing fast," yelled Terry in near panic.

Adrenaline surged through the pilots.

Don bolted erect in his seat. Time dilated. Seconds became minutes. He intently scanned the inky blackness and could see only starlight. He focused straight ahead in the direction that posed the most danger. And then he saw it. A light bigger than anything in the backdrop of stars. And it was stationary, meaning it was approaching head-on.

The two planes were each traveling at 450 knots, which meant that their closing speed was 1,058 mph, giving the pilots in each plane roughly thirteen seconds to react.

Don studied the oncoming light. Two additional lights were on either side of his peripheral vision. One was above to the left, the other below and to the right. But the center light didn't budge. It just kept coming, kept getting bigger.

"We're on a collision course," Jim yelled over the radio. "We're going down."

The major plunged the plane into a dive. Don realized in an instant that Jim was looking at the wrong light. He'd fixated on the jet above and to the left, and didn't see the center light coming head-on. Diving was the wrong maneuver.

Don instinctively reached for the yoke and desperately wanted to override the major's orders and issue a new radio call. But his training and the chain of command made him hesitate. The big plane was already committed and beginning a stomach-fluttering drop. The only thing to do now was watch.

The planes came together faster than a rifle shot. But for Don and his adrenaline-flooded mind, time unfurled in ultraslow motion.

The oncoming light spread into two—one for each wingtip—and a great, gray shadow filled the windscreen as the other plane appeared to be flying directly into the cockpit. Don stared at the fuel tank that hung under the plane's right wing. It was headed straight for his face.

His mind raced through a series of emotions. First was denial. This was surely some sort of surreal dream from which he would soon wake. His second was anger. Who the hell thought a three-sixty maneuver was a good idea? His third was acceptance. That fuel tank would be in the cockpit soon. There was no escape. But at least it would be quick, hard, and painless. Zap. And then nothing. After acceptance, he felt total peace. It was as though he were out of his body, watching with complete fascination his own death.

B-52s are anything but nimble and are very slow to respond. Though Don's plane had only just started reacting to its dive command, the oncoming B-52 had been plunged into a dive perhaps two seconds sooner. And so the fuel tank fell from Don's view, and the great, gray plane floated beneath him like a whale passing in the dark of an ocean depth. To his right, Don watched the towering tail fin glide gracefully by, thinking, "Whew, that was close."

And then the plane bumped like a car hitting a pothole. Lights flickered, and the cockpit went black.

"Well, I guess I'll be dead after all," Don's mind thought. "So far, death doesn't seem so bad. And it doesn't appear there'll be any pain."

The two B-52s had almost averted collision, except that the huge tail—or vertical stabilizer—on the oncoming plane sliced off the outer third of the right wing on Don's plane, cutting open the fuel tank.

A blinding flash filled the cockpit. The plane rumbled and shuddered. An orange fireball bloomed in the night sky and could be seen by trailing B-52 cells from over two hundred miles away.

Don instinctively grabbed the yoke to get a feel for the plane. His first thought was to bank ninety degrees left and head for Clark Air Force Base north of Manila in the Philippines.

"If we're missing just a wingtip, we could make it," he thought.

He looked for the flight instrument panel to see whether the plane was still level, but the flash from the explosion had temporarily blinded him.

"Still," he thought, "there's a chance to keep it airborne long enough to get back to Clark and land at the airstrip."

Such thinking, however, is almost always fatal for pilots. A cardinal rule of flying is to never stay with an out-of-control plane. Yet Don wasn't certain that the plane had been severely damaged and began pulling on the yoke. He didn't yet know that the entire right wing had been blown off by the fuel tank explosion.

His vision returned enough to make out the outline of the plane's altimeter. From that reading, he could determine which way was up. Don leaned forward and peered at the dial.

A loud bang shook the cockpit. The sharp smell of cordite—a smokeless gunpowder—filled the air, and the instrument panel fogged instantly. The major had ejected. And Don should have already ejected, too. His first thought was that he felt bad for Jim because the major hadn't buckled into his seat and was now free-falling thirty thousand feet into the ocean without a parachute. His second thought was that he may have already cost his own life by squandering precious seconds trying to fly a mortally wounded plane.

Don resorted to his pilot training. He bolted upright in his seat, flight helmet hard against the head rest, butt firmly against his parachute, back straight, legs tucked, hands on the armrest ejection handles.

He took a deep breath and pulled up on both handles. Only the left handle moved into position. He squeezed the ejection trigger and waited to be slammed by the fifteen g's of force that would catapult him into the night.

But there was nothing.

Don squeezed the left trigger again. Still nothing. He squeezed yet again. The ejection mechanism wasn't firing.

He swallowed his panic and cursed the plane's maintenance crew. He pulled hard on the right handle, but it wouldn't budge. He squeezed the left trigger one more time, and still nothing happened.

He thought of one final option. Inside his armrest was another handle that would release his parachute from the back of his seat. He would have to leave his survival kit, which was built into the seat, but could grab the parachute, climb downstairs, and jump out of one of the navigator's hatches. No one had ever manually bailed out of a jet at thirty thousand feet and lived. And once he did land in the water, he'd be exposed in the ocean without a raft, food, water, or supplies. His mind quickly nixed the idea. There simply wasn't enough time, and the odds against him were astronomical. No, he would press the eject trigger one more time and then calmly await death. Again.

Don looked down at the trigger in his hand. He gave it a desperate jerk. With a bang and a hiss, the seat rocketed him through an overhead hatch and into the dark.

CHAPTER THREE

DON ACCELERATED ONTO THE ON-RAMP OF INTERSTATE 80 HEADING east from Sacramento. His right hand wore a black lambskin driving glove and held the narrow stick-shift knob like an egg. The engine whined. Don worked the clutch and gas in unison with his feet and pulled the stick into second. The engine gave a low-throated rumble and pressed Don farther into the seat. He jammed the shift up to third, held the gas to the floor, let up, and then pulled the shift down to fourth. The MG jumped to eighty-five miles per hour and its engine settled into a high-pitched thrum. The convertible streaked past palm trees that flew by like telephone poles, and the spoked wheels gleamed in the bright winter sun. A chilled wind drowned out the radio and blew through Don's hair, but he was plenty warm in his brown leather bomber jacket along with the knowledge that while it was a crisp forty-five degrees in Sacramento, it was fifteen below in his hometown of Pocatello, Idaho. His gloved hand reached to turn the radio to full volume. The song "Downtown" blared in counter to the wind. It was February 8, 1965, and you couldn't listen to an AM station for fifteen minutes without hearing that peppy Petula Clark tune. Don, who could've been a professional drummer, tapped his hands to the beat on his steering wheel. He had two days of leave, and it was good to be young, handsome, and driving fast with the top down in California.

In quick succession, newly built ranch homes gave way to tilled fields. The farmland then gave way to the rolling hills, brown grassland, and scattered oak of gold country. The interstate climbed and twisted, and the oak gave way to a forest of ponderosa. Patches of snow appeared on the ground. Don stopped to put his convertible top up, and by the time he reached Emigrant Gap, snowbanks loomed four feet high on either side of his low-slung car. Through the trees and tunnel of snow, he could occasionally catch glimpses of the jagged white peaks of the High Sierra. The snowbanks were eight feet high when he reached Donner Pass. He stopped to get coffee at the Donner Party Memorial, where he craned his neck to see the top of the forty-foot obelisk that represented the snow depth during the ill-fated winter of 1846. Tourists milled around the foot of the memorial, shook their heads, and commented about the Donner Party's bad luck. But Don held a degree in mathematics from Idaho State University. He didn't believe in luck. The pioneers were simply victims of a cascading sequence of probability. Each event taken by itself was almost inconsequential and easily manageable. But strung together by chains of chance, the events became glaringly obvious and fell like an avalanche of crushing disaster. Had the wagon train started three days earlier from Independence, Missouri. Had the pioneers not argued and splintered. Had a wagon wheel not broken. Had they not taken the ill-advised Hastings Cutoff through the rugged Wasatch Range and the Great Salt Lake Desert that sapped their strength, killed their oxen, depleted their supplies, and cost them time. Had they decided to simply winter near Reno when they reached the precipitous eastern slope of the Sierra Nevada in late October. A couple of bad decisions are an annoyance. But if you daisy chain together a series of million-to-one events, then the probability of disaster grows exponentially until it is only a coin flip away.

Don pulled back onto to Interstate 80 and could soon see Reno, the Truckee Meadows, and the brown, sage-covered expanse of the Great Basin spread out below him. Twenty minutes later, he drove down Virginia Street, crossed the bridge over the Truckee River, and pulled up to the valet stand in front of the Mapes Hotel. He thought briefly that the Donner Party likely set camp on this very spot over a century ago. If only they'd stayed for the winter, he mused.

The Mapes was the world's first hotel-casino and the first high-rise built in the western United States after World War II. It was a symbol of America's postwar prosperity and a pent-up national yearning for mobility, entertainment, divorce, and materialism. Before the gaudy gambling and entertainment complexes like Caesar's Palace, the Bellagio, and the Wynn rose from the Las Vegas desert, there was the Mapes.

Four years earlier, the Mapes was at the epicenter of one of Hollywood's great disasters—the filming of *The Misfits*, a movie starring Clark Gable, Marilyn Monroe, and Montgomery Clift. The film was directed by John Huston and written by Arthur Miller—Marilyn's husband *du jour*. In spite of all the high-voltage star power, the movie flopped at the box office. Gable, Clift, Miller, and Huston spent their days in the scorching desert heat on a nearby dry lake bed shooting horse-roping scenes. They spent their evenings in a drunken stupor at the Lamplighter, a bar off the Mapes's ground floor lobby. Marilyn passed her time in a booze-and-pill-induced haze, taking two weeks off in midproduction for a quick trip to a detox facility. Ten days after filming concluded, Gable died of a heart attack. Eighteen months later, Marilyn died of a drug overdose. One Hollywood era had ended; another was about to begin. America was hurtling toward a similar fate. Everyone had a vague sense that change was coming, but few knew what form it would take and what ultimately it might mean.

Don carried that same nagging sense as he stepped out of his car and looked up to see the Sky Room on the twelfth floor atop the Mapes. The air was dry and cold. Don could see his breath, though it was almost noon. Later in the day, he would glimpse America's future, and the troubles that lay ahead would come into sharp focus. But for now, he was just another pilot on leave in one of the country's most permissive cities. He grabbed his duffel bag from the passenger seat, slung it over his shoulder, and tossed his keys to the valet. He strode into the lobby and picked up a pay phone to call my mom, who was living in nearby Carson City.

"Hey, sis," he chimed.

"Don!" my mom replied excitedly. "Did you make it? Are you in Reno?"

"Ee-yep. Just got here. I'm gonna check in, stow my things, and see if I can count cards well enough to cover the dinner tab for everyone tonight."

"Okay. Well, good luck. My friend Sandy is looking forward to seeing you. She's never met a pilot before. We'll be in the lobby at six."

"I'll be there," said Don. "I'm just hoping your friend is half as good looking as you say she is."

"Oh, don't worry, she is. I also told her you were a perfect gentleman. Behave yourself and don't make a liar out of me."

Don laughed. "Sorry, but I'm on leave. And no telling if or when I'll be back this way. Carpe diem and all that stuff."

"See you at six," said my mom, shaking her head.

By the time Don made it back to the casino floor, it was almost 2:00 p.m. He wore slacks and a crisp tan shirt. He'd just showered and shaved. He wore a precise part in his hair and a bracing dash of cologne.

Don peered through the smoke that curled up from cigarettes held by middle-aged women in beehives and old men wearing dark suits, white shirts, and narrow black ties. He strolled past the craps tables and the clattering wheels of roulette. He thought to himself that roulette had the best odds. A smart player could push his chances to just under fifty-fifty, but really no more. The house always held the hammer, no matter what. But if a player enjoyed gambling and knew what he was doing, he could stake ten dollars and sit at a roulette table all night.

Craps, Don thought, was a little worse. A smart player could always go on a streak and make a nice run. But, again, the house was always in the driver's seat, even though the allure of craps rested on the player harboring an illusion of control.

And that's why Don hated most forms of gambling, with the exception of the few games of chance in which he could work to stack the odds in his favor. He couldn't stand losing at anything and had a deep-seated need to be in control. He was appalled that so many people—the ladies in the beehives and the men with the black, narrow ties—thought themselves so special that the laws of the universe would bend just for them—Fortune would smile and the ball would clatter and drop into a spinning slot marked "red 26," or the dice would tumble across the green felt and settle, showing fours exactly when they were needed.

It reminded him of the old military joke.

"Men," the sergeant barked. "This is a suicide mission. There's no other way to put it. Nine out of ten of you won't be coming back."

The big private looked to either side at his nine comrades and then shook his head in dismay.

"Poor bastards," he muttered.

No, for Don there was no mystery to gambling, no great smiling goddess of Fortune in the sky. The universe turned endlessly like a giant machine, without thought, without concern. Events happened. And because they happened, other events followed in sequence. Decks were shuffled and cards dealt.

Don walked slowly and carefully through the cluster of tables where twenty-one was being dealt. He passed the tables where only one gambler sat, clinking the ice in his Scotch and soda. He also passed the tables where giddy novices bounced in their seats as they hit on sixteen. He eventually took a seat at a table that was nearly full with five players and a seat open at third base. He'd be the last person to receive cards each hand and had the advantage to see as many cards as possible before having to make a decision.

Yes, Don hated gambling, but he loved puzzles, especially those with mathematical complexity. He had a sharp mind and a memory that bordered on photographic. He approached games like poker and twenty-one not so much as gambling, but rather as opportunities to outwit the house by bending the odds whenever possible in his favor and patiently snatching small victories from amid the large waste heap of losers. Don was almost always the smartest guy in any room and had a dispassionate devotion to being the best at whatever he pursued.

He settled into his seat at the twenty-one table and handed the dealer a ten-dollar bill. The dealer looked sternly at the green paper lying on the felt, picking it up with both hands. He held each edge between a thumb and index finger and gave the bill a crisp snap to remove any wrinkles. He then waved it with a flourish and slipped it into a slot on the side of the table. Like a magician, he placed his right hand on the table in front of Don, deftly moving it to the side to reveal a stack of red $1 chips. With a quick wave, the dealer spread the chips in an arc on the table, pausing for a moment so Don could see there were ten. He then waved his hand back, and the chips stood in a perfect column where they'd begun. The dealer leaned forward, sounding like an English butler, and said, "Ten dollars, sir. Good luck."

A cocktail waitress holding a tray bent down next to Don and in a breathy voice said, "Excuse me, sir, may I bring you a drink?"

The dealer shuffled his deck. The cards zipped and shussed, zipped and shussed. Don smiled and admired the waitress's ample cleavage.

"Thank you, sweetie. Just a club soda and lime, though, please."

She nodded and stood straight.

Don turned his head over his right shoulder and watched her walk away in her short skirt. He never drank when he wanted to keep his mind sharp. And that included before and after missions, while gambling, and when picking up women.

The air in the casino was cool, dry, and smoky. But half a world away, in the steaming jungle of South Vietnam's Central Highlands, the gears of the universe began to turn. At a remote helicopter outpost called Camp Holloway, a group of American men played poker, smoked cigarettes, and drank Scotch inside a barracks beneath the dark Indochina night. A light-bulb dangled from the ceiling. Smoke hung heavy in the room, and the air dripped with humidity. The nasal, sing-song, clicking sound of Vietnamese wafted through the damp night as South Vietnamese soldiers patrolled the perimeter. An American took a deep drag from a Marlboro, laughed, and laid down three kings. A mortar shell shrieked overhead, and an explosion knocked him from his seat. The outpost erupted in the yelling of a cacophonous language the Americans did not understand. Footsteps could be heard splashing through the mud outside the hut. Gunfire began to blaze from the dark, leafy border surrounding the outpost. Another mortar shell shrieked, another explosion rumbled. Screams burst from the jungle and descended upon the outpost. The Americans dove to the floor and fumbled with their side arms. Bullets tore through the thin plywood walls. With a hard kick, the door flung open and gunfire rained down.

Don was a patient gambler—the kind the casinos hate. If he had a bad hand or the conditions weren't right, he didn't press the issue; he simply bailed and waited for better odds to be delivered. He was down four dollars, and the dealer was getting near the end of his deck. Don was dealt a pair of eights. The dealer had a four of clubs showing. Don made his move. He split the eights and placed an additional bet. The dealer flipped down a two of hearts. Don surveyed all the other cards on the table and recalled what had previously been dealt that he knew of. He calculated that about 80 percent of the cards left in the deck were an eight or higher. He doubled down on his bet and drew a queen of spades. He hit on the next card and drew a nine of diamonds. The dealer flipped over a ten of hearts, drew an eight of clubs, and then busted. Just like that, Don was up two dollars.

"Ha!" he laughed out loud, rubbing the palms of his hands quickly together and pulling his winnings toward him. He always got a thrill whenever he was able to successfully bend the odds in his favor, even if it wasn't for the big money and simply for the thrill of the chase.

An electronic voice from above broke in.

"Lieutenant Harten, please see the house operator. Lieutenant Harten, please see the house operator. You have a phone call, Lieutenant Harten."

Puzzled, Don instinctively looked up at the ceiling as though he might divine what the page was about just by looking at the intercom speakers. Annoyed, he pushed two chips toward the dealer for a tip, grabbed the remaining chips in his fist, and shoved them into his pocket. He stood and explained to the dealer, "That's me."

Without speaking, the dealer nodded toward him slowly as though to congratulate him on a good game and to grant him permission to leave the table. The dealer then shuffled his cards, asked a player to cut the deck, waved his hand regally over the bets that had been placed, and continued gracefully flinging cards toward his charges. Dealers dealt. Gamblers gambled. The world kept turning for everyone but Don.

"Don, this is Ellen," my mother said urgently. "Your base called and said for you to get back a-pass."

"You mean ASAP?" Don replied.

"Yeah, that's it. They said to hurry and that the highway patrol had been notified so you can drive as fast as you need to."

"Ha, maybe we're going to war," Don joked.

"That's not funny," replied my mom. "The man was real serious and said you should get there as quickly as you can. He also said to 'drag your bag,' whatever that means."

"Was his name Jim Gehrig?"

"Yes, that's it. A Major Gehrig called."

"Don't worry. They're just playing some silly war games. But it still pisses me off; I was looking forward to meeting your friend."

"We'll get together another time. She'll understand. Call me when you can."

It's not often that one gets a free pass from the highway patrol, and Don took full advantage, pushing his MG as hard as he could across the Sierra. He was back on base in less than two hours, wearing his flight suit and carrying his mobility bag.

Chapter Four

A BLAST OF AIR SLAMMED HARD INTO DON. IT TORE AT HIS FLIGHT suit, causing his arms and legs to whip wildly. Don's neck seared with pain; he'd been looking down and to the side when the seat ejected. The force whiplashed his helmeted head. He should've been dead from a broken neck. But instead he tumbled violently through the sky like a wayward astronaut.

Don fought to spread his arms and legs in order to stabilize his fall. He looked down and could see his one-winged plane plummeting about five hundred feet beneath him. Two successive explosions flashed blindingly and released a mighty "Whump, whump," that reverberated through his chest and head. A third, smaller explosion sent shrapnel knifing into his left calf.

Don scrambled to orient himself as his mind became overwhelmed with a surge of surreal sights and sensations. Panic raced through every nerve, and Don fought to suppress it. Panic was a killer. Don knew that for certain. He swallowed his fear and let his training take over.

Don plunged through the clouds with no sense of up or down. In the darkness he couldn't tell he whether he was floating or falling. The sense of time had escaped him. How long or how far he'd fallen was a mystery. His parachute opened automatically with a hard jolt. Don grabbed the risers with both hands. He couldn't breathe, so his first order of business was to get oxygen. He fumbled with the valve on his emergency oxygen canister but couldn't get the air to flow. Panic again began welling up inside him. He pulled on the canister as he reflexively gulped to find a breath. He became frantic, thinking that he'd survived the crash only to suffocate on the way down. It then occurred to him that he was no longer at thirty thousand feet. His chute was programed to open at fourteen thousand feet. There was plenty of oxygen at his current altitude. Don removed his mask and took a deep breath. Cool, humid air filled his lungs. The panic subsided.

He left his mask to dangle along the side of his cheek and looked down between openings in the thunderheads to see the ocean burning where his plane had gone down. He wanted to simply relax and hang beneath his parachute to watch the spectacle, but he needed to keep focused to stay alive. He pulled the lanyard to open the automatically inflating life jacket called the Mae West. Flaps of yellow rubber rolled down either side of his chest as flat and flaccid as the ears of a hound dog. The CO_2 cartridges responsible for inflating the Mae West had failed. Don reached for the tube to blow up the life jacket with his mouth. He looked down in time to see a tremendous explosion and a heat-fueled cloud mushrooming toward him. It had been caused by the fifty thousand pounds of jet fuel that had just ignited on the water. The heat and turbulence would sear Don and rip his parachute apart.

Panic again gripped him. He thought about his training and managed to suppress the terror. The cloud roiled closer.

"Think, damn it, think," he said to himself out loud.

He remembered the "four-line cut" that the Air Force had taught him. There wasn't time for a textbook maneuver, so he just grabbed two risers, pulled hard, and slipped the chute sideways. Don skidded across the sky. He felt the heat from the fireball rush to the side of him.

He'd literally dodged a bullet. He relaxed and let the risers go. The parachute came to a sudden stop, but Don didn't. He swung up in the air, then down, then up again. It felt as if he were on a swing set. The typhoon raged, the winds grew fierce, and the ocean lay black beneath him. Pockets of flame sprawled for a mile or more atop the surface. Don swung like a pendulum and began gathering momentum. He pulled on the risers to try to make the swinging stop, but nothing worked. If this continued much longer, he would be in danger of swinging over the top of his parachute, becoming tangled in its lines and plummeting to the ocean. Exasperated by death's relentless pursuit, he tried to think his way out of yet another dilemma. He remembered from one of his physics classes that the longer the arm of a pendulum, the slower it would swing. He reached down and pulled a handle that released his life raft and survival kit. The yellow raft inflated and dropped fifty feet beneath him, suspended by a lanyard. The survival kit dropped another thirty feet below the raft. Don held the risers tight, and the oscillation stopped as quickly as it had started.

Don noticed that the fires below had been nearly all consumed by the sea. The night grew black once more. Don knew he would again have trouble telling which way was up or how close to the water he might be. He turned his sore neck in each direction to see whether any of his crew members might've made it out of the plane, too. About a half mile away he spotted a white parachute with Day-Glo orange panels drifting through the storm. He wondered who it might be.

Don yanked his risers in opposite directions in order to turn the parachute toward the other survivor. He hoped to chase it down and land as close as possible. His parachute spun quickly but then wouldn't stop. Don started twisting in the opposite direction. His parachute cords began twining together and pulling his parachute into a ball.

"Holy mother of Jesus," Don screamed into the sky. "Not again."

Panic welled up once more. Another few seconds of this, and Don would begin dropping like a stone. He pulled against the twisting lines with all his strength, and the spinning stopped. Briefly. Don then began twisting in the opposite direction, only faster. When he got to the bottom, he popped the risers as hard as he could, and the spinning stopped. He vowed to cease tinkering with his parachute. It only led to trouble.

Lightning flashed, and the ocean loomed a couple of thousand feet beneath him. Between intervals of blackness, the electric flickers sporadically revealed the menace that lay in wait. Huge waves foamed white. Luminescent plankton churned in the storm, and the water glowed turquoise in places. Don clung to his risers in terror. As bad as his parachute had been, he wanted to stay with it forever—just a guy and his parachute, floating in the air for as long as it took to get rescued. Anything to stay out of the ocean. Anything.

But still Don descended. In the lightning flashes, he could see mountains of waves undulating beneath him. Sea foam blew from crests and scudded white across the black surface. He was maybe one hundred feet from splashdown. He remembered his training. Arms tucked, legs tucked, stare at the horizon. Arms tucked, legs tucked, stare at the horizon. Terror overwhelmed him. He gritted his teeth to suppress an involuntary yell. The water rose fast to greet him. He slapped hard into a black wave and sank beneath the surface.

Chapter Five

The briefing room at Mather Air Force Base overflowed with flight personnel. Pilots sat in rows at college lecture hall–style desks. Others leaned against the walls and crowded into the exits. Every B-52 crew on base was jammed into a room that typically held only ten flight crews.

The Strategic Air Command emblem sat on an easel atop the briefing platform. Depicting an Orwellian image of peace through war, the SAC shield had an armor-clad forearm and clenched fist clutching an olive branch and three lightning bolts. This was emblazoned against the serene backdrop of a robin's-egg-blue sky and two cottonball-white clouds.

"Ten-HUT!" boomed a voice from the front of the room.

Every man snapped to attention, back rigid, chest thrust, arms to the side, chin level.

Col. Van Parker strode onto the platform wearing a scowl; Don instantly knew they were all headed for Vietnam.

Col. Parker was tall, broad shouldered, and imposing. To young pilots like Don, he was a demigod. The pilots' attention was riveted to anyone who had survived as many combat missions as he had. They listened raptly to his stories. They watched his mannerisms. They asked questions of men who knew him. They hoped to find small nuggets that might someday be useful in a future mission. Perhaps they might be able to take away something that could help build their own aura and mystique—a protective cloak that might keep them alive in the days, months, and years ahead.

Col. Parker flew B-29s throughout the Pacific Theater in World War II. He led the US "Show of Force" mission over Tokyo Bay in September 1945 as the Japanese signed articles of surrender aboard the USS *Mis-*

souri. He flew B-29 bombing missions again in the Korean War before switching to B-52s during the Cold War and Cuban Missile Crisis. And now here he was, preparing to brief his air squadron about a seemingly insignificant strip of land in Indochina.

Typically, such briefings were conducted by a couple of staff colonels. But Col. Parker didn't take combat lightly. He knew the lives of the men in his squadron would soon change forever. It was best if they heard from him directly.

"At ease," the voice in the front calmly drawled.

Col. Parker stood at the lectern, cleared his throat, and scanned the faces of the men in the room.

"Men," Col. Parker said in a solemn greeting. "As you may know, the Vietcong have begun their Communist spring offensive by attacking a US helicopter airfield and advisory compound in Gia Lai Province, South Vietnam. Seven American soldiers were killed and another 126 wounded."

An aide pulled down a large canvas map of Indochina and the Western Pacific. The aide pointed to Vietnam and the location of the attacks. Pilots leaned forward and craned their necks to study it. They could recite from memory just about every river, bay, mountain, town, glacier, and sea in the Arctic. They'd spent hundreds of hours poring over flight plans in that region and had personally flown over the area on dozens of missions. But Southeast Asia? To these men, it was as mysterious as the seemingly impenetrable jungle that covered it.

"President Johnson yesterday convened a meeting of the National Security Council. It was attended by our commander in chief, secretaries of state and defense, the director of the National Security Agency, and the Speaker of the House and Senate Majority Leader. The council was unanimous in recommending retaliatory air strikes against the Vietcong.

"Furthermore, our SAC planners have put forth a recommended combat mission that we believe will be effective in halting Communist aggression in Vietnam."

The aide then pulled down two side-by-side maps. One showed the entire Pacific hemisphere; the other was an enlarged section of the South

China Sea with a focus on North and South Vietnam. Red lines tracked from the West Coast of the United States across the ocean.

"Men," Col. Parker continued, "this mission is classified. You may tell your families only that you're deploying to the Western Pacific. Lt. Col. Jones will now brief you on your mission and your route. Godspeed."

Lt. Col. Jones was tall, rangy, and matter-of-fact. As he spoke, the aide followed his geographic descriptions with a long wooden pointer.

"At sixteen-hundred today, the B-52s on this base were taken off nuclear alert for the first time since January 1, 1960. These planes will be configured into conventional bombers and will depart Mather Air Force Base at oh-eight-hundred hours on February 10. A wing of thirty B-52s and twelve KC-135s will follow a course north of San Francisco. We will aerial refuel off the coast of California before following a great circle route, nonstop, to Andersen Air Force Base on the Island of Guam. Our tankers will land at Hickam Field, Hawaii, refuel, and continue to Kadena Air Base, Okinawa.

"Men," Lt. Col. Jones continued, "you will have only a brief stay in Guam. You will rest and eat while our maintenance crews refuel your planes and load them with bombs. You will depart Guam within twelve hours of your arrival and meet your tankers for aerial refueling once again above the South China Sea."

Every pilot in the room followed the lieutenant colonel's words and his aide's wooden pointer with rapt attention.

"After refueling, you will fly to Tiger Island, off Vietnam's Demilitarized Zone. At Tiger Island, you will descend to five hundred feet over the ocean and follow the coastline north. You will then turn northwest and overfly Hanoi at five hundred feet before rising to fifteen hundred feet and dropping your entire payloads on key military, industrial, and transportation targets in and around the city, including the North Vietnamese MiG airfield at Phúc Yên, about ten miles northwest of Hanoi. You will then descend back to five hundred feet, make a wide left turn, and exit North Vietnam just south of Thanh Hóa before climbing to forty-five thousand feet and flying directly back to Guam."

The pilots sat back in their seats, stunned. This was a bold gambit. Everyone in the room knew it. It was shock and awe before shock and awe. Only their professionalism and rank prevented them from standing and cheering. The Strategic Air Command was proposing to hit North Vietnam with roughly 1.4 million pounds of bombs, decimating within minutes virtually all of the country's airpower as well as most of its will to fight. It would be America's opening, and perhaps final, move of the Vietnam conflict—the largest US bombing raid ever.

The men of the Strategic Air Command were all inveterate card-sharps. Marathon poker games were rampant and proved one of the only reliable ways to fight the boredom that accompanied a continuous state of nuclear alert. The pilots in the room could practically smell a winning hand—and Cols. Parker and Jones had just dealt them one.

Chapter Six

THE HOWLS OF THE WIND CEASED WITH A SPLASH. DON FLAILED IN THE watery blackness. He could only hear the distant churning of waves passing overhead. Darkness was total. And again, he had no sense of up or down. Perhaps this is where death would finally greet him. He held his breath and floated in the abyss.

"No sense in trying to swim to the surface," he thought. There was a risk he could expend all his energy and remaining breath swimming deeper. "Best to just float and let the surface find me."

Within seconds, he was yanked by his harness and erupted from beneath the waves. Winds from the typhoon blustered across the ocean's surface, catching Don's parachute and sending it ripping across the water like a plastic grocery bag caught in a gale. A layer of ocean spray hurtled above the surface and made it difficult to breathe.

Don flew into the air and bounced on the water several times. The parachute hauled him the way a speedboat might drag a downed water skier who refused to let go of the towrope. He zipped facedown along the surface—forced to take gulps of seawater between frantic breaths of air.

He clung to his parachute risers and thought to spread his legs in hopes of reducing his violent bouncing. It worked. Don then flipped onto his back with his legs spread wide. He could now breathe without having saltwater forced down his throat.

Don reached for the release pins located near each collarbone. He unlocked both covers, and pull rings flipped into position. He gave each ring a tug and neither budged.

"Shit," he thought. "The maintenance crew on my survival gear better hope that I drown, because if I live . . ."

Don locked both his thumbs into the pull ring on the right. He jerked with all his remaining strength. Nothing.

He thought about all the times he'd seen the maintenance crew sitting on the white sand beaches of Guam drinking beer and talking about rendezvous with nurses at the nearby hospital. His anger grew to fury.

He screamed into the storm with murderous intent as he pulled the ring once more.

The right riser snapped loose and whistled past his ear like a bullwhip. The parachute dropped flat against the water, and Don came to a sudden stop.

Chapter Seven

The tule fog squatted heavy and thick atop California's Central Valley on the early morning of February 10, 1965. Stretching 450 miles from Redding to Bakersfield, the fog enveloped a kidney-shaped swath of the state's interior farmland and was hemmed to the east by the Sierra, hemmed to the west by the Coast Ranges, and pressed low by a high-pressure ridge and clear, cold skies above.

Don's B-52 idled on the tarmac. Perched in his copilot's seat some twenty feet above the ground, he could barely see the reflective markings below or the lights from the plane ahead. But he stared intently into the shapeless, gray purgatory, excited that his life as a combat pilot was finally about to begin.

A cell of three KC-135s, each carrying two hundred thousand pounds of transfer fuel, rumbled and whined onto the runway. A deep, distant roar shook through the fog, and the faint smell of jet exhaust seeped into the cockpit. The mission was under way.

Major Gehrig responded to instructions from the control tower. Don called out fuel and engine readings. Major Gehrig pushed full on the throttle, and the eight jet engines roared in unison. The brakes released with a chirp, and the plane slowly began to gather speed, its long wings flexing from small undulations in the runway and its fuselage reverberating from the tremendous thrust.

Major Gehrig kept the plane true as it rolled down the center of the runway and picked up speed. There was barely a sense of motion due to the fog, but Don could feel the wings grow taut and the engines more efficient. The front wheels lifted off the runway, but the back of the plane seemed hesitant to release contact with the ground. Major Gehrig held the throttle steady until the long wings finally caught hard on the heavy, damp air, pulling the plane steep into the sky.

Don was pressed back into his seat as the plane climbed. A deep gray filled the cockpit windscreen, and small beads of water streamed across the glass. At about four thousand feet the fog turned smoke white for several seconds before the plane rose into a brilliant sky.

With the sun at his back, Don surveyed the view. An ocean of white clamped low and flat on the Central Valley and stretched all the way to the hills east of Napa. The plane rose quickly to thirty thousand feet, and Don could see waves rolling in parallel white lines to the California coast. The deep blue of the Pacific opened beneath him. To his left, the Farallon Islands stood as a small, jagged outpost amid the expanse. The islands glided slowly beneath the plane and out of view; Don understood that they were his final glimpse of US soil.

Toward the horizon, he spotted his cell's KC-135. He could see the lead B-52 approach beneath the tanker for refueling, marveling at the sight of the two behemoths flying in umbilical tandem.

After topping off the lead plane, the KC-135 began drifting back toward Don until it loomed large overhead, looking like a mechanical grasshopper dangling an ovipositor from its abdomen. Major Gehrig slid into position, and the boom operator in the KC-135 maneuvered the fueling tube until it snapped into what looked like a whale's blowhole atop the B-52.

Don recorded all the fuel readings and then settled in for the grinding monotony of a Pacific crossing. The KC-135 banked left and set a course for Hawaii. Major Gehrig pulled up to forty-five thousand feet and followed the eight white contrails laid parallel in the sky by the jet engines in the cell's lead plane. He would follow them like aerial railroad tracks all the way to Guam.

High in the stratosphere, Don could make out a slight curve in the earth. Everywhere in the world over the middle of the Pacific, there was blue. There was the golden blue of the water directly below that reflected the glare of the overhead sun. There was the metallic blue of the water that stretched beyond the sun's reflection and toward the horizon. There was the powder blue of the sky above the water and below the plane. And there was the cobalt blue of space that arced high above the horizon and over the cockpit.

"Midway Island is just off our left," declared navigator Terry Lowry over the plane's intercom. "We're coming up to take a look."

No one on the crew with the exception of Maj. Gehrig had ever flown this route before. It was a change of pace from the Arctic missions, and each person was eager to see the site of the Battle of Midway, which occurred there almost exactly twenty-three years earlier, thus changing the tide of World War II. Eastern Island and Sand Island make up the Midway Atoll, which is roughly equidistant between North America and Asia. Each spit of land is barely big enough to hold an airport runway, yet its location was important enough for American and Japanese forces to fight savagely for its domain.

Both navigators and the electronic warfare officer crowded into the cockpit to take a look at the impossibly remote islands.

"Crap," said Terry. "There's a spot of cloud cover. Doesn't look like we'll get a peek today."

The men shook their heads in disappointment and shuffled back to their stations.

A little under three hours later, Terry called out over the intercom, "We're abeam of Wake Island. Is it worth coming up to take a look, copilot?"

Don and the major leaned over to check the view out of the port side of the plane. They scanned the waters, but at forty-five thousand feet, it's difficult to see a small atoll, even if you know where you're supposed to be looking. The sun had passed in front of the eastbound jet, and Wake Island was lost somewhere in the golden glare coming off the water.

"Save yourself the trouble," Don replied. "The sun is blinding. We can't see anything on the surface except glare."

The men were disappointed by their lost chance to see two landmarks from World War II. But the crew was quietly nervous about their own upcoming combat mission. They knew that within thirty-six hours they would join those who had come this way two decades earlier and who had fought so valiantly amid the jungles and islands and water. They had hoped for some inspiration but got only cloud cover and reflective glare. But no matter. They were from a different time and off to fight a different foe in a different place. Perhaps it was best to let the past lie.

High above the Pacific, the B-52 droned on.

Chapter Eight

For the first time since his ordeal had started, Don was free from panic. For a moment, he allowed himself to think that he might actually survive. But he knew that he was far from safe. There was still no time to relax, no time to be contemplative. Only the immediate future mattered.

Don calmly swam to his bathtub-sized life raft. He draped his arms over the side, threw his right leg over the rubberized-canvas bladder that ringed the small craft, and rolled, exhausted, into his only sanctuary from the elements.

The raft was teardrop shaped and large enough to hold only one man sitting upright with his knees bent. The back of the raft was wide enough for a man's hips and arms; the front narrowed to the width of a pair of feet. It seemed like a wholly inadequate vessel in which to ride out a raging typhoon, but at this point Don was thankful for small victories and glad to be aboard.

In spite of his exhaustion, there was no time to rest. Don focused his mind and quickly assessed his current situation. He was in the ocean, being pushed by a relentless wind and pelted by continuous ocean spray. The most obvious menace, however, came in the form of huge, seemingly infinite waves. Like a roller coaster that never stopped, Don was lifted slowly upward. As he crested, he became briefly weightless before skidding down the wave's steep back slope. He waited several seconds in a flat trough before ascending and then descending. Over and over, without end, the ride continued. He counted ten seconds to traverse up the face of the wave and ten seconds to descend down the back. He calculated the waves to be between thirty and fifty feet. Each new wave was as terrifying as the last.

After taking several minutes to adjust to his surroundings, Don went back to the business of survival. He grabbed a piece of parachute cord, threaded it through an eyelet in the raft, looped it through a strap in his flight suit, and tied himself securely.

He reached over to the thin nylon lanyard that connected his survival kit to the raft and pulled the black, floating bag toward him, hand over hand. The kit was almost as long as the raft. Don pulled it out of the water and balanced it on his lap, with either side of it drooping over the raft and into the water. He pulled on a waterproof zipper that stretched diagonally across the thick rubber that sealed the top of the kit. The zipper didn't budge. Don wasn't sure whether this was due to another equipment malfunction or because he'd been completely sapped of strength and was now too exhausted to open a simple zipper.

Regardless, there was no time to wonder. Don reached inside a pocket on the inner thigh of his flight suit and pulled out an orange switchblade survival knife. He opened it with a flick, slit a gash across the cover, and tucked the knife back into its pouch.

Don reached into the kit and began pulling out a puzzling assortment of objects. Of course, it is important to remember that B-52s were built to confront and deter Russia, America's Cold War adversary. As such, the planes were designed with the Arctic in mind. This intensified with the launch in 1960 of Operation Chrome Dome, in which squadrons of B-52s remained airborne in continuous succession. At any hour of the day or night, at least one or two dozen thermonuclear-armed B-52s were aloft above the Alaskan and Canadian Arctic. The program was designed to counter Russia with nuclear deterrence through the omnipresence of armed bombers circling near the North Pole. The operation lasted until 1968, when a B-52 crew near Thule Air Base in Greenland was forced to ditch its plane—nuclear weapons and all—into the sea ice above Baffin Bay. Though the hydrogen bombs didn't detonate, several conventional explosives did, scattering parts of atomic weapons and radioactive material throughout the area. The dirty bomb cleanup took years.

From the end of World War II until the discontinuation of Operation Chrome Dome, there had been numerous high-profile crashes in the Arctic. Pilots and mission planners feared the cold, the ice, and the rugged, remote terrain. A number of crew members had survived crashes only to ultimately die of hypothermia, frostbite, or starvation. A few had even been attacked by polar bears. As a result, the survival kits stowed in B-52s were designed to keep crash survivors alive in Arctic extremes. Steamy jungles and tropical typhoons were hardly a consideration.

Don first pulled out two pieces of what appeared to be metal tubing. Each section was about a foot and a half long. He screwed the pieces together and saw that it was an ingeniously designed rifle. The stock of the gun comprised a quarter-inch-diameter tube with a small pad at the end. The weapon would've been ideal for either fending off a polar bear or shooting a seal for food. But in the Pacific tropics, it was entirely useless. Don held it away from the raft and released it, barrel first, into the ocean.

Next he pulled out an item that was about one foot square. Each side was covered by a thin piece of fiberglass that sandwiched what appeared to be nylon fabric. A screw and a wingnut clamped the fiberglass together and kept the cloth tightly compressed. Thick, black lettering read: "One each, Arctic sleeping bag." Don marveled that they had been able to fit a sleeping bag into a one-foot-by-one-foot-by-two-inch space. On the top of the next large wave, he set the fiberglass square onto the water. It skied fast down the watery slope before settling into a trough and sinking beneath the surface.

More items amazed and confounded him. He pulled out a large pair of wool socks and a gray ski mask. As he inspected the mask, he began to shiver from the wind and the wetness. For a moment, he thought it would be nice to take off his flight helmet and exchange it for what appeared to be a warm, comfortable mask. Then he thought about the possibility of death. It would simply be too embarrassing to be found dead wearing a wool ski mask in the tropics. Overboard it went.

He next removed an Arctic survival book, complete with paintings of flowers and plants that grew in the tundra. Each plant was described in detail. The book pointed out those that were edible and warned which of them were poisonous. There were also instructions on how to build a snow cave and an igloo as well as how to properly skin a seal.

Don pawed through the kit in a quest to find just a single item that might be useful in his current predicament. He couldn't find one. He simply kept tossing military property overboard, one item at a time.

His hand reached to the back of the kit, where he noticed a series of broken flanges. It was likely that the section had once been a compartment containing communication gear. But the equipment was gone, likely having detached during ejection. He had hoped to at least find a radio or a flare. Instead he floated up and down, the wind rippling his flight suit. As though he were dumping a useless carcass overboard, he heaved the remains of the survival kit away from the raft and was left floating in the South China Sea with only his wits and his hope.

Chapter Nine

Major Gehrig tapped Don's shoulder and nodded slightly left.

At about eleven o'clock, amid the golden shimmering ripples of the Western Pacific, lay the hourglass-shaped island of Guam, the first piece of land the pilots had seen in thirteen hours of flight. About thirty miles long, Guam sat east of the Philippines on the suboceanic precipice of the thirty-six-thousand-foot deep Mariana Trench and was the United States' westernmost territory. It was first settled by the Chamorro people around 2000 BC before becoming an important stopover, after discovery in 1521 by the explorer Magellan, for Spanish galleons traversing the Pacific from Manila to Acapulco.

Ghosts of World War II still haunted the island as Don flew overhead in 1965. Guam had been overrun by the Japanese the day after Pearl Harbor, and the native Guamanians were held in brutal, lethal occupation for nearly three years. When the Americans returned in 1944, the Japanese occupiers fought to the death; over eighteen thousand Japanese soldiers were killed, and less than 2 percent of their force on the island surrendered.

The B-52 began its descent from the stratosphere into the hot, heavy humidity of the tropics. After more than a dozen cold-soaked hours at forty-five thousand feet, the plane's transition back to earth had some unexpected side effects. The cabin fogged during the descent into the troposphere, and Don could barely see out of the windscreen. He opened ventilation ducts and ran the cockpit fans on high. Metallic parts crinkled as they expanded from extreme cold to warm. Water beaded on the ceiling and dripped from metal tubes overhead. The plane made a sweeping turn, dropped to one thousand feet, and approached the island from the southwest. To Don, the tropical air smelled heavy and sweet. Then it began to rain inside the cockpit.

The sun, which the squadron had chased from its morning rise in the California dawn, began to sink amid scattered columns of coral-colored clouds on the western horizon. The water beneath the plane ended abruptly as Maj. Gehrig glided softly up the island's narrow length toward the airstrip on its northeastern edge. Palm trees waved gently in the late afternoon breeze. Church steeples jutted above the jungle, and small homes with corrugated metal roofs and whitewashed walls glowed flamingo pink from the tropical sunset. Dark green foliage was held back by a chain-link fence, and a black asphalt runway stretched long and narrow beneath the plane. The B-52 floated down to the surface, rolled to the end of the runway, turned left, and came to a stop in front of a man in a flight suit waving a pair of signal flags. Don powered down the engines, which gave a final, low whine, and for the first time in 5,900 miles, the great plane was still and silent.

Don was the fifth to land. Behind him was the remaining squadron from Mather Air Force Base as well as an additional squadron that was on approach from Barksdale Air Force Base in Louisiana. For over an hour, B-52s streamed from the sky—single file and one per minute—over the length of the island. Children ran into the streets to wave at pilots and to marvel at the big jets that kept coming, one by one by one. Older Guamanians looked up from doorways or sat quietly on stoops, recalling with trepidation the bloody days of World War II. The locals weren't quite sure why, but there was no mistaking that the Americans were staging the largest display of air power in the Pacific since 1945.

A young, gangly airman with a fresh buzz haircut met the crew at the plane. He snapped to attention and gave a sharp salute as Maj. Gehrig stepped to the tarmac. The crew flung their travel bags into the back of an open-top transport jeep with three rows of seats. They left their flight gear in the plane since they would likely be back in less than six hours to embark on their mission to Vietnam.

The airman spoke loudly and excitedly over the rush of the wind and the sound of the incoming planes as he drove across the airfield toward a row of buildings on the edge of the base. He knew something big was afoot but attempted to make small talk anyway. The crew was tired from the flight but also tense from the thought of their imminent combat mission.

"Where are you folks from?" the airman called out to no one in particular as he drove.

There was no answer. The mission was top secret, and there was no need to fill in any blanks for a curious nineteen-year-old driver.

"The States?" he ventured.

Major Gehrig silently shook his head at the driver's awkward persistence. Don felt bad. The kid was only trying to be polite.

"I've never seen so many B-52s," he continued.

There was more silence until Don finally broke the awkwardness by saying, "Neither have we."

"But you fly them all the time," said the airman, happy that he'd broken through.

"Yeah, but never so many all at once," said Don.

Major Gehrig gave Don a nudge to the ribs, thus bringing any further conversation to a close.

The driver dropped the men off at a two-story concrete barrack that stood only yards from the dark, dense jungle that pressed against the chain-link fence forming the perimeter of the base. Don walked into his assigned room and tossed his travel bag onto a bunk. Because an entire armada of B-52s had arrived somewhat unexpectedly at the base, Don would be sharing the room, which was about the size of a college dorm, with five other officers. He didn't much care, though, since he'd only need the bunk for a few hours after rising before dawn for his first combat mission.

Major Gehrig returned from a short meeting with the air base commanders and told Don and another group of pilots that they'd been cleared to have dinner at the Officers' Club. The men walked about one hundred yards to a large hall and sat down to a meal of steak and potatoes. Voices inside the club were low and solemn. No beer or wine was served because flight crews were prohibited from drinking alcohol within twelve hours of flying.

While Don thoughtfully sliced his steak and ruminated on the specifics of his imminent combat mission, political turmoil roiled the capitals of the two Cold War adversaries, the United States and Soviet Union.

In the United States, President Kennedy had been assassinated fourteen months earlier. President Lyndon Johnson spent all of 1964 staving off action in Southeast Asia due to the upcoming election and stiff-arming the myriad military solutions to the crisis that arrived from the Pentagon weekly. But Johnson had been inaugurated into office for his first elected term only three weeks earlier. He'd decided that the time to act was now. After the Camp Holloway incident, he said of the Vietcong aggression: "I'm tired of this. We're not going to take it anymore from the Vietcong."

The turmoil in Moscow was perhaps even more severe. Premier Nikita Khrushchev had been deposed less than four months earlier and had been replaced by a troika of leaders: Alexei Kosygin as premier, Leonid Brezhnev as first secretary, and Nikolai Podgorny as chairman. Each was vying for consolidated power and none had the stomach for war in Southeast Asia. Their predecessor, Khrushchev, had repeatedly told North Vietnamese chairman Ho Chi Minh that the Soviets would not send antiaircraft batteries and surface-to-air missiles to protect Hanoi, nor would they provide *carte blanche* shipment of armaments to North Vietnam. Khrushchev had been actively seeking an exit from the conflict. On February 5, 1965, Premier Kosygin traveled to Hanoi to personally tell Chairman Minh of his country's plans to cease military aid to North Vietnam and to disentangle from Southeast Asia.

Yet the biggest battle of 1964 and early 1965 was not between the Americans and Russians or the Americans and North Vietnamese. It was between two tremendously powerful men in Washington, DC, who were polar opposites in style, demeanor, and thought. Each would develop and propose very different strategic plans for the United States in Southeast Asia. And President Johnson would have to choose between one or the other. Like all the other disasters that came before, the crisis in Vietnam traveled a path of seemingly insignificant events that became intricately linked until doom hung over the entire venture, only a fifty-fifty coin flip away.

Robert McNamara was the original Whiz Kid. Educated at the University of California and Harvard Business School, McNamara was a number cruncher extraordinaire. He embraced the concept of statistical process control and believed that any endeavor could be explained, managed, and improved by the tight discipline and application of numerical values. During World War II, he dramatically boosted aerial bombing rates and effectiveness. After the war, he swooped into the Ford Motor Company and saved it from corporate implosion. He was tapped by Kennedy as secretary of defense. During the Cuban Missile Crisis, he backed the president in averting another potential disaster that came down to a fifty-fifty coin flip. The choice was to either aggressively bomb Cuba and the Soviet missile installations there or to run a naval blockade of the island and negotiate a face-saving political settlement with the Russians. The head of the Strategic Air Command advocated for the former; McNamara advocated for the latter. Kennedy in a coin-flip decision chose McNamara. The gambit worked. Nuclear war was averted. History later showed that Khrushchev had ceded control of more than twenty nuclear missiles to commanders on the ground in Cuba. And those commanders had a free hand to launch the warheads at US cities along the Eastern Seaboard should the Americans attack. Kennedy made the right gamble. Had he chosen the plan presented by his air force general, over twenty million Americans would've died, along with over one hundred million Soviet citizens in a retaliatory response.

General Curtis LeMay was that general—the man who almost brought the world to an end. He was the Chief of Staff of the Air Force and the youngest American four-star general since Ulysses S. Grant. The son of an ironworker, LeMay was a midwesterner educated at Ohio State. He fearlessly flew and commanded bombers during World War II over Europe, the South Pacific, and Japan. He directed the Berlin Airlift and was the person most responsible for the creation of the Strategic Air Command, a twenty-four/seven airborne force of nuclear-armed B-52s. Few people on the planet understood war better than LeMay, and perhaps no one better understood the proper application of aerial bombardment in modern warfare. He once stated: "Flying fighters is fun; flying bombers is important." His men feared and respected him, calling him either "Big Cigar" for his omnipresent stogie, or "Old Iron Pants," for his rigid, hard-assed style of command. He subscribed to the Civil War military genius of Confederate General Nathan Bedford Forrest, who proclaimed, "Get there first with the most." And with that, he told Lyndon Johnson that his B-52 pilots could put an end to the Southeast Asian conflict quickly with hammer blows to military targets in and around Hanoi.

—◆—

While the power struggle ensued between LeMay and McNamara in Washington, DC, Army Specialist Bob Marshall stood on the third-floor balcony of a hotel in the South Vietnamese port city of Quy Nhơn. The air was warm, heavy, and humid. It had just rained. He pressed the butt of his M14 rifle to his shoulder and scanned the dark, wet streets below after having just heard gunshots crackle through the night. He spotted two Vietcong soldiers running from the hotel, which housed over one hundred American advisers. Marshall, a trained sniper, set his gun sights on the lead soldier and calmly pulled the trigger. The soldier dropped. His comrade stopped to provide assistance. Marshall squeezed the trigger again, and both Vietcong lay dead in the street. Marshall surveyed his handiwork, heard a deep rumble from the base of the hotel, and then dropped three stories into a heaping pile of broken concrete, twisted metal, and choking dust. Twenty-three American servicemen died in the hotel bombing and twenty-two were seriously injured.

Within hours, nearly one hundred Navy F-4 Phantoms, F-8 Crusaders, and A-4 Skyhawks launched, from the USS *Ranger*, *Coral Sea*, and *Hancock* just off the South Vietnamese coast. Air Force F-100 Super Sabre fighters scrambled from Da Nang Air Base just south of the Demilitarized Zone. Most of the sorties targeted Vietcong supply routes through the jungle as well as Vietcong military barracks just north of the border between the two countries. A handful of sorties targeted military installations near Hanoi. Bombs fell only blocks from where Soviet premier Kosygin was holding talks with Chairman Ho Chi Minh. The Soviets were furious. Instead of backing away from the conflict in Vietnam, Premier Kosygin reversed course and promised Ho Chi Minh all the materiel he would need for the duration of the war, as well as a sophisticated system of Soviet-made surface-to-air missiles ideal for shooting down American jets and protecting the city of Hanoi.

———

Little of this was known to Don at the time, nor was it his particular concern. His job was to fly a massive bomb-laden plane up the coast of Vietnam and destroy the war-making ability of an American nemesis. He reviewed the flight in his mind, memorizing names of cities, geographic formations, and coordinates. He was tired and wanted to finish his meal quickly so that he could get at least four hours of sleep before having to buckle himself back into his plane for the twelve-hour flight to Hanoi and back.

A colonel Don had never seen before strode into the Officers' Club, stood on a chair near the bar, and asked for silence. He barked official orders from a document he held in his hand. Don heard only the colonel's final few sentences: "Your mission has been canceled. You are to maintain readiness. New orders will be forthcoming. But until then, the bar is open."

Cheers erupted in the Officers' Club, and within minutes something akin to a raucous fraternity party broke out. A fellow pilot handed Don a tall glass of beer. He guzzled half of it. The tension of imminent combat vanished. He leaned back in his chair, closed his eyes, and let the alcohol mix with exhaustion.

CHAPTER TEN

NAUSEA GRIPPED DON'S BODY AND FURTHER WEAKENED HIS MENTAL state. He leaned over the side of the raft and began retching all the sea-water he'd swallowed earlier. The waves were relentless. He kept thinking about how he would gladly give away all his earthly possessions for just a moment of flat sea. But Don knew he had to keep fighting through the seasickness. He had to be alert and to keep thinking. He scanned the horizon atop the next wave and noticed that the clouds to his right were beginning to glow. Dawn had arrived. Perhaps the day would bring relief from the savage storm. He'd also gained his bearings and a sense of direction. Although being able to accurately point north held almost no practical value, it did provide him a sense of inner comfort and accom-plishment. At least he was no longer adrift in a directionless black void.

Don continued to scan the horizon through the lifting darkness. Atop a wave, he caught a glimpse of a huge ship. He slipped down the wave and wondered whether he were already hallucinating. He rode up the next wave in frantic anticipation. There it was again. He studied it, five seconds at a time, each instant he crested a wave. He then thought about what he'd seen and analyzed what it meant during the ensuing twenty seconds or so until he reached the next crest. The huge ocean freighter was black and orange and plowing through the waves like a bulldozer. It was only about four hundred yards due north and was heading west.

Don crested another wave and instinctively screamed for help and waved his arms. He did the same on the next crest and the next. Finally, he felt ashamed and idiotic in his desperation. There was no way his voice would carry through the wind and onto the ship's deck, which towered sixty feet or more above the crashing seas. To make matters worse, there was no sign of life on deck. The ship appeared to be nothing but a great machine, oblivious to the elements, pushing relentlessly toward its destination. There was no need or desire to keep an eye out for a desperate speck amid the nearly infinite, undulating expanse. Don grabbed the lanyard attaching the emptied survival kit to the raft. He hauled the kit back toward him and frantically searched inside for a flare. Perhaps he'd missed something in the dark. There had to be a flare somewhere. How could a survival kit not have a flare? He groped and groped, but there was nothing. He tossed the kit overboard once more in disgust.

Don crested a wave again and caught sight of yet another oceangoing ship. It appeared to be all white. It was located only about half a mile east of him and was headed due north on a perpendicular path toward the black ship. From Don's vantage point atop the wave crests, it appeared that the ships were on a collision course. He realized that they were likely farther apart than they seemed, but given his recent experience, it wasn't something he was going to rule out just yet.

He then saw a pencil flare streak orange into the dark gray of the clouds. It was the other parachutist he'd seen on the way down. There had been at least one other survivor, and he was apparently in a raft only yards from the white ship. Another flare streaked into the sky. And then another, and another.

But the white ship plowed mechanically through the heavy seas. There was no sign of life, no flicker of lights, no acknowledgment of the downed pilots. Don's hope of a quick rescue sank with each slide down every ensuing wave. The black ship continued west, the white ship north. They didn't collide, and Don spent the next twenty minutes watching them each grow small on the horizon.

Chapter Eleven

WAR AND DISASTER OFTEN SWEEP US ACROSS CONTINENTS AND OCEANS as we march inexorably toward our own destinies.

Of course, death closely stalks such migrations and plucks multitudes from the ranks long before they can reach foreign shores. It is by the vagaries of chance—fought against long odds—that we become who we are in our own time and our own place. Were it not for historic calamities, Don would not be sitting in a bathtub-sized raft, lost in the ocean in the aftermath of a great disaster on his way to a great war.

This was not the first time death's jaws had snapped at Don. Nor was it the first time a Harten had been moved by the sweep of history.

Don could recall first sparring with his own demise at the age of four. As my grandfather Kenny Harten sped along a highway outside of Pocatello, Don sat on his mother's lap in the front seat, while the back of the car was packed with cousins and my three-year-old mother. The old, black Packard had what was called a "suicide door," meaning that the front of the door opened outward, while the back of the door was hinged. There were no seat belts, and the door opened by pushing down on the handle rather than pulling up. Automotive safety was an afterthought in the pre–Ralph Nader days. Don squirmed in my grandmother's lap and gave the handle a kick. The door flew open and Don tumbled out as my grandmother lunged to grab an arm or a leg.

Don rolled down the street at fifty miles per hour like a barrel of beer that had dropped from the back of a truck. After about thirty yards, he came to a stop, sat on the pavement for a moment, and then ran after the skidding car, which was already a quarter-mile away, yelling, "Mom! Dad! Don't leave me. Don't leave me."

Don came away with only a few bumps and bruises, thus initiating his near mystic ability to cheat death.

Shortly after my family had learned that Don was missing in action, the phone rang at our home in Carson City. A reporter from the *Reno Evening Gazette* had somehow found my mother and asked her what she thought of the incident, to which my mother replied with incredulity: "I still can't believe that he was flying jets. My dad hardly trusted him with the family station wagon, which he wrecked when he was sixteen, and now the US government trusts him with multimillion-dollar airplanes?"

The quote ran on the front page of the paper. The Associated Press picked up the story, and my mom's wrought words appeared in virtually every newspaper in the country. It wasn't exactly the kind of eulogy a combat pilot would've hoped for.

For the Hartens, the journey to America was circuitous. It began in northern Germany in the late 1600s, when a mercenary soldier likely named William Hartenstein took up arms to join the great Protestant crusade of Dutch king William of Orange, whose mission was to defeat English king James II and drive the perceived scourge of Catholicism from Britain's shores.

William Hartenstein boarded a Dutch warship, which sailed into Ireland's Belfast Lough and laid siege to the castle at Carrickfergus in August 1689. In July of the following year, King William III marched his largely mercenary force of thirty-six thousand troops to the Boyne River north of Dublin. There he met King James II and his army of twenty thousand, most of whom were Catholic Irish, French, and English. At the Battle of the Boyne, William Hartenstein was a small cog in a great struggle for the British crown. The fight was ultimately won by King William III and would forever cleave Ireland into a Protestant north and a Catholic south.

For his troubles, William was given money and land near Belfast, where he settled, shortened his name to Harten, and made an effort to fit in.

Thus, the Harten clan thrived in Belfast for over two centuries until the vagaries of history, tragedy, and fate reached out, touched Don's grandfather—also named William Harten—and swept him off, like so many other Irish, to the distant shores of the United States and the even more unlikely town of Pocatello, located in the remote vastness of the American West.

Don grew up next door to his grandfather William and his grandmother Sarah. He relished listening to his grandfather's stories. That's because William, with his soft Irish brogue, could make a short walk to the grocery store sound like the medieval quest of a noble knight.

When asked how he came to live in America, he would always begin, "She was a grand ship—the grandest ever."

William would go on to paint a larger-than-life portrait of 1910 Belfast. He made it sound like the center of the universe on its best days or a global hub of commerce and culture for the fading British Empire on its worst. It was a place where the shipyards clattered and clanged with construction of great seagoing vessels during the day and the dance halls reverberated with the melodious blare of late-night horns, fiddles, and Irish crooning.

"There was no better place to be a young man with skilled hands," William would say as he drifted into his nostalgic reverie. "The lasses all wore fine, long dresses, the likes of which can't be seen in America.

"We lived on Jaffa Street, and from the road that led to Belfast Lough, I could see the huge gantry over Thompson Dock where the *Titanic* was taking shape. I was a ship's carpenter for Harland and Wolff. We were all very proud. It was the most important work any of us had ever done—the most important we'd ever do. The woodwork inside the ship was grand. It was the finest ever attempted in the history of shipbuilding, and we were honored to do our part. The inside was modeled after the Ritz Hotel in Paris. We installed intricately carved wooden panels, sweeping oak staircases, and dozens of stately doors. That was my specialty—the doors. I installed delicate gold inlays that could be ruined by the slightest scratch. It took hours and hours and the patience of Job. But no expense was spared, and every job had to be perfect. When working with metal, you'll come to find that each person has a different chemistry. Some people have sweaty hands, some people don't. Some people can touch a brass plate and leave a dark tarnish. Some people don't. The head carpenter soon discovered that my hands never sweated and that I could work with brass and gold all day and never leave a tarnish. So I was given the job of installing doorknobs and hinges throughout the ship. I didn't leave behind so much as a fingerprint. And when I finished polishing my work, the doors and hallways gleamed like the palace of King Midas. Oh, my, yes, she was a grand ship."

His voice would then grow somber as he recounted how in the spring of 1912 he'd been working on the HMHS *Britannic*, the *Titanic's* Olympic-class sister ship.

"As I walked home for lunch that Monday morning, a boy on a bicycle passed by hollering something about the *Titanic*. I arrived home, and soon another boy on a bicycle came pedaling up the way, hollering louder than the first. People leaned out their windows and gathered outside. I stopped the boy and asked him for details. He said he only knew that the *Titanic* had struck an iceberg near Newfoundland and that telegrams had been sent from the ship saying she was sinking.

"I ran back to the shipyard, where a crowd had begun to gather. Every half hour or so, a man would emerge from the telegraph office and give us updates, which became more and more desperate by the hour. The entire city was in a state of shock and grief. We'd been told a thousand times that the *Titanic* was unsinkable. And now, all our hard work and pride had been swallowed by the ocean.

"After the sinking, I was furious at the stupidity of the men whose carelessness had caused that grand ship to sink. I milled around Belfast for a few months, but the sorrow was everywhere. We were no longer the best. We were no longer revered the world over. We had helped send passengers to their deaths. All our work and pride was for naught."

Construction on the *Britannic* was immediately halted as teams of marine engineers gathered to perform a postmortem on the *Titanic* in an effort to determine how something unsinkable had just been sunk.

Out of work and with wounded pride, William telegraphed one of his daughters who had been lured to southern Idaho some years earlier, having answered the siren call of Mormon missionaries, who regularly trolled Belfast for converts, having found rich hunting grounds in and around the city's deplorable linen mills, where young women worked twelve-hour days on their feet in the dank, noisy, pestilent textile factories. Life on a tidy, spacious Utah or Idaho farm seemed like nirvana by comparison.

The *Titanic* sank in April, and William sailed for America in June, never again to return.

Years later, he would find himself on a Pocatello porch, regaling his grandson with stories of the great ship—stories Don never tired of hearing.

By the age of five or six, Don had memorized nearly every facet of the ship and its doomed voyage. He knew its length (882 feet), height (175 feet), and weight (46,328 tons). He knew the cascade of events that had conspired perfectly to send 1,514 souls to watery graves, along with sending a wondrous feat of engineering twelve thousand feet to the bottom of the Atlantic.

Like nearly all disasters, the *Titanic* was undone by a litany of events that kept stacking higher and higher until they were tipped by a common cause.

It was the ship's maiden voyage. None of the crew or equipment had made a transatlantic crossing under those specific circumstances.

The ship had tremendous speed and power for its class. The crew had no experience in running this particular vessel at full steam.

J. Bruce Ismay, chairman of the White Star Line, which operated the *Titanic*, made several last-minute ornamental design changes to the ship. Additionally, the *Titanic*'s sister ship, the *Olympic*, came into dock for repairs from a minor collision just prior to the *Titanic*'s completion. Both incidents delayed the launch of the *Titanic* by weeks.

The *Titanic* was designed with sixteen watertight compartments and was thus dubbed "practically unsinkable." The ship could withstand a breach of up to four compartments; the iceberg ripped an open gash in five.

While there was a criminal shortage of lifeboats aboard, many of the boats left the stricken mothership filled to as little as a third of their capacity. Even the boats that had been boarded to capacity could've safely accommodated an additional five to ten passengers, especially in the glassy, calm seas. This mistake cost the lives of more than five hundred people.

And, finally, there was the incident with the SS *Californian*, a steamship that was less than ten miles from the *Titanic* when she sank. The telegraph operator on the *Californian* wired his counterpart that the *Californian* had stopped for the night because it had spotted icebergs and was surrounded by floating sea ice. The *Titanic* operator was busy clearing out a backlog of telegrams from VIPs and wealthy passengers and replied to the *Californian*, "Shut up, shut up; I'm busy." With that, the *Californian* operator went to sleep. Ten minutes later, the *Titanic* had its infamous collision. Throughout the night, spotters on the *Californian* reported seeing flares fired from the *Titanic*. They advised their captain, but he assured the lookouts that those were merely company flares not intended to signal an SOS. He, too, went to bed.

And so it was that something so improbable and avoidable became inevitable. On the surface, all human disasters are different. At their core, they're all the same. It was something Don certainly contemplated as he fought for his life in the South China Sea. He thought of his grandfather. He thought of the *Titanic*. And the only consolation he could take away was that the water in the tropics was warmer than it was in the North Atlantic.

CHAPTER TWELVE

DON FLOATED IN DESPERATE MONOTONY. UP, THEN DOWN. UP, THEN down. Up, then down.

He looked at his feet and noticed that they were, for some reason, underwater. On closer inspection, the entire front of the raft was submerged. He floated into a trough and began the ascent up another wave. With a tremendous yank, he was dragged beneath the surface.

Don flailed in the watery darkness. His hand grabbed a riser that was still attached to his harness. His parachute was, yet again, plotting his demise. He'd been so relieved to successfully detach his right riser after he'd landed that he'd forgotten all about the left one. At the time, it seemed inconsequential. That's because nothing in his Arctic training told him that a parachute soaked in water could eventually act like an anchor, sinking beneath the surface before billowing open and latching onto the tremendous underwater pressure, thus acting as though it had been caught on a boulder.

Don frantically reached for his survival knife. He knew he had only seconds. He thought briefly that it might already be too late. One act of carelessness in such a hostile environment can be the difference between life and death. Perhaps the parachute had already won. He pushed those thoughts away and swallowed the panic that welled up within him. Don fumbled for the switchblade, trying to keep calm so that he wouldn't lose his grip. He could imagine the knife squirting from his hand and sinking silently to the bottom of the ocean as life was snuffed from his body. He flicked open the blade, held the handle tight, and started slashing a handful of wet, taut cords.

"Damn," he thought. "This is going to take too long. I've dodged death half a dozen times in the past few hours, but it looks like this is it."

His lungs were bursting with the impulse to inhale. He fought his reflexes and continued slashing. He became angry at his own stupidity. Angry at the careless flight maintenance crew. Angry at the mission commanders. Angry that he would never see the United States again. Angry that he'd never be with another woman. His fingers bled, but he slashed with a fury that had been renewed by anger. He made a final cut, and the cord snapped like a rubber band, with Don rushing upward, pulled to the surface by his raft. He gulped for air and coughed out seawater. He wasn't sure what had compelled him to tie himself to his raft earlier, but he was certainly thankful that the notion had entered his mind; otherwise, he'd be wrapped up beneath the waves in his parachute, sloshing dead, under the sea, as though he were in a giant washing machine.

Don swam to what remained of his raft. The underwater pressure had forced most of the air from it, leaving a crumpled yellow mass about the size of a basketball. Don pulled it toward him and found the manual inflation tube. He treaded water and slowly inflated it with his mouth. In spite of his travails, he was never more thrilled to be alive. His near-death experience and anger at the incompetence that surrounded him had given him renewed focus and determination.

Once the raft was fully inflated, he climbed into it, slumping down with exhaustion and thinking about what to do next.

CHAPTER THIRTEEN

THE FINE CORAL SAND OF GUAM'S TARAGUE BEACH FEELS POWDERY AND cool beneath the feet and blazes brilliant white under a high tropical sun. Large open-ocean waves crash on a reef a mile from shore and can be seen as a distant white ridge on an aqua horizon. By the time the thundering sound reaches the beach, it is nothing more than a rhythmic hush. Small remnants of waves ripple across a crystalline lagoon before lapping gently on the packed, wet sand.

Don floated face first in the water, breathing slowly and loudly through a snorkel, and watched, mesmerized, colorful parades of fish gliding synchronously in front of his mask. Every couple of minutes, he would slowly swish his swim fins just beneath the surface and continue his directionless tour of the lagoon. Don would paddle lazily for two to three hours at a time, alone without thought, responsibility, or care. The fish were wondrous and came in dazzling hues of banana yellow, midnight purple, jet black, iridescent green, electric crimson, and royal blue.

A Col. Kline had told the airmen that their mission had been suspended "indefinitely." Pilots and crew were free to wander the island wherever and whenever they liked as long as they made sure to log out before leaving the air base.

And so Don drifted. Breezes blew. Palm trees swayed. And day melted into day.

There was no such serenity in Washington, DC. Secretary of Defense Robert McNamara had the full ear of the president and Gen. Curtis LeMay had been relegated to the rear of the bus. From the political back rooms of the Capitol to the smoke-filled war rooms of the Pentagon, a strategy for the Vietnam conflict emerged. McNamara waxed eloquently and professorially about his new theory of "gradualism." It was a war plan that fit neatly within the flowcharts and statistical analytics of the Whiz Kid number geeks whom McNamara had brought in tow to Washington.

Tossed overboard was the brutish but brilliant insight of the military genius Gen. Nathan Bedford Forrest as well as the long-and-deep strategic bombing expertise of Gen. LeMay.

"Get there first with the most" was replaced with "tit for tat."

McNamara's doctrine of gradualism had emerged as a concept in 1964. By the fall elections, McNamara and his minions had fluffed the concept into something bigger. They added facts, figures, timelines, and casualty projections. They crafted a short, simple story that had a beginning, a brief middle, and a quick end. They gave the notion of gradualism a heft of muscle and gravitas. And by the winter of 1965, gradualism had become a full-fledged doctrine, slithering from the bowels of Washington and coiling around the whole of the American military like a constrictor.

Oddly, in the blinding struggle for power that serves as daily sport in the US capital, few could see McNamara's doctrine for what it really was—namely, one of the greatest military blunders in the history of warfare.

In addition to his cavalier assumption that it would be best to tip-toe into battle, he fatally compounded that error by attacking his foe's geographic strength, which in North Vietnam's case was its thick jungle canopy. Instead of delivering a crushing blow to the north's fragile and exposed head, which resided in Hanoi and its nearby harbor and sur-rounding airfields, McNamara opted for body blows to the serpentine country's midsection.

There's a reason the armies of maniacal leaders Napoleon and Hit-ler lay in ruins following ill-advised thrusts into the flat, expansive cold of the Russian steppe. It's difficult enough to battle a people; it's often impossible to battle geography.

In early February 1965, McNamara convinced Johnson to retaliate for the Vietcong attacks on Camp Holloway and Quy Nhơn by launching Operation Flaming Dart. On February 7 and 11, American air force and navy fighter jets flew a total of 148 sorties into North Vietnam, targeting an army outpost along the central coast as well as communications and supply centers in the deep jungle near the Demilitarized Zone. The jungle swallowed most of the American bombs, and Flaming Dart succeeded only in escalating the war.

On the edge of the water near the outskirts of the Guamanian capital of Agana stood the South Seas Club, a cinderblock cantina with a corrugated metal roof, where Rachel San Nichols tended bar and waited tables.

Rachel had high cheeks and long, thick black hair, which she pulled back and let drape over her left shoulder. She had inviting, dark eyes, a broad smile, and white teeth that contrasted sharply with her smooth, brown skin. She smelled fresh and wore a yellow plumeria above her right ear.

A gunner named James Davidson had discovered the South Seas Club and had made the mistake of mentioning the stunning beauty of Rachel San Nichols to a crewmate. James had been lunching at the South Seas Club daily for a week and had begun working to convince Rachel San Nichols to be his girlfriend.

Several pilots had thrown in together and for the month rented a Guam Bomb—an early 1950s, American-made, four-door sedan with a weathered paint job and an ample number of dents. The island was full of such cars. Up to eight men could squeeze into the Guam Bomb, which was used to shuttle a steady stream of servicemen to the South Seas Club from late morning to early evening.

The men would drink San Miguel beer served in brown, squat bottles and gorge themselves on such Chamorro specialties as barbecued pork ribs, fried balls of Spam drenched in Tabasco, smoked fish and tinaktak, a kind of beef and coconut milk stew. Shuffleboard seemed to be the national pastime in Guam, and the men played for money, with spectators laying down side bets on each game.

The first time Don sat at a table at the club, he ignored the menu and watched Rachel San Nichols's every move. She glided gracefully from table to table. She could balance and carry three plates on each arm and could squeeze the necks of up to four San Miguels between her fingers. She smiled incessantly, and after she'd clunked the bottles of beer down on the table in front of each pilot, she stood next to Don, placed her small hand gently on his back between his shoulder blades, and suggested that everyone try the fresh dorado, which her brother was cooking in the kitchen.

Rachel glided to the bar and glanced back to flash a big smile at Don. Her stout brother stood at a wooden chopping block next to a cast-iron grill vigorously hacking fish, taro, and plantain with a long, slightly curved blade. He looked up, glowered at Don, and continued chopping at full force.

Over the course of the next two weeks, Don rarely spoke to Rachel San Nichols. Instead, he sat and watched her fill the room with energy, ceaseless movement, and charm. He was perfectly sated from the beer, pork ribs, and her presence. That was enough. Plus, he fully expected to be gone within the next couple of days, so why ruin a good thing by acting like an idiot?

Another day passed without a new mission materializing. Most of the regulars at the South Seas Club had decided to play golf instead. Don drove the Guam Bomb alone along the precarious, jungle-lined road that snaked from the flat-topped limestone plateau that made up most of the island before dropping abruptly some six hundred feet to the beaches below.

Rachel San Nichols set a cold beer on the table in front of Don. He watched it sweat in the humidity, water beading heavily on its sides and running down into puddles that encircled the base of the bottle above the polished dark wood.

It began to rain. Big intermittent drops fell on the metal roof and filled the cantina with a hypnotic drumming. Don took several gulps of San Miguel and reveled in the sound of the rain and the sight of Rachel San Nichols.

She walked over and slid a plate of pork ribs in front of him.

Her long hair brushed against his neck as she placed her hand on his back.

"Enjoy," she said softly, so that Don had to strain to hear it.

Don stiffened and smiled. He ate slowly and deliberately, savoring each bite.

Outside lightning flashed, thunder rumbled, and the rain fell ever harder. Inside, the metal roof reverberated until its blunt cacophony drowned out all else. There were no conversations, no outside world, no war in Vietnam.

Don glanced up at the roof.

"Don't worry," said Rachel, almost yelling to be heard. "It'll stop soon. It always does."

Don nodded. Rachel smiled.

By early March, McNamara's doctrine of gradualism was rapidly unfolding. Johnson had approved an eight-week bombing campaign that McNamara had assured would halt Vietcong aggression in its tracks. Dubbed Operation Rolling Thunder, it called for incremental aerial bombing of supply depots, transportation lines, industrial sites, and materiel moving south of Hanoi and north of the Demilitarized Zone. Hanoi and surrounding areas would be off limits, as would the Demilitarized Zone and a thirty-mile buffer along North Vietnam's border with China. The beauty of Operation Rolling Thunder, McNamara told anyone who would listen, was that by attacking trivial sites, destruction would be minimized, thus sparing important locations while holding the entire country hostage. The operation would be tightly controlled from the top down, with each target personally preapproved by either McNamara or Johnson, including the day and hour of the attack, the bomb tonnage, and even the types of aircraft to be flown.

The goal of the strategy was to apply pressure on the North Vietnamese leadership in Hanoi, bringing them to the table for peace negotiations where they would eventually promise to end all hostilities toward the south. All this would be accomplished without having to send significant American ground forces into the fray.

The original plan for Operation Rolling Thunder called for only the use of air force and navy fighter jets. America's huge fleet of B-52s—perhaps the most fearsome and effective war machines on the planet—sat idle and on the sidelines in the Central Pacific.

Ultimately, McNamara's eight-week campaign would stretch into forty-four months.

———

The rain stopped as quickly as it had started. Don finished his meal, left a small tip, and ventured away from the restaurant, down a narrow, sandy path to the nearby lagoon. He stripped to his boxer shorts, tossed his clothes in a pile on the sand, and plunged into the warm, calm water. The late afternoon light was soft and orange, and thunderheads billowed far off on the eastern horizon. Don gracefully glided toward a flat wooden raft anchored a quarter-mile out near the reef where the big open-ocean waves were breaking with silent thunder.

Once on the raft, he lay on his stomach, looked over the edge, and watched the sea life swim by. It was like peering into an aquarium. Urchins with purple-black spines crawled across the lagoon floor, and teeming schools of colorful fish twisted and turned in unison. Don lay in reverie until a large black-tipped fin glided not more than three feet away. "Holy shit!" he yelled, reflexively springing to his feet. He ran across the raft, away from the shark, and dove into the lagoon, churning through the water as fast as he could back to shore.

There likely wasn't anything in the world that terrified Don more than sharks. He'd been neighbors in Pocatello with a sailor who had survived the sinking of the USS *Indianapolis*, which went down during the final days of World War II. The ship had just delivered half the world's supply of uranium-235 to Tinian, an island north of Guam, where final preparations were being made to arm Little Boy prior to its detonation above Hiroshima. Guam would be the last port the *Indianapolis* would ever call on. After loading up with new supplies and fresh sailors, the ship was torpedoed by a Japanese sub en route to the Philippines. Some three hundred men went down with the ship. But over nine hundred floated in the Pacific for four days before rescue ships arrived. Those who didn't drown were eaten alive by sharks. A few more than three hundred survived. Don first heard the story when he was six or seven. It was like a real-life monster movie. As a result, sharks terrified him as a child and terrified him even more now that he was in the water near where those attacks took place.

Don reached the shore and dragged himself onto the sand, exhausted. He looked up to find Rachel holding two beers.

"You weren't out there very long," she observed, handing him a cold beer.

"Shark," Don huffed. "There was a big shark out by the raft."

She smiled.

"*Halu'on unai*," she said reassuringly. "Reef shark. Don't worry about him. He's not out to bother anyone."

Don and Rachel sat in the sand, sipped their beer, and watched the sun—large and orange on the horizon—flatten and then sink surprisingly quickly into the sea. Don was mesmerized by the sunset and was no longer thinking of sharks.

Over the horizon, a war was racing toward crescendo. But in Guam, there was only a warm breeze, a calm lagoon, and the beauty of Rachel San Nichols.

Chapter Fourteen

Alone, alone, all, all alone,
Alone on a wide wide sea!
And never a saint took pity on
My soul in agony.

The many men, so beautiful!
And they all dead did lie:
And a thousand thousand slimy things
Lived on; and so did I.

—Samuel Taylor Coleridge,
"Rime of the Ancient Mariner"

Don looked to the eastern horizon. Darkness had lifted, the roaring wind had subsided into a stiff breeze, and the monster waves had dampened to ten-foot swells. The wall of clouds broke, and between the openings, the sun blazed orange for minutes at a time. Don winced and shielded his eyes like a drunk taking his first step out of a bar well after sunrise.

Typhoon Dinah had been traveling due west, ripping into the jungles of the Luzon Peninsula before its western edge had begun spilling into the South China Sea. Don had fallen through the southwestern quadrant of the storm. Had it continued on its westerly course, it's likely that the eye of the category 5 typhoon would have stampeded over him, providing an oceanic trampling that simply wouldn't have been survivable—not in a small, inflatable raft. But as the great storm crashed into the Luzon Peninsula, it glanced northward and wheeled toward Taiwan.

The clouds continued to break, and Don watched solitary columns of thunderheads glow pink and orange in the morning sun, sweeping north like rearguard sentries protecting the southern flank of a massive army on the march. The sky overhead grew pale and blue. The water turned dark green with a white froth at the crest of each wave. Don stretched his legs and let them hang into the water. He laid his head back, dangled his hands over the side, and stared at the sky. He thought of what he might do to further his odds of survival. Nothing came to him. He was a speck in a vast ocean. The South China Sea is roughly half the size of the continental United States. Finding a solitary person in a small raft—even if you knew where to look—would be like hoping someone flying over Chicago could spot a man standing in a wheat field in Kansas. Don calculated the odds. They weren't good. If he were in a casino, it wasn't a wager he'd put his own money behind. And so he floated. Up and down. Up and down. Up and down.

He looked at his watch. It was still ticking and read 0800 for his time zone. He felt for his service revolver. It was still strapped snug to his hip. He remembered that he'd stashed in a pouch of his flight suit a packet of M&Ms his mother had sent him in a care package. He excitedly reached down his leg and dug through a variety of pockets. The thought of unexpectedly finding some candy thrilled him. He searched frantically but quickly realized that everything he'd placed in his pockets had been blown out during the ejection. Deeply disappointed, he went back to floating and staring at the sky.

He began to retch again. Over and over and over. Like the infinite waves, the nausea wouldn't stop. His lips and mouth and throat were raw from all the saltwater he'd ingested. Each time he vomited, the acidic bile burned, leaving him in agony.

Don hated the ocean. He'd grown up in Idaho and had never set foot in it until only a few months earlier, when his squadron had been sent to Guam. But a white sand beach and a calm, shallow lagoon are one thing. Deep, open water is something else altogether. It is one of the most inhospitable places a human can be. Given the choice, Don would rather be in the air. Flying was exhilarating, serene, and life affirming. Both the air and the sea were almost equally unforgiving of mistakes. And both were isolating and solitary. But Don found the ocean to be savage and terrifying. He preferred the sky any day.

Don came from a family of storytellers and talkers. He had five brothers and sisters and dozens of cousins. The house was never quiet, and Don was perhaps the loudest and most opinionated of them all. A small raft in the middle of the ocean was an uncomfortable place for more reasons than the obvious.

With no one to talk to, the only thing remaining was to stretch out and be alone with his thoughts. How long would he live? Another day? Two days? Three?

He'd grown up with God and religion everywhere. In church. At home. All over the town of Pocatello. But when you're a speck in the middle of the ocean, what does God really mean, anyway? You're nothing special—just a small morsel of fish food that will soon be reunited with all the molecules of the sea. Don had always suspected himself of agnosticism; it's just that floating in the ocean has a way of making you confront and acknowledge such a belief.

What would it be like to drown? Would it hurt? Would it be better to just inhale a big blast of seawater and get it over with, or would you owe it to yourself to fight to the bitter end, holding your breath until you'd almost passed out?

Would they ever find his body? Would he wash up eventually on some island? Or would he slip below the waves and join his place in the food chain?

Don stared at the sky, which was growing whiter as the sun rose higher. The waves continued to subside, with swells of maybe six feet. His arms and legs were splayed across the raft and hanging in the water. He no longer bothered with the effort required to vomit over the side. He simply turned his head and retched onto his right shoulder. The next wave would just splash over him and wash it off anyway.

Don continued to think, but something in his peripheral vision jolted him upright. He pulled in his legs and grabbed his knees with his hands. His eyes scanned the surface around the boat. He wasn't yet sure whether he'd actually seen something or just imagined it. From beneath a wave, a large fin sliced the water and came again to the surface. It passed along the side of the raft and turned behind him before slipping again out of view. Don's heart raced.

"Crap," he thought. "I'm not even going to get a chance to drown. I'm going to be eaten."

He visualized death by shark. Would the shark be patient and wait for him to die of thirst before dragging him from the raft? Or would it eventually figure out that there was something large, tasty, and worth eating on top of that floating object? It could surely smell the blood and vomit. Perhaps it would brush against the raft and puncture it with its sandpaper-rough skin. Or perhaps it would just bite into the raft, leaving Don to tumble into the water so that the shark could then take its time biting chunks from his flesh with each thrashing pass.

The fin rose again, slicing a wide arc near the foot of the raft. Don slowly pulled his .38 from its holster. He held the gun, opened the chamber and inspected the six brass bullet casings. Already the pistol was beginning to rust because of the saltwater and humidity. He surmised that it would be just about impossible to seriously wound or even scare the shark with a handgun. Plus, that would likely just attract more of its friends. No, Don was practical. The gambler in him knew when it was time to fold. He concluded that the best use of the gun would be to turn it on himself if he had to. He'd faced a number of forms of death over the past several hours, but getting eaten alive by a wild animal was by far the most terrifying. If the shark managed to breach his raft, Don decided that he'd try to empty five bullets into the shark, saving the sixth bullet for himself, if necessary. After all, a bullet to the brain would be a better way to go, he thought. And it wouldn't be cowardice, he rationalized; just call it a personal preference. He removed a single bullet from the chamber and carefully placed it in a breast pocket on his flight suit, where it wouldn't fall out. That was the bullet he'd use on himself if it came to that. He didn't want to risk leaving it in the gun and forgetting how many shots he'd fired. There was no way that shark was taking him alive.

Don continued scanning the water around the raft in vigilance for the fin. It would rise briefly and unexpectedly, glistening a dark greenish gray before disappearing as quickly and quietly as it came. Don wondered where the most effective place to shoot himself would be. After considering all the options, he concluded that just behind the right ear would be best. He then thought about where his body would end up. Most of it would be eaten, but perhaps some would fall to the ocean floor and become part of the primordial ooze. His blood would disperse through the water, carried by the ocean current. Theoretically, the molecules of himself would eventually be distributed throughout the world's oceans, and he would be broken down into the smallest of elements.

The thought of death now brought only peace. There was no fear. Don was resigned to it. He bobbed in his raft in the ocean, clutching his gun and on the lookout for a fin. The breeze that blew over his soaked flight suit made him shiver, but the sun had grown bright and warm.

Chapter Fifteen

Col. Kline was frantic. He'd spent a full month watching the world's best-trained bomber pilots grow soft from an endless diet of beach going, eating, drinking, fishing, snorkeling, golfing, tanning, loafing, and womanizing. This was the United States Air Force, damn it, not Club Med. There was a war going on, but you certainly got no sense of that from looking around Andersen Air Base.

Col. Kline advised that, starting immediately, there would be a daily briefing at 0900. Attendance was mandatory.

At the first briefing, Col. Kline gave an update regarding the pending status of the squadron's next mission. He said that Operation Rolling Thunder had begun and was being executed by small fighter jet wings from the air force and navy. The brass in Washington had assured him that the operation would last only until early May and that there would be no likely need for B-52s in the Vietnam conflict. He told the men to enjoy the warm weather because by summer, most of the flight crews would be back to flying Chrome Dome missions over the Arctic. However, he reminded the men that they were on alert and near a war zone; they could be called into action at any minute, so readiness was essential.

The briefing lasted thirty minutes. Pilots gathered afterward and chatted about the wisdom of Rolling Thunder. To a man, they agreed it was FUBAR—effed up beyond all recognition. There was no way fighter jets could bring even a small country like North Vietnam to its knees by punching at its jungle midsection. The consensus was that the jet jockeys needed to step aside and let the big boys take out Hanoi in one or two missions.

The men glanced at the rows of bombers parked at the edge of the base. They shook their heads and muttered. Then they immediately returned to their daily dose of beach going, eating, drinking, fishing, snorkeling, golfing, tanning, loafing, and womanizing.

The *Red Rooster* was a sportfishing boat that the US Air Force had recently commandeered to help boost troop morale. The pilots supposed that this was part of the readiness to which Col. Kline had referred in his briefing.

A pod of dolphins swam ahead of the bow's wake as the boat headed for open water north of the island. The dolphins arced gray and glistening, seemingly leading the ship to its destination. The vessel would startle schools of flying fish, causing them to periodically erupt from beneath the surface. The men could hear the buzz of their fins as they flew in bursts and then glided a couple of feet above the water before plunging their short, narrow bodies back into the ocean with barely a ripple.

Though the airmen on the stern were supposedly trolling for marlin and dorado, they seemed more interested in drinking San Miguel. About a mile and a half from shore, directly aligned with the end of the runway at Andersen Air Base, was a fishing trawler bristling with radio antennas. It had appeared over a month earlier and had been plying the same waters ever since. Romo, the stocky Guamanian fishing boat captain, instructed the men to reel in their lines. He throttled up the *Red Rooster* and chopped through the waves toward the trawler. He passed at full speed within twenty feet of the ship and made a sharp starboard turn, kicking out a huge wake that crashed into the trawler's port broadside. The trawler tilted twenty degrees and then began rocking hard, side to side. Half a dozen men emerged from the bridge and below decks and were cursing loudly in a foreign language. Romo throttled down, made a sharp turn, and prepared for a slow second pass along the trawler's starboard side.

The seamen lined the rail of the trawler to get a close look at the rogue sport fishing boat.

"Privet amerikanskim comrades!" they yelled, smiling and waving.

"Fuck you, Russian scum!" the airmen yelled back, each holding their middle fingers high.

The Russians laughed and stood in mock salute. One of the airmen tossed an empty bottle of San Miguel that splashed two feet short of the trawler.

"We trade you vodka for beer," the trawler captain offered cheerfully. He seemed amused and genuinely happy to see other people—even Americans—after so many weeks at sea.

The airmen laughed and for a moment seriously considered the trade. A few bottles of genuine Russian vodka—though clearly contraband—would be like gold back at the base.

Romo slowly increased the throttle and began to maneuver away.

"Do svidanya," waved the Russians. "Do svidanya."

"Have fun in Vietnam," yelled the trawler captain in near-perfect English.

Romo pushed the throttle toward full. The *Red Rooster*'s bow lifted off the water and the engine churned a tail of white foam. As the Americans sped away, the trawler continued rocking wearily from side to side.

By the middle of March, Col. Kline could see that his daily briefings were having little impact on base discipline. With no orders except "continue to maintain readiness," Col. Kline felt as though he'd been marooned at a tropical country club. At his morning briefing, he introduced a new plan meant to busy idle hands. Pilots and their crews were required to fulfill annual training checklists for a variety of maneuvers and procedures. With an abundance of downtime, Col. Kline declared that this would be the perfect time to check some boxes.

Every morning, Don and his crew would hurtle down the runway and launch into the Pacific sky. They would always look for the Russian trawler and were sure to buzz it whenever possible. The crew would fly to the nearby islands in the Northern Marianas, bank hard, return to base, fly several touch-and-goes, buzz the Russian trawler yet again, and then bring the big plane in for a final landing. They were usually back in time for lunch at the South Seas Club.

By mid-April, every flight crew member in the bomber wing had fulfilled his training regimen for the entire year. Col. Kline was out of ideas for keeping the men busy. Even his enthusiasm for the daily morning briefings began to wane.

But far over the western horizon, a war began to fully take form. Rolling Thunder was nearing the end of McNamara's promised eight-week run without any discernable progress. In fact, things in Vietnam were only getting worse. Much worse. The South Vietnamese government had collapsed. The Vietcong had raided a number of American strongholds with impunity. The Soviets had flooded the country with antiaircraft batteries and deadly surface-to-air missiles. The Americans were shocked at the number of planes that had been downed and the number of pilots who'd been lost. By the end of the year, Soviet MiGs and surface-to-air missiles (SAMs) would notch an astounding 170 kills of US aircraft.

In April, the United States asked North Vietnamese premier Pham Van Dong if he'd had enough. He quickly replied that he hadn't and said he would sit for peace negotiations only if the Americans ceased their bombing and removed all troops from Indochina.

McNamara was perplexed. So he talked Johnson into extending Rolling Thunder and doubled down on the number of sorties. The air force and navy were now flying at a rate of over four thousand combat missions per month as May arrived. Pilots pinpointed coordinates for over two dozen SAM firing locations that had been responsible for downing the majority of American planes. The air force requested permission to take the missile batteries out. McNamara denied the request because the batteries were too close to city centers. Instead, he called in ground troops, ostensibly to protect American bases and airfields.

Andersen Air Base was quiet. Palms bent gently in the trade winds. Over five dozen B-52 tail fins towered in silhouette above the tarmac. The Russians bobbed in a trawler off the north point of Guam, drinking vodka and reporting little. Back on base, even Col. Kline had taken up the game of golf.

Chapter Sixteen

Don felt hot and cold at the same time. The sun blazed large and pale directly overhead. His raft was filled with seawater and vomit. He was weak with exhaustion, and his head began to throb from dehydration. He wondered how long he could continue to vomit and lose fluids before he would fade into unconsciousness. One hour? Three? Six? Twenty-four? He felt an urge to sleep but remembered the shark and didn't think he could risk it—not necessarily because he worried so much about dying, but because if the shark attacked him while Don was sleeping, he might not have time to put a bullet in his own head and thus would be eaten alive. It seemed that now his primary mission was to avoid getting eaten alive by a shark. His secondary mission was to stay alive long enough to perhaps get rescued. Don thought that as a gambler, the safe bet right now would be to put everything on the shark. He reached into the left breast pocket of his flight suit and pulled out the sixth bullet for his revolver. He held it up to the sun, and the brass gleamed. He rolled it between his index finger and thumb and thought how easy it would be to sleep forever.

The fin rose closer and cut effortlessly through the waves. There was no black tip, and it was much, much larger than the fin that belonged to Don's friend, the harmless *halu'on unai* that haunted the placid lagoons of Guam. He wondered about Rachel San Nichols and whether she'd cry when she discovered Don had died. He hoped she wouldn't take the news too badly. He was sorry he'd visited this misery upon her. He wondered what the Chamorro word was for "hammerhead" or "great white" or "tiger shark." He was pretty sure his visitor was one of those three. He made a mental note to be sure to describe the fin to Rachel San Nichols so that if he ever made it out of this alive, he would at least have a name to give the fin that would likely forever haunt his dreams.

Don kissed his bullet and carefully placed it deep into his breast pocket. His eyelids grew heavy. The shark circled. The world went black.

—⁕—

The sky roared. Don startled back to consciousness. He felt the rubber sides of his raft. Inside, seawater and vomit sloshed. For a few seconds he wasn't sure where he was. At home in Sacramento? At base in Guam? He squinted at the sky. The roar turned into a shriek, and the shadow of a massive KC-135 tanker jet passed over. The plane was maybe two hundred feet above the water. Don kneeled in his shaky raft and screamed, waving his arms above his head as the big jet rose toward the sun.

The tanker jet flew toward the horizon and disappeared over the waves. Don slumped back into his raft. He shook with guarded excitement. He wasn't sure whether the pilots had spotted him and hoped against hope that they had. It was silent except for the sloshing. Each time Don crested a wave, he scanned the northern horizon. The shark fin reappeared, and for the first time in hours he thought a smart gambler might place money on Don rather than the shark.

Water sloshed. Waves rose. Waves fell. Don trembled. He strained to listen for a jet engine. He waited.

Don crested a wave and caught a glimpse of the KC-135 coming in low from the north. The engines filled the air with a deep, rising rumble. The plane came overhead, not more than one hundred feet off the water. Don could hear the metallic whine of the jet's turbines. A large hatch on the back belly of the plane was open. A round, orange, ten-foot-diameter raft was shoved out. It spun and wobbled to the ocean's surface, landing about fifty yards from Don.

"I'm saved! I'm saved!" he thought.

Or maybe he'd yelled it out loud. He wasn't sure. It didn't matter. He was euphoric.

The KC-135 throttled up and disappeared into the sky.

Don kneeled and paddled with his hands toward the new raft. He imagined all the survival gear aboard: water, food, dry clothes, blankets, flares, radio, and medicine for sea sickness.

Don paddled furiously but didn't seem to be able to close the distance between the two rafts. Because of the shark, he only dared use his hands to paddle. He could see the new raft only when he crested a wave. He paddled himself to complete exhaustion. The distance between the rafts grew. After about twenty minutes, the new raft disappeared behind a wave, some two hundred yards out. Don never saw it again.

He sank back into the bile, dejected but hopeful. Every muscle in his body shook. The smart money, once again, began to lean back toward the shark.

CHAPTER SEVENTEEN

DON HAD NEVER SEEN A COFFIN DRAPED IN AN AMERICAN FLAG BEFORE. After he'd completed a B-52 training run at Andersen, the driver of his air crew slowed as they crossed the tarmac. More than two dozen coffins were being hoisted into the cargo bay of a KC-135, which was scheduled to soon depart for the States. The men passed in silence.

"Holy shit," Terry Lowry whispered in awe. "I thought we were supposed to be in and out. What the hell's going on?"

"Well, for starters," said Don, "they've had us here cooling our heels for three months. This thing would've already been over had we just flown our original mission."

The men all nodded, and another coffin was hoisted aboard.

Death is a familiar companion of any military pilot, even in peacetime. Don already knew two pilots who had died in crashes back in the States. But in wartime, death is omnipresent. The good pilots can hear death's constant whisper and not mind. The others? They live with a relentless fear, a tension that never eases. That alone sometimes gives death an open door.

Pilots were being shot down at a dizzying rate. Everyone at Andersen knew someone who had been killed or captured or lost.

The golf and the swimming and the drinking became less fun. It was quickly apparent that in war, there was no such thing as a quick little skirmish—no in and out. This was serious. It was life or death. It was bloody and brutal. Anyone could die at any time. It was war. And they were in it.

"Men," Col. Kline began. "Welcome to the daily briefing of 17 May 1965. Your country thanks you for your patience in these trying times. You have been without a clear mission for over three months. And I know you are all eager to help put a quick end to communist aggression in Indochina and to support your brothers in arms. That chance has come. I have here your new orders. It is a mission called Operation Arc Light."

CHAPTER EIGHTEEN

Whereto answering, the sea,
Delaying not, hurrying not,
Whisper'd me through the night, and very plainly before daybreak,
Lisp'd to me the low and delicious word death,
And again death, death, death, death,
Hissing melodious, neither like the bird nor like my arous'd child's
heart,
But edging near as privately for me rustling at my feet,
Creeping thence steadily up to my ears and laving me softly all over,
Death, death, death, death, death.

Which I do not forget,
But fuse the song of my dusky demon and brother,
That he sang to me in the moonlight on Paumanok's gray beach,
With the thousand responsive songs at random,
My own songs awaked from that hour,
And with them the key, the word up from the waves,
The word of the sweetest song and all songs,
That strong and delicious word which, creeping to my feet,
(Or like some old crone rocking the cradle,
swathed in sweet garments, bending aside,)
The sea whisper'd me.

—WALT WHITMAN, "OUT OF THE
CRADLE ENDLESSLY ROCKING"

DON LAY LISTLESS IN HIS RAFT, SLOSHING UP ONE SIDE OF A WAVE AND
sloshing back down the other side. Sloshing up. Sloshing down. Sloshing

up. Sloshing down. Sloshing up. Sloshing down. Up. Down. Up. Down. Up. Down.

It was growing difficult for Don to discern where the ocean ended and the sky began. He was soaked in seawater and crusted with salt. It felt as though the vast ocean would soon absorb him. He thought about Fick's laws of diffusion, which describe how a mass of high concentration eventually diffuses into a mass of low concentration until, overall, an equilibrium, or steady state, is achieved. He recalled some of Fick's formulas and mathematical equations and let them dance momentarily in his head. He imagined his blood, urine, tears, and sweat seeping into the water before being sucked into a current and perhaps spreading across the surface of all he could see, unfurling toward the horizon in a sheen maybe a couple of molecules thick.

Sloshing up. Sloshing down. Sloshing up. Sloshing down. Sloshing up. Sloshing down. Up. Down. Up. Down. Up. Down.

But then the wind blew stiff and cool and the sun glowed warm and pale, and his face burned, and his lips cracked. Maybe, Don thought, the sky would claim him instead. He was a pilot after all. Soon the winds would calm, the seas would flatten, and the sun would blaze. Instead of being claimed by the sea, his blood, urine, tears, and sweat would evaporate into the sky, molecule after molecule rising into the canopy of hot, tropical air. His skin would stretch brown and tight across his protruding bones. His eyes would sink, and his teeth, bleached by the sun, would gleam dull and white.

Sloshing up. Sloshing down. Sloshing up. Sloshing down. Sloshing up. Sloshing down. Up. Down. Up. Down. Up. Down.

Don was never really sure when he'd lost his fear of death. He still feared sharks. But he didn't fear dying. And, for certain, he never thought of death in the same way again. Not after it came lapping and sloshing across his body, so certain of its victory over him.

Sloshing up. Sloshing down. Sloshing up. Sloshing down. Sloshing up. Sloshing down. Up. Down. Up. Down. Up. Down.

And, of course, this changed him. Forever. He felt at one with the ocean. At one with the sky. His strong sense of self had diffused and he was now part of something bigger. Something omnipresent. Something omnipotent.

Sloshing up. Sloshing down. Sloshing up. Sloshing down. Sloshing up. Sloshing down. Up. Down. Up. Down. Up. Down.

Don closed his eyes and listened to the wind. He crested a wave and heard a faint gurgle. He sloshed into a trough, crested, and again heard a gurgle. His eyes flashed open and his body reflexively tensed. He listened intently to the wind and the sloshing water. He crested another wave and heard a gurgle and a sputter. The sound came on—then off—in rhythm with the waves, as though someone were playing with a radio dial. He sat upright and scanned whatever he could see of the horizon. The sound grew louder and less intermittent.

Don crested another wave and then spotted it—a twin-engine sea plane was spluttering through choppy seas, perhaps two hundred yards away, picking its way toward him. The rescue plane, an HU-16 Albatross, was struggling, its nose tilting skyward as it climbed each swell before plunging back down, its tail now tilting up. The plane rocked its way across the surface, two pontoons at the end of each wing keeping its propellers high and out of the water, with the plane's midsection acting like a large canoe.

Don kneeled as best he could in his sad, sagging, soggy, vomit-filled raft. His heart soared and euphoria electrified his body. He tried to control his emotions but found himself laughing maniacally. He raised his arms and waved them in a crossing motion overhead. He could see the crew in the cockpit, and they began waving back. The pilot maneuvered the plane as close as he could to Don's raft. The propellers whined and sharp whiffs of exhaust swirled in the wind. The pilot tried to keep the plane steady, but it rocked violently, the waves slapping hard against its aluminum skin. Don worried about getting inadvertently sucked into one of the propellers. The plane now loomed large beside him, and he could see more of the crew waving to him from an open door behind the left wing. Don could feel a blast of air from the nearest propeller. He saw a tie-down ring on the left pontoon only a few feet away and dove for it. He felt surprisingly weak as he tried to swim, but as soon as he was able to grasp the ring, he gripped it tight with his right hand and put his left arm through it for good measure. There was no way he'd be alone in the ocean ever again.

A head popped up out of the water next to him. Don was confused by the commotion and wondered if he were hallucinating this entire sequence. Perhaps he was still in his raft dreaming of mermaids or Neptune. The bobbing young man had a crew cut, a broad smile, and a square jaw. He was a parajumper, or PJ, the air force's equivalent of the navy SEALs.

The PJ grabbed Don's forearm and motioned for him to wrap his arms around the PJ's back. Don clung to the tie ring, his first contact with anything safe since his collision. He couldn't, wouldn't let go. The PJ motioned again. Don clung tighter.

The PJ pulled closer and yelled into Don's ear over the whine of the propellers.

"Lieutenant, it's okay. Let go. You're okay. Let go and hang on."

Don loosened his grip, and the PJ pulled him away from the pontoon. Don thrashed in the water, frantically grabbed the PJ and wrapped his arms tight around his chest. The PJ seemed almost twice as big as Don and glided effortlessly toward the plane's open door. Several hands grabbed Don, yanked him from the ocean, and pulled him up and into the plane.

Don, still tethered to his raft, turned and began pulling the tether hand over hand. He lifted the raft out of the water and started hoisting it into the plane's cabin. The PJ noticed what he was doing, pulled out a knife, and severed the cord.

"Hey," Don yelled. "What are you doing? I need that."

The raft had saved his life. And though it was an inanimate object, Don felt a sense of connection and gratitude. He couldn't just leave a trusted comrade floating in the South China Sea.

The PJ lifted his knife overhead, stabbed the raft, and sank the blade deep into its yellow bladder. He pulled the knife toward him, leaving a foot-long gash. He then stabbed and slashed the final inflated bladder on its other side.

"What are you doing?" Don cried out in near anguish. "That's my raft."

The PJ didn't seem to understand. None of the men on the plane seemed to understand. They had to restrain Don from jumping back into the ocean to save his now-deflated raft, which the PJ had balled up and shoved away from the aircraft. Don mournfully watched the bright yellow ball shimmer and waver as it sank farther and farther beneath the pale green water. A wave rose and the yellow shimmer ceased. Don resigned himself to its loss and dropped his head in frustration.

"C'mon, Lt. Harten," a crew member said, gently putting an arm around him, turning him away from the open door, and guiding him toward his seat. "Let's get you stripped down and wrapped in some blankets. Just be calm. You're safe now. You're safe."

Chapter Nineteen

The PJ buckled Don into a passenger seat. He'd been stripped down to his underwear and a T-shirt and was wrapped in a large, thick, wool blanket.

Don turned his head and saw another blanket-wrapped figure seated across the aisle from him. The figure sat hunched and had skin that appeared deathly white. Don leaned closer to get a better look. He worried that he, too, looked that bad. The man retched into half of a Mae West bladder the PJ had thoughtfully cut open for him.

"Lt. Col. Chuck Andermann?" Don thought.

Don leaned closer, thrilled that there had been at least one other survivor, even if it was from the other B-52.

"Col. Andermann?" Don exclaimed, still unsure.

The man lifted his head from the Mae West bladder and turned toward Don.

"Gaaaathpphhh," he said. "Gaaaathpphhh."

"How are you feeling, Col. Andermann?" Don asked in a lower, more-concerned voice. "You okay?"

"Gaaaathpphhh," he repeated. "Gaaaathpphhh." He then turned back to his Mae West and retched.

"Whose crew are you on?" Don asked after Andermann was done retching. He was curious as to whom he'd crashed into.

The man lifted his head, labored to form words, and then lurched back down to his Mae West and resumed retching.

The PJ tapped Don's shoulder and pointed toward the cockpit.

"Capt. Joe Robertson," the PJ yelled over the noise of the plane, which had resumed taxiing through the choppy waters, searching for more survivors.

"Aircraft Commander Joe Robertson?" Don thought. So that's whose crew they'd collided with. Capt. Robertson was seated in the jump seat and appeared to be helping the crew spot survivors. Don knew Joe's copilot, Jim Marshall, well. He hoped that Jim had made it and wondered how Capt. Robertson could look in decent shape while Lt. Col. Andermann appeared close to death. Regardless, he was again thrilled to see even one more person still alive.

Don was strapped into a seat next to a small porthole that afforded him a view of the left wing and propeller. The PJ handed him a cut-open Mae West bladder and instructed him, almost cheerfully, "Lt. Harten, you can barf into this."

Don smiled, nodded his head and promptly retched into the Mae West. He stared at the propeller, which whirred silver and mesmerizing in the afternoon sun. He tried to scan the horizon to see whether he could spot anyone or anything, but the surface of the South China Sea, in the wake of Typhoon Dinah, was a rambunctious sprawl of swells that rose and fell between six and twelve feet. Don peered out the porthole for a minute, quickly became queasy, and again retched into his Mae West. Nevertheless, he couldn't remember ever being so happy.

Don looked out the porthole again and spotted something bobbing in the waves. He tapped the PJ, who nodded and replied, "Yes, we're taxiing up to another raft."

Don's euphoria returned. He was anxious to discover which of his comrades had made it. He ran several names through his head, but that exercise became stressful—sort of a Solomon's choice. Each time he hoped to see a specific colleague, he felt mortally sad for the other men he'd excluded. He finally just cleared his mind and stared down at his Mae West.

The plane taxied up to the raft, Don peered through the porthole, and euphoria once again swept through him.

"Jim Erbes," Don said aloud. "It's Jim Erbes."

Erbes was the electronic warfare officer on Don's crew. He was glad to know someone else had survived from his plane and hoped there might be others.

Erbes floated toward the back hatch of the plane, and Don waved excitedly from his small porthole.

"Jim Erbes," he thought. "Well, I'll be damned. I'm so happy for him. Now, let's keep taxiing until we pick everyone up."

The PJ pulled Erbes into the plane, stripped him down, bundled him up, and strapped him in a seat across from Don.

Erbes laughed, shook his head, and waved at Don. Don laughed and waved back.

The Albatross resumed taxiing in its continued quest for survivors.

As soon as Erbes had settled into his seat, Don caught a glimpse of another raft, bobbing on the horizon.

"Oh, man," he thought. "This is great. At this rate, we'll have found everyone in just an hour or two. It's amazing that you can fall into a great big ocean and in less than twelve hours communication is sent halfway around the world and crews are quickly dispatched to find you and pluck you out of an impossible situation. It's so great to be an American."

The Albatross spluttered toward the new raft, and soon Don could see that the survivor was Jay Collier, the navigator from Don's crew.

Don again was elated. At this rate, he became convinced that they would quickly find everyone, though he harbored the dark secret of Maj. Jim Gehrig, who'd failed to buckle into his seat and thus had ejected without a parachute—a secret Don had already determined he'd keep from any official reports or accounts of the accident. He'd rather Maj. Gehrig be remembered for dying a hero, thus saving him the indignity of perishing due to something as simple as failing to buckle a seatbelt. A family knowing that their son, brother, husband, father had perhaps been lost at sea was bad enough, but the image of that man falling thirty thousand feet through a typhoon and into the ocean was altogether a different level of horror. It's something Don wanted to save the family from. He'd already replayed the image in his head dozens of times and could only imagine Gehrig's children replaying the image, too, for decades hence. Their father falling, falling, falling. The wind rippling his flight suit. His arms and legs flailing in the darkness. His screams swallowed by the enormity of a great typhoon. The surreal sight of jet fuel burning on the dark, churning water. All of it rushing toward him during a free fall that would take nearly three full minutes. And, of course, at times, three minutes can pass in a flash. But at other times, and Don was certain that this was the case with Maj. Gehrig, three minutes can be an eternity, especially when you're amped on terror and adrenaline with the full knowledge that death is unavoidable and imminent. Three minutes can indeed be a world of time.

Don shuddered and chose to turn his attention back to Jay Collier, pushing thoughts of the unfortunate Maj. Gehrig to a part of the mind that every combatant in every war learns to store and contain all the assorted horrors they've managed to accumulate.

Don saw Collier board the plane and became euphoric again. He still couldn't believe his luck and, until now, still wasn't sure he was really going to survive and make it out of the South China Sea. But his confidence in the future grew. How great is it going to be, he thought, to get together with both crews from both planes and drink beer and tell tales of how they'd all cheated death? What stories they'd all have.

Don shook his head, smiled, and again thought, "It's great to be an American."

The Albatross taxied for another hour. No other life rafts were seen. Don's euphoria faded. He looked down and noticed seawater swirling around his bare feet. He looked toward the center of the cabin and saw a large, red disc in the center of the cabin floor. The disc had begun rising and dropping with each wave. Water gushed from beneath it and had started sloshing through the cabin.

A young captain named Dave Haines, the Albatross's copilot, walked back from the cockpit with a clipboard and a pen. He asked each person on the plane for their name and service number. He then went back through and asked each person again, careful to double check so that he wouldn't report back any erroneous information.

Don had become worried about the water in the cabin and pointed out the obstreperous red disc.

The copilot nodded and leaned toward Don.

"That's our bilge cover," Haines noted. "It means our bilge is full, and if we don't take off soon, we're going to sink."

A sense of dread again rushed through Don.

"Sink?" he thought. "We might sink?!"

Don had never been in a seaplane before, and in spite of the elation he'd felt about getting rescued, he was leery about all the waves and bilge-water. He wasn't confident about the plane's capabilities.

Haines clapped Don on the shoulder and yelled over the noise, "Don't worry, we'll be airborne here in a minute or two. As soon as we lift into the air, we'll dump the bilge, and all this water'll be gone."

The copilot took his seat in the cockpit, and the engines revved. The Albatross taxied forward and turned into the wind. The captain throttled up the engines. The propellers whirred, the plane accelerated and began skimming violently over the choppy seas, much like a loaded-down pickup truck rambling altogether too fast over an impossibly rutted dirt road.

Don bounced hard in his seat and clasped his seatbelt harness with both hands. The red bilge cover shot up and water intermittently sprayed into the cabin like a geyser. Don looked over at the PJ, who'd flown in such planes dozens, if not hundreds, of times, to see whether he should be worried or not. The PJ was stoic and showed no sign of emotion or concern.

The Albatross whined louder, and Don could feel the plane starting to lift.

Bam!

The plane's flat belly and pontoons smashed the face of a large wave. The propellers, perched high on the wings in order to avoid contact with water, sliced hard into the crest of the big swell. The engines chugged with a deep-throated rumble. The props sprayed pellets of water, machine-gunning the side of the plane, which pinged with the tattering din of what sounded like a blast of hailstones. The crew and passengers were jolted hard, and the entire cabin shook.

The plane stabilized and floated back downward, unable to get airborne due to the choppy water and full bilge.

Bam!

The plane hit another wave.

Bam!

Another.

Bam!

Again.

The pilot throttled down and the plane bucked to a stop on the water.

"Jesus," Don thought. "I've never piloted a seaplane, but I don't think these guys can get us out of here in these conditions."

He looked toward the cockpit and could see the pilot and copilot conferring.

The plane drifted in the waves before the pilot again revved the engines and turned into the wind. The plane rumbled and slapped and bounced along the surface. Again, it gained speed and began to lift skyward. Again, the bilge cover lifted and ocean water spewed into the cabin.

And again: Bam! Bam! Bam!

Don feared the plane would break apart.

The pilots, frustrated, throttled back down, drifted in the waves, and continued to confer. The PJ sat stoic.

The pilots turned into the wind, throttled up, and were met again with Bam! Bam! Bam! as waves slapped violently into the plane's underbelly every time it threatened to become airborne.

This occurred on six straight attempts.

On the seventh, the pilots turned the Albatross into the wind and gunned the engines to full throttle. The plane skimmed and bounced along the surface. The wind caught the wings and pulled the plane skyward.

Don counted: "One, two, three . . ." They were airborne. At last.

But then he could feel the plane sinking back to the surface of the sea. Bam!

The underbelly of the Albatross slammed into a wave that felt like concrete. It was the most violent of all the bumps, and Don expected that the plane would break up and he again would be dead. The engines paused, strained mightily by the propeller's collision with the water. But then they coughed, rumbled, and revved.

And with that, the plane's nose lifted. The Albatross rose skyward, picking up speed.

But once again, it slowly drifted back to the surface, and Bam!

The plane shuddered. The crew and passengers were jolted hard in their seats. Don expected the aircraft to blow apart.

But the plane angled skyward, picked up speed and began, finally, to lift away from the ocean in earnest.

Don again counted, "One, two, three, four, five, six . . ."

The bilge began to spew its contents back into the sea, and as the plane grew lighter, it rose higher. A sucking sound beneath the red disc created a sloshing swirl above it, pulling water out of the cabin much like an unplugged bathtub.

Don was again elated. Each second the plane was airborne was another second he was closer to ever seeing home again.

He peered out of his porthole and could see the expanse of a pale green ocean, choppy with white-capped waves. The plane was one hundred feet, maybe two hundred feet off the surface. It was gaining speed but straining to gain altitude.

Don heard the right engine cough, and he was thrown forward. The plane slowed and banked hard right.

"Holy mother of god," Don thought. "This can't be happening."

The plane continued to bank.

"C'mon, engine. C'mon, engine," he begged.

The South China Sea rushed toward him.

Don put his head down and gripped his seat belt harness tightly.

The plane slammed violently into the water, bouncing and spinning and tearing in places like an aluminum can. It sloshed to a stop, and Don opened his eyes, amazed that he was once again alive.

The bilge cover was up, and water gushed into the plane at a frightful rate. Don looked out his porthole and could see the left propeller rotating slowly and aimlessly on its spindle. He looked across the cabin and could see that the right propeller was bent and mangled. Don surmised that it had been damaged by one or more of the waves prior to takeoff, thus putting enough strain on the engine to cause it to fail in midflight.

"Jesus. Sweet Jesus," Don thought. "How is this possible?"

He looked at each of his comrades' stunned faces as they struggled to assess their situation. Lt. Col. Andermann was ghost white, and his dread was palpable. No stranger to calamity, he'd been shot down in a B-17 over Austria in World War II and had spent time in Stalag Luft III, site of the "great escape." But now he appeared to have neither the stamina nor the inclination to get back into the water.

Don locked eyes with Jim Erbes, who normally had a calm demeanor. But he, too, looked panicked.

The red bilge cover floated by, and Don knew then that they were going to sink. He cursed the PJ for slicing up his raft and began searching for anything that might float.

The PJ, meanwhile, had already unbuckled himself and had set calmly and professionally about doing his job, which primarily entailed dealing with disaster. The PJ approached Don and checked him for any severe injury.

"I'm moving everyone toward the back hatch," the PJ said, "in case we need to abandon the aircraft."

Don got out of his seat and sloshed knee-deep through the water. He turned back and saw that Joe Robertson was still seated in the cockpit jump seat.

Don tugged on the PJ's arm and pointed back toward the cockpit.

"Hey, isn't Joe Robertson coming back here?"

"Lt. Harten," the PJ said matter-of-factly, "Capt. Robertson is dead."

Chapter Twenty

Don huddled in the back of the plane with the two pilots, the PJ, and the other three crash survivors. He was frantic and terrified about having to jump back into the ocean, this time without a raft or survival gear. Between that and the sharks, he was sure that death was now certain should the plane go beneath the waves.

The PJ stuck his head out the door, pointed, and then invited Don to take a look. Don gripped a handle near the door and gingerly stuck his head outside of the plane, which was still rocking wildly in the choppy swells.

It had been such a surreal daisy chain of events that he was prepared for anything. Sea serpents. A great white whale. Neptune with his trident. Reality had long ago taken leave, and this could all be a grand hallucination anyway.

Don looked up and saw the big black and orange freighter that had passed near him in the night. He'd already pretty much convinced himself that the ship had been a hallucination the first time he'd seen it slip effortlessly through the storm, off in the distance, powering through monstrous waves, horizontal rain, howling wind, and flickers of lightning as though it were a phantom. And now that it was floating only a quarter mile from his wrecked seaplane, as seemingly large and solid as an island, Don had no idea what to think.

A wooden longboat crested a wave, its oars flailing briefly in the air, before the vessel dropped back down. The oars again caught water and continued stroking in unison. The boat pulled up next to the hatch, and Don could hear the half-dozen men crewing it speaking a Scandinavian language.

"Vikings," Don thought. "We're being rescued by Vikings in a long-boat?"

The Norse sailors reached their hands out and pulled each of the American airmen from the stricken plane, seating them on planks inside the long, narrow rowboat.

Don sat on his plank, stunned, as the big Norwegians worked their oars and muscled the boat through the waves back toward their mother ship, which now towered before them.

Don looked back toward the mangled Albatross, and a sense of loss and finality washed over him. This was it. There would be no other survivors. The hope Don had initially felt after his own rescue had been completely dashed. And in its place sat a feeling of emptiness that was, in fact, the cold, hard reality of war.

The longboat pulled alongside the giant freighter, a seeming minnow next to a whale. The relentless waves bashed the longboat repeatedly against the freighter's hull. Don noticed the large block letters high up on the ship's prow. ARGO. The ship's name was *Argo*.

"Fitting," Don thought. He knew his Greek mythology and was fairly sure that while Jason and his Argonauts had indeed had themselves some adventures aboard their *Argo*, they never had one quite like the one Don had been immersed in for these past sixteen hours.

A thick rope with knots tied at regular intervals was tossed down from the deck, about thirty feet above. The rope wriggled, snapped, and then swayed against the hull. One of the oarsmen grabbed the rope and pulled it taut. Another oarsman helped Don to stand, pointed him toward the rope, and motioned for him to climb up to the deck.

Don looked up, looked at the rope, and then looked back at the oarsman.

"I'm supposed to climb this? You guys don't have a ladder?"

The oarsmen shook their heads in unison and pointed back up the rope.

Don imagined himself falling from the ship as he neared the railing, his survival from this ordeal once again thwarted at the last moment. Don could think only of the story his uncle Billy Harten had told him dozens of times. Billy had been aboard the USS *West Virginia* during the attack on Pearl Harbor. He'd been running along the deck with a shipmate when a concussive blast knocked Billy off his feet and sent his fellow sailor overboard. Billy lunged to help the man, looking over the rail to see him thrashing in the water between the doomed *West Virginia* and its tender ship. Another bomb exploded in the water nearby, creating a huge swell that lifted the tender and slammed it against the hull of the battleship. The wave swept backward and pulled the tender away. Uncle Billy could see only a large, red stain against the battleship's hull. Another wave surged against the hull, and like that, all traces of the man had been erased from the earth.

Don trembled, unsure of his ability to climb a rope in his weakened condition. The big Norwegian shook the rope toward him and implored him to climb. Don didn't want to appear a coward, so he grabbed the rope with both hands, placed his feet against the side of the hull, and walked his way up, terrified to look down and thinking of nothing but Uncle Billy's unfortunate shipmate the entire way up.

As Don neared the rail, his knees wobbled and his arms burned. Several hands reached down, grabbed him tight, and hoisted him over the weathered, wooden rail, which scraped Don's side, leaving his skin filled with splinters. His hosts stood him upright on the deck, and for the first time since this ordeal had begun, Don found himself standing on something solid.

"I'm saved," he thought. "I'm really, truly saved."

He shook his head, thanked his rescuers, closed his eyes, and trembled with exhaustion and joy. He stood naked except for his wet, nearly see-through skivvies and stomped his feet atop the deck of the *Argo*, thrilled by the hard surface.

CHAPTER TWENTY-ONE

NAVIGATORS JAY COLLIER AND TERRY LOWRY SAT TOGETHER IN THE B-52's cramped section beneath the cockpit, listening to radio chatter, deciphering electronic signals, and keeping a wary eye on their radar screens. Tailwinds from Typhoon Dinah had pulled them north and pushed them too quickly toward their designated refueling location. This anomaly threw the mission, which had been meticulously planned for months, into chaos. It was a small thing. Nine minutes. Yet radios crackled, radar pinged, notations were furiously scribbled, and multiple recommendations were handed down, some at cross-purposes with each other. Yes, it was only nine minutes, but Collier and Lowry could see the stream of events snowballing dangerously before their eyes.

The US Air Force had never flown the B-52 in combat, nor had it flown this many bombers in a single formation since World War II. And now it showed.

When the command came to roll their plane into a 360-degree turn, Collier and Lowry looked at each other, shook their heads, and relayed the order to the cockpit. They then sat with a tense foreboding, fairly certain that danger lurked ahead but unable to buck the chain of command.

They both stared at the green, glowing radar screen as the plane tilted into a steep bank. Just as the B-52 leveled out, flying directly into the trailing planes of their own squadron, the navigation electronics bristled, erupting into a cacophony of flashing lights, warnings, and radio static. Lowry shouted his desperate warning to the cockpit. Collier felt the plane drop in reaction to Lowry's call, and though his stomach had left him, he couldn't take his eyes off the radar screen. He prayed for the best but couldn't help wincing in anticipation of impact and death.

The plane bumped, the walls shook and they could feel that they were no longer sailing aerodynamically through the sky but rather rumbling, grinding, and scudding through the stratosphere.

"Twenty-nine," Terry called out over the interphone as the plane began to drop into a full-throated plunge. "Twenty-eight, twenty-seven, twenty-six . . ."

When the plane reached twenty-five thousand feet, Jay and Terry looked at each other in near disbelief. They gave each other a thumbs-down sign, signifying that the aircraft was doomed and ejection was the only option.

Jay reached below his seat and grabbed a large ring. He took three quick breaths, held the last one, tensed his body, closed his eyes, and hesitated for just a second in disbelief about what was happening and what he was about to do. He then gave the ring a hard yank.

His seat blasted with a sharp bang, and he shot downward like a cannonball through a hatch in the belly of the crippled plane.

A wall of wind slapped him across the sky, and he tumbled through the night, still attached to his seat. He rolled and twisted violently and had no sense of up or down. Jay fell through the clouds and wind and rain for what seemed like an eternity, the whole time thinking that his parachute should automatically open any second. It didn't. He was finally able to grope around his torso and find a large D-ring. He gave it a yank and a small chute, designed to stabilize one's fall—but not slow it down—streamed upward. The rolling and tumbling quickly stopped and he settled into a facedown free fall.

In places he could see through the big storm where an inferno of jet fuel burned atop the ocean's surface. He surmised that he was at about fifteen thousand feet above sea level and, thus, had about a minute and a half to figure out how to deploy his main chute. He waited a few seconds more. Still no chute. A desperate urgency set in, and Jay worked hard to keep that sensation from spilling over into sheer panic.

He groped at the gear strapped to his back and was prepared to dig and claw the parachute out of its pack with his fingernails if that's what it took. He then felt something big and bulky, which made him realize that he was still strapped to his seat, thus preventing his parachute from deploying.

Jay reflexively reached down, placed his hand on his lap belt connector and prepared to give it a tug before realizing at the last second that such a maneuver would release his entire harness, separating him from not only the seat but also his parachute and survival gear, sending him into free fall. He calmly removed his hand from the clasp as though it were a pin on a grenade.

Jay stared down at the flames that were growing closer and larger with each passing second. The inferno blazed atop the undulating blackness, and Jay could see streaks of whitecaps from over two miles up. He reached down to the bottom of his seat and felt a handle on either side. Amid the mayhem of the crash, he couldn't remember which was the proper handle to pull. One handle was designed to separate the survival gear from the parachute, should an airman need to get out of his seat, leave his survival gear behind, and bail out of the plane manually. The other handle was designed to disengage the seat's integrated harness, causing the seat to fall away from the airman and allow his parachute to automatically deploy. For Jay, one handle was certain death (no one was surviving in this ocean and this storm without a raft), the other was life. It was a coin flip.

The wind roared, the surface rushed closer, and Jay tried to calm his mind. He visualized the B-52 flight manual in his head. He could see its cover title: *Dash One*. And he could see the title for chapter 3: "Emergency Procedures." He mentally flipped through the pages and could even remember specific subject headings and their placement on the page. He was now at maybe five thousand feet and could see clearly the ferocity of the ocean's surface. He continued trying to mine the flight manual for any clues, but there was nothing that would jar his memory. Four thousand feet. He thought back to his early B-52 flight school, sifting through three months of both classroom academics and in-flight training. Three thousand feet. He remembered there was a sequence for manual bailout. Two thousand feet. And that sequence began with the right handle and then the left. Mountainous waves rushed upward, filling his entire vision and lunging toward him wildly. One thousand feet. That meant only the left handle remained as an option. There was no time to even hope he was correct. He gave the handle a hard yank. He was so close to the water, he could see the spray blowing off the tops of the waves. He closed his eyes and braced for a deadly smack onto the ocean's surface. His seat fell away, and the chute unfurled. Hurricane winds howled into the nylon, snapping it open and pulling Jay violently sideways a mere fifty feet above the water. He splashed hard into a wave, reflexively unleashed his parachute harness, and followed his tether to his raft, hardly believing he was still alive.

Chapter Twenty-Two

Captain Joe Robertson was a six-year air force veteran and a pilot's son. His father flew KC-135 refueling tankers, the very planes Capt. Robertson and his squadron were on the way to meet for their nighttime rendezvous over the South China Sea.

Robertson had broad shoulders as well as a square jaw, big smile, and strong handshake. He was football-star handsome and sported a Vince Lombardi flattop. He hailed from Salinas, California—Steinbeck country—where he was a multisport athlete and no stranger to farmwork. Robertson had been fascinated with airplanes since he could remember, having learned to fly at the age of twelve, when he'd joined a local chapter of the Civil Air Patrol as a cadet.

Though he was an experienced, by-the-book pilot who'd grown up amid the fastidious regimen of an air force officer's family, he was slightly nervous and alert on this, his first combat mission.

"Uh, Captain?" came the voice of radar navigator Chuck Andermann. "One of our squadrons up ahead is rolling into a 360, so be alert."

"Roger, navigator," Robertson replied. He hesitated for a moment as the information sank in. "Uh, navigator?"

"Yes?"

"Could you repeat?"

"Our lead squadron is rolling into a 360. We might come close to intersecting. That's what I've been told. Be alert."

"A 360? Who on god's green earth gave that order?" Robertson barked at no one in particular.

Robertson sat erect in his seat. He scanned his instrument readings, cinched his parachute straps, checked his seat harness, and inspected his ejection pins. He peered into the dark that pressed against his cockpit windscreen, trying to discern any oncoming lights in the night sky, which at thirty thousand feet was ablaze with bands of stars.

Nervous anticipation filled every crew member on the plane. And then the cockpit intercom blared, bringing their fears to life.

"Beacons, captain," proclaimed Andermann. "I've got beacons. Closing fast."

Andermann was thrown into near panic by the three oncoming blips on his radar screen. He quickly cinched his parachute straps, checked his seat harness, and glanced at his ejection pins.

"I've got a visual," Robertson blurted. "Full dive. Full dive."

Andermann's stomach fluttered, and blood rushed to his head. Sweat beaded on his forehead, and he felt as though he were about to vomit. He was transfixed by his radar screen and tried to think of something constructive to tell Capt. Robertson. But there was no time and no solution other than to dive and pray.

Robertson saw the oncoming lights grow large quickly. He was focused solely on the middle aircraft of the three-plane squadron. Time slowed. Seconds became minutes. He instantly thought, "Oh, shit, they're diving, too."

The light from the oncoming B-52 grew from a distant bright point to a large series of lights that spread from wingtip to wingtip, with the cockpit serving as a focal point. Robertson thought for a split second about how he didn't want to die. In the next split second, he resigned himself to the fact that there was no escape and his life would end in a massive fireball. He mostly felt bad for his wife and family.

The oncoming B-52 spread dark and gray before him. Robertson's plane was accelerating as it plunged. Its wing flaps grabbed the air, shoved the nose down and tilted its four-story tail up. The wing of the oncoming B-52 whooshed above Robertson's cockpit. He could hear the sonic roar of eight jet engines just above him. He felt a slight vibration in his seat and prepared to exhale.

In the radar room, Andermann sat frozen. His eyes stung from the sweat that had begun to trickle into them. He could see that the beacons on his screen were on an intractable collision course. He fingered his eject button and prepared for the worst. This wasn't his first air crash. He'd once bailed out of a wounded B-17 over Austria in 1945 and knew how things in a plane could go so wrong, so quickly. As a result, he was never one to suspend disbelief and waste valuable seconds hoping for the best.

From his windowless compartment, he heard a roar that came suddenly and left quickly. Concurrently, there was a metallic scrape and then relative silence.

Both Andermann and Robertson exhaled, startled that they were still alive. They didn't yet know that their B-52's massive vertical stabilizer had been clipped. And without a tail fin, the plane, now completely rudderless, fell victim to physics. It entered into one of the most dreaded of all aerodynamic phenomena: the flat spin.

The big jet, its eight powerful engines still thrusting, began to rotate through the sky. Slowly at first. And then quick. And quicker. And quicker. Soon it would be a jet-powered centrifuge, subjecting its occupants to gravitational forces of five g's, ten g's, fifteen g's before breaking apart and exploding, in midair, into a massive fireball.

Andermann was instantly slammed sideways. His helmeted head bashed into the metal wall of the fuselage next to his seat and stayed there, pinned. His thumb was on the eject button, but if he pushed it now, with his head tilted, he'd be decapitated as he blasted his way through the hatch. He struggled to sit upright, fully aware that every tenth of a second counted. His peripheral vision went dark as blood rushed to his head. His eyes began to bleed, and the plane spun wildly. He closed his eyes, clenched his teeth, pulled his head as close to upright as possible. Then, deciding to let whatever was going to happen, happen, he pressed his eject button.

Andermann was spat from the belly of his aircraft and into the night sky. Nearly unconscious, he tumbled into the maw of Typhoon Dinah. Helpless, he closed his eyes and waited for his parachute to automatically deploy.

In the cockpit, Robertson could immediately see the Milky Way begin to swirl. He reached for his eject button, but his left arm flung outward as the big plane began to spin. He fought to pull his arm back but couldn't. In desperation, he reached with his right hand, gripped the eject button on his left seat handle, and pressed. He exploded awkwardly through the cockpit hatch and into the night. His left arm, which had been extended during the ejection, felt numb. It had slammed the hatch's metal edge during the blast into the stratosphere.

It's unknown whether any other crew members made it out of the plane. Perhaps they'd hesitated for an instant, hoping for the best, and, having squandered those few tenths of seconds, were eventually consumed by terrific g-forces, which had rendered them unconscious. Or if they were able to fend off the centrifugal motion and grip their eject buttons, it's likely that they were awkwardly propelled from the bomber, perhaps breaking a neck or losing an arm or a leg on their way out of the aircraft.

For seconds after Andermann and Robertson had ejected, their B-52 spun faster and faster until, finally, its aluminum skin tore at the midsection of the fuselage. Air flowed into the rupture at near supersonic speed, cracking the aircraft in half. In split-second succession, catastrophic failure ensued. Both wings ripped away, as did what was left of the plane's tail section. The night sky erupted into a fireball of jet fuel and exploding ordnance.

Andermann and Robertson, each barely conscious, felt the whump-whump-whump of the exploding plane. Their parachutes rippled open automatically as they descended beneath fifteen thousand feet. Captain Robertson's left arm felt wet and sticky beneath his flight suit, and he hoped that there was a tourniquet in his survival kit.

Barely two hundred yards apart, the pair floated into the typhoon, carried almost gently by the howling winds.

Chapter Twenty-Three

Charlie don't never see 'em or hear 'em, but it'll suck the air out of your damn lungs.

—Mr. Clean, *Apocalypse Now*

On the horizon west of Saigon, a red-orange sun began shouldering its way into a hazy, tropical dawn that wavered with heat and humidity even at this early hour.

And then the sky shook.

A deep, low thunder concussed the morning and rumbled over the low-slung sprawl. The air reverberated, windows rattled, and walls shuddered. Residents, half awake, took to the streets and looked to the skies, expecting, perhaps, to see a great tropical electric storm. But the skies were clear. Yet the thunder kept coming in waves, so deep and low that one could feel the thrums in their chests and on the bare skin of their arms and legs.

The Vietnamese were no strangers to war. But this was altogether different from the intermittent pop and crackle of gun and mortar fire that the people had grown used to. For it rode through the sky accompanied by a sense of world-ending doom.

During the near-decade of war that spanned from 1965 to 1973, the US Air Force dropped millions of tons of bombs on Southeast Asia, more than all the Allied Forces had dropped during World War II on Germany and Japan combined. Each B-52, the workhorse of America's Vietnam War effort, could drop a dozen times the payload of one of its predecessors, the B-17, which was the workhorse of World War II. And so it was that the B-52, originally built for a war with the Soviets that had never come to pass—built, in fact, as a nuclear deterrent—had begun its transformation into the world's most feared conventional bomber. The B-52 would fly over 126,000 combat missions during the Vietnam War. This was the first.

As Don fought for his life in the raging waters of the South China Sea, pummeled by Typhoon Dinah, his squadron flew on. The big bombers raced west into a half-dark sky of fading stars, chased from behind by the spreading light of a tropical dawn. The squadron dropped to an altitude of twenty thousand feet. The dark flat of the ocean butted against the sandy sliver of shore that changed abruptly into a broad expanse of jungle. The squadron passed high above Saigon without notice and banked north. The air crews had been flying nonstop for seven hours, but their adrenaline surged as they neared their target. The sun rose to their right, bathing the jungle treetops in a soft light and transforming the world beneath them into a deep green that stretched, seemingly endless, to each horizon.

Twenty-eight miles northeast of Saigon, in the heart of the Bình Dương Province, lay the Bến Cát District. According to US Army Intelligence, the Bến Cát was a haven for the Vietcong. The air force had been given precise coordinates of a forward Vietcong military outpost harboring thousands of enemy troops firmly entrenched beneath the jungle canopy.

The formation now numbered twenty-seven B-52s, down from its original thirty. Two had collided in midair and one had been forced to turn around and land at Clark Air Base in the Philippines due to an electrical malfunction that had thwarted its midair refueling attempt.

The formation had been directed to bomb a one-mile by two-mile "box" in the jungle, which was approaching fast just ahead and beneath them. The box was indiscernible from any other part of the jungle. From twenty thousand feet, none of the crew could tell whether they were flying over the Vietcong army or an empty jungle. A sea of green stretched in every direction.

The bomb bays on each of the B-52s opened. The squadron flew steadily. The bombs fell. They streamed from beneath each plane. Over 1,200 in all. The jungle flashed and thundered below. By the time the planes had banked right and had begun flying into the rising sun, the one-by-two-mile box of jungle had been shattered, flattened, and denuded.

––—

Some four months after the B-52 squadron's surprise attack on Hanoi had been abruptly waved off, the aircraft's first wartime bombs had been delivered near a remote rubber plantation in the jungle. This was hardly what Gen. Forrest had in mind with his doctrine of "getting there first with the most." For the Americans, precious days, weeks, and months had been squandered by political squabbling and infighting in Washington.

Most of the surviving B-52 pilots Don flew with will tell you, if asked, that the Vietnam War wasn't lost in the jungles and rice paddies of Southeast Asia. It wasn't lost in the skies over Laos, Cambodia, and North and South Vietnam. And it wasn't lost in 1975 when the last marine helicopter lifted from the rooftop of the US embassy in Saigon.

Rather, it was lost in the White House, the halls of Congress, and the Pentagon in Washington, DC.

Specifically, it was lost in February 1965. That's when General Curtis LeMay lost a titanic political battle with Defense Secretary Robert McNamara and was ousted as chief of staff of the US Air Force.

Though separated by nearly a century, LeMay and Forrest had more in common than one might suspect. Both were born poor—LeMay in Ohio to an ironworker father, Forrest in Tennessee to a blacksmith father. Both had a common touch, were natural leaders, and possessed a deep understanding of their fellow man. They also spent much time studying and understanding their enemy. And they both believed in quick, mobile forces.

When asked why he chose the cavalry, Forrest explained that he preferred to move fast, strike hard, and keep the enemy off balance. He also liked the numerous strategic options that a mobile army enabled. Forrest's tactics and strategies presaged the highly mobile warfare that would fully emerge in the twentieth century. And, of course, these were similar to the reasons why LeMay was such a devotee of aerial combat.

The two generals also had an innate feel for war. They'd both fought in vicious battles. Forrest had killed dozens of men in hand-to-hand combat. And both had proclaimed often that they'd never send their men into a battle in which they wouldn't readily volunteer to ride on either the lead horse or in the lead plane. Importantly, they were both ruthless in war. As a strategist, Forrest could sit in the saddle and look out over the hills and swales of Tennessee and watch an impending battle play out in his mind. He always seemed to know what his enemy might do and when they might do it. And he always seemed to have an answer for their every move and countermove. Likewise, LeMay could study a map or aerial photos and know exactly where and when to send his squadrons.

When asked by President Lyndon Johnson and McNamara for a plan to defeat the North Vietnamese, LeMay stated that the strategy should be fairly simple. It should be one of decapitation. It should be lightning quick and hammer hard. He advocated an early heavy bombing campaign against North Vietnamese cities, railways, harbors, ports, and bridges. In February 1965, Hanoi was a completely defenseless city. American bombers and jet fighters could have their run of the place. LeMay's initial plan called for the complete and total destruction of the Phúc Yên air base just north of Hanoi as well as all railways leading in and out of the city, along with all manufacturing centers, military installations, and the industrial port of Haiphong. Without Hanoi or Haiphong, North Vietnam was nothing. Its war-making capability would be thoroughly nullified.

As Johnson weighed competing strategies for what to do in Vietnam, he worried about the provocation of either the Soviets or Chinese, thus potentially drawing them directly into the conflict with a massive bombing in and around Hanoi.

LeMay countered that the Soviets were three thousand miles and a full year away from mustering enough forces to be effective in a North Vietnamese conflict. Further, due to economic conditions, the Chinese lacked both the materiel and the will to enter a foray in Vietnam. The Chinese had been bitter enemies with the Vietnamese for well over a millennium. They weren't likely to come to their rescue now. And, finally, with air, transportation, and military bases destroyed, neither power would be able to gain a foothold in Southeast Asia from which to launch a counterattack against the Americans.

McNamara vociferously argued against LeMay's plan. He believed in constricting and containing the North Vietnamese by deploying a body-blow strategy rather than one of decapitation. He believed that the North Vietnamese could be stopped in the jungles—their supply lines into the south could be severed, their armies decimated, and their will to wage war crushed. He espoused a doctrine of gradualism. US forces would be deployed in the manner of a python, slowly constricting the enemy until it has no choice but to eventually surrender.

Of course, LeMay could hardly believe the folly inherent in McNamara's plan. And he warned both Johnson and McNamara in blunt terms. LeMay's sentiments were summed up by a statement he made to a biographer after leaving his command: "[The North Vietnamese have] got to draw in their horns and stop their aggression, or we're going to bomb them back into the Stone Age. And we would shove them back into the Stone Age with air power or naval power—not with ground forces."

It was the very antithesis of the McNamara approach to Vietnam.

And as President Johnson, always the master politician, weighed each strategy, he stated that he preferred to avoid images of the wealthiest country in the world dropping bombs on the capital city of a largely impoverished third-world country.

And with that, McNamara was in and LeMay was out.

The massive February 1965 bombing raid of Hanoi was abruptly canceled. Johnson declared all ninety-four of LeMay's critical bombing targets in North Vietnam off-limits. No American planes could approach within thirty miles of Hanoi or ten miles of the Chinese border without direct approval from the president.

Of course, McNamara and Johnson were suckered into Vietnam by a classic rope-a-dope. For nearly a decade, they would flail ineffectively at Vietnam's jungle midsection, exhausting their precious reserves of blood, treasure, and materiel while doing little to quash the north's will to make war.

In reflecting on his strategic blunder in Vietnam late in his life, McNamara said, "We were wrong, terribly wrong. We owe it to future generations to explain why."

Certainly in private moments, Johnson and McNamara rued their failure to listen to the brilliant, ruthless LeMay.

The Americans did not get to Hanoi first with the most. By the time of this first Arc Light mission on June 18, 1965, Hanoi's air defenses had been fully fortified. Its environs—thanks to Soviet and Chinese support—bristled with batteries of Soviet-made surface-to-air missiles. An attack now on Hanoi would be extraordinarily dangerous, difficult, and costly.

And so the Americans delivered their first body blow to the jungles of the Bến Cát District. Military spokesmen at the Pentagon immediately declared the mission a success. They told the Associated Press, which distributed the Pentagon's glowing quotes to millions of readers throughout the United States, that the destruction of Vietcong forces by the B-52 raid had been precise, effective, and total. They lauded the B-52 force for its use of dazzling new technology that enabled massive bomb loads to be directed on target from stratospheric heights. And they predicted that the B-52's entrance into the war would serve to "harass the VC, to disrupt his normal activities, to permit him no respite from danger even in his jungle redoubts, and to wear him down psychologically."

Following the bombing mission, the US Army sent reconnaissance teams into "the box." They did find that the destruction had been impressive and total. But what they didn't find was what really mattered. They didn't find any Vietcong casualties. They didn't find any loss whatsoever of Vietcong weapons or strongholds. Their enemy's ability to wage war hadn't been diminished at all. Military planners mused that the Vietcong must've been tipped off about the coming air raid and had quickly evacuated the area. Or perhaps it was just delusional to think that one could successfully bomb an army hidden beneath a dense jungle canopy into submission from twenty thousand feet.

Either way, the Americans were undeterred. It was simply one B-52 mission down, 129,000 to go.

Chapter Twenty-Four

The pale moon was rising above the green mountains,
The sun was declining beneath the blue sea
When I strayed with my love to the pure crystal fountain
That stands in the beautiful vale of Tralee,
She was lovely and fair as the rose of the summer,
Yet 'twas not her beauty alone that won me.
Oh, no! 'twas the truth in her eyes ever dawning
That made me love Mary, the Rose of Tralee.

In the far fields of India, 'mid war's dreadful thunders,
Her voice was a solace and comfort to me,
But the chill hand of death has now rent us asunder,
I'm lonely tonight for the Rose of Tralee.
She was lovely and fair as the rose of the summer,
Yet 'twas not her beauty alone that won me;
Oh no, 'twas the truth in her eyes ever dawning,
That made me love Mary, the Rose of Tralee.

—"The Rose of Tralee" (Irish ballad)

William Harten was lost in America.

He stood barely five feet three, had a thick, wavy head of hair and smoky blue eyes, and sported an elegant mustache that was waxed and tightly twisted at each end. He often wore a bowler and never ventured into public without a suit and tie.

On the bustling streets of Belfast, he would've looked like any other Irishman, and it would've been difficult to pick him out of a crowd. But in Pocatello—a quintessential city of the American West, founded by a confluence of French fur trappers, cavalrymen, pioneers, prospectors, railroadmen, and Mormon farmers—a city that sprang naturally at a fork in two westward trails, one that jotted northwest to Oregon, another that veered southwest to the gold fields of California—he stood out. He was never comfortable. It was as though he were perpetually trapped in an ill-fitting suit.

And it wasn't just his appearance. It was also his essence. His life experience. He came from a country that had its roots in a people whose history stretched back to before the Bronze Age. He'd been raised in a great capital of Europe. He was educated, smart, worldly. He was a classically trained musician. He'd read everything written by Yeats, Wilde, and Joyce, as well as Shakespeare and Dickens. He didn't think much of American writers, though he thought Twain was a hoot. He was a master storyteller with a lilt in his voice and mischief in his eye. He could hold a single person or an entire room entranced by even the simplest story. He could play the fiddle, as many Irishmen did, with a jaunty confidence— sometimes delivering mercurial joy, other times, a soulful melancholy. And he could sing. He was unabashed about tippling through high, soft notes if that's what a song required. Or he could belt out an operatic roar—something completely out of proportion with his diminutive size. If people wanted to sing in Belfast, they had to be prepared to cut through the dense cacophony of a smoky pub. They had to fill a crowded room—grab a crowd by its scruff and never let go. Irish singing was not for the faint of heart or timorous.

Yet in spite of this trove of talent—and deep beneath the songs, the laughter, the music, the stories—William Harten was haunted by a searing sadness. He hailed from a country torn asunder by centuries of war, strife, and famine. Inescapable trauma tumbled through the years and the generations. It had visited everyone and left no one unscathed. Life in Ireland was often brutish and short. He'd lost four children, three siblings, and his first two wives to a variety of epidemics, the most prevalent of which was tuberculosis, which ravaged the island in the late nineteenth and early twentieth centuries. In addition, an economic maelstrom blew relentlessly across the land, scattering friends, relatives, and countrymen to the far corners of the earth in a most desperate quest for work and the security of food, shelter, and family survival. He was bitter that he'd had to leave the land he loved in exchange for a job in a distant place not of his choosing. But such was his lot, as was the lot of most Irishmen and Irishwomen.

His wife, Sarah McDonald Price Harten, had also been touched by tragedy. Her parents had both been born into the Great Hunger, the potato famine that had shattered the island in the 1840s and 1850s. It was an epic calamity that had killed over a million Irish in both the north and south and caused another million to flee into a global diaspora, the likes of which the world had not yet seen. Sarah's parents told of going to bed and looking out over summer fields green with blossoming potato plants only to awaken the next day to a sick countryside, putrid with wilted, blackened foliage. Children went hungry and sat quietly in stoops with eyes sunken and bellies distended. Parents foraged in the trash heaps and often died in the streets. Disease lurked everywhere and stalked everyone. In Ireland, there was only a time before the Great Hunger and a time after. It was a force that did as much to cleave the country as any.

Sarah's parents, sisters, and brothers had all left for the United States, but she'd chosen to stay out of love for one Jack Price, a striking man from a well-to-do family in Belfast. He owned an entire wardrobe of fine, hand-tailored suits from London. His social and economic status was such that it promised to buffer Sarah from the poverty and despair that had so frequently enveloped young women in Ireland. And when Jack had been offered a job in Cape Colony (now Cape Town), South Africa, managing construction projects in and around the diamond and gold mines that had been disrupted during the Boer Wars, he took it. There he could earn in one year what it took ten men to make in Ireland.

So Jack and Sarah married and set off for their great African adventure. For six years life was idyllic. Jack and Sarah dressed in finery, he in his tailored suits and silk ties, she in elegant gowns trimmed with Irish lace and draped with the exoticism of an ostrich boa. They had two daughters, whom Jack and Sarah enjoyed dressing up on Sundays and parading through the city streets. Together they marveled at how the temperate sun of Cape Colony contrasted sharply with the damp gray of Belfast.

But, of course, no Irish story is ever a happy one. And as much as Sarah prayed every day that hers might be an exception, the doom that forever hovered over her people finally and inevitably brushed against her.

Jack had been overseeing construction of a new sewage system at a nearby diamond mine. He tripped and fell into an open reservoir of raw sewage. One small stumble. One seemingly innocuous mistake. His construction foreman fished him out, stripped him naked, and hosed him off on the spot. But the damage had been done. A fever gripped him in the night, and by morning he was dead.

Sarah and her daughters were grief stricken. But there was no time for mourning. An Irishwoman, or any woman for that matter, in South Africa then had few rights. She couldn't buy, own, or sell property. She couldn't hold a bank account or withdraw money, even if it had belonged to her deceased husband.

She quickly sent a letter to Jack's parents, informing them of the news and asking them for help releasing money to Jack's account so she could pay for passage back to Belfast for herself and her daughters. But in Ireland, women were a burden. The island was half devoid of men, who'd all either died or had left for work in foreign countries. A widow and two daughters? Who would want to take on a financial responsibility like that? Jack's brothers took control of his bank account and hired an agent to sell his house and property. Jack's parents wrote to Sarah, condoled her for her loss, and advised her to stay in Cape Colony, find whatever job or new husband she might, and pray to the Father above for come what may.

Sarah was shocked and bitter, even though she had no time to be afforded the luxury of wallowing in her own sour despair. Her survival and that of her daughters depended upon her steely resolve and resourcefulness. And Irishwomen were nothing if not resourceful.

Sarah gathered her husband's entire collection of fine suits and made her way to the city center. There she sold each one to passersby until she had enough money for a voyage back to Belfast. She couldn't bear to part with her own dresses and gowns, and even though she knew they were now the extravagance of a past life and likely useless in her life to be, she packed them all neatly in a steamer trunk and shipped them half a world away to Belfast.

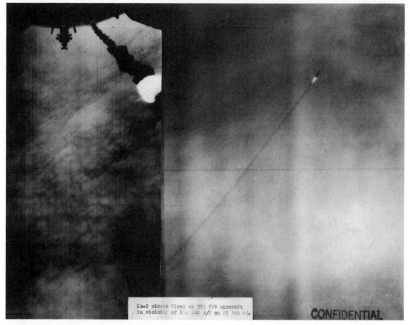

Left: A Russian-made SA-2 surface-to-air missile passes at a speed of Mach 3.5 only a few feet beneath Capt. Don Harten's F-105, which was flying over Hanoi on February 22, 1968, on its way to bomb the nearby Hòa Lạc Air Field. The missile detonated just behind the F-105's tail. In a mission report, military aviation experts stated that the plane was well within the missile's "kill zone" and were puzzled at how the jet escaped unscathed. (Official USAF photo) *Right:* US Air Force reconnaissance photo showing one of three successive SA-2 missiles fired toward Capt. Harten's four-plane Bison One formation on February 22, 1968, over Hanoi. (Official USAF photo)

Another view of the SA-2 passing Capt. Harten's F-105. (Official USAF photo)

Lt. Don Harten arriving at Andersen AFB, Guam, June 21, 1965, after his rescue from the South China Sea, following his midair B-52 collision three days earlier. (Official USAF photo)

The four survivors of a midair collision between two B-52s at 30,000 feet above the South China Sea on June 18, 1965. Photo taken at Andersen AFB, Guam, June 21, 1968. From left: Lt. James Erbes, Lt. Don Harten, Lt. Jay Collier, Lt. Col. Chuck Andermann. (Official USAF photo)

A formation of F-105s on a training run streak along the escarpment of the Eastern High Sierra, California, just below the summit of Mt. Whitney. (Official USAF photo)

Lt. Don Harten, second from left, poses with his six-man bomber crew in front of their B-52, *Parker's Pride*, at Mather AFB, Sacramento, California, April 18, 1966. From left: Capt. Pete Nichols, Lt. Don Harten, Lt. Col. Chuck Andermann, Capt. Bernie Dowes, Lt. Jim Erbes, Capt. Charlie McCarthy. (Official USAF photo)

Lt. Don Harten's B-52 bombing a Vietcong stronghold in North Vietnam, 1966. (Official USAF photo)

Telegram from US Secretary of State Dean Rusk, containing a signed personal note from Sec. Rusk, regarding Lt. Don Harten's survival of a midair B-52 collision, June 21, 1965.

Don Harten, age three, after his first "ejection" in 1943. During a Sunday drive in his family's Packard, he accidentally pushed down on the car's "suicide handle," a dangerously designed door latch that pushed down instead of pulled up, and fell out of the car, which was traveling between 40 and 50 mph on the highway. He rolled like a barrel along the asphalt before jumping up and giving chase to the car, which had skidded to a stop. He survived with only minor cuts, scrapes, and bruises. (Harten family photo)

Don Harten, age three, with a bandaged head following his "ejection" from the family Packard. From left, Ellen Harten, author's mother; Lucille Harten, mother; Don Harten; Kenneth Harten, father.

Don Harten, age four, feeling jaunty, dressed as a military officer, 1944. His sister Ellen Harten, the author's mother, is on the right. (Harten family photo)

Don Harten was a professional musician and expert drummer. Here, at age seventeen, he's playing at a high school dance in Pocatello, Idaho. (Harten family photo)

Don Harten with his favorite pooch, Ladybug, in Pocatello, Idaho, 2003. (Harten family photo)

Second Lt. Don Harten's official US Air Force portrait taken in January 1965. (Official USAF photo)

Portrait of William Harten, Don Harten's paternal grandfather, 1915. William was a ship's carpenter for Harland & Wolff in Belfast, where he was a craftsman on the *Titanic*. Distraught by the great ship's sinking, he emigrated to America three months later. (Harten family photo)

The runway at Andersen AFB, Guam, 1965, as seen from the cockpit of a circling B-52. (Don Harten photo)

A B-52 on approach at Andersen AFB, Guam, 1965, following an Arc Light mission over North Vietnam. (Don Harten photo)

The Mekong River Delta in South Vietnam, as seen from the cockpit of a B-52 at 30,000 feet in 1965. (Don Harten photo)

From February to June 1965, B-52 pilots, crewmembers, and commanding officers awaited orders on Guam as the Vietnam War began its heavy escalation to the west. Left to their own devices and bereft of direction, the American servicemen whiled away the hours playing golf, sunbathing at the beach, snorkeling in the Pacific, and drinking in the local clubs and restaurants. That would all change abruptly on June 18, 1965, with the first-ever B-52 bombing mission, dubbed Arc Light One, over North Vietnam. (Don Harten photo)

Top and bottom: Maj. Don Harten performing high-speed contour flying in an F-111 through the Laotian Highlands near the North Vietnamese border in 1972. The F-111's advanced radar systems enabled it to maintain consistent altitudes as low as 100 feet above ground level while flying at supersonic speeds. Here, Maj. Harten flies above a jungle-clad, limestone pinnacle created by a geological formation known as karst. This particular pinnacle was dubbed "Godzilla" by American fighter pilots. (Official USAF photo)

Gail Johnson Boyatt, Don Harten's uncle, in his official World War II US Army portrait. Boyatt served as an ordnance officer in North Africa, Italy, and the South Pacific during the war. He was also an expert poker player who taught Don the finer points of that game of chance. (Official US Army photo)

Lt. Col. Chuck Andermann at work as a radar navigation officer aboard a B-52. Lt. Col. Andermann was one of four survivors of the June 18, 1965, midair collision of two B-52s above the South China Sea. (Official USAF photo)

Kenneth Harten, Don's father, 1972. (Harten family photo)

Lucille Harten, Don's mother, 1944. (Harten family photo)

Don Harten, left, and his nephew, author Craig K. Collins, following a speech by Harten to a group of retired Naval aviators in Van Nuys, California, March 2014. (Craig K. Collins photo)

Capt. Don Harten's patch for flying one hundred combat missions over North Vietnam aboard an F-105. (Craig K. Collins photo)

Maj. Don Harten's patch designating him as a member of the US Air Force's 474th Tactical Fighter Wing, dubbed the Road Runners, based at Takhli Royal Thai AFB, Thailand. (Craig K. Collins photo)

Don Harten's Strategic Air Command patch. (Craig K. Collins photo)

Capt. Don Harten posing in front of his bomb-laden F-105, dubbed the *Pink Pussycat*, at Takhli Royal Thai AFB, Thailand, 1968. Photo is autographed by Harten and addressed to his "sweetheart"—his mother. (Official USAF photo)

She then purchased passage aboard a rusty ship that regularly trawled up and down the west coast of Africa, carrying both passengers and cargo, with stops in the ports of Luanda, Pointe-Noire, Port-Gentil, Libreville, Lagos, Abidjan, Monrovia, Freetown, Dakar, Casablanca, and Tangier before finally reaching the British port of Gibraltar, which offered a direct connection to Belfast.

The two-week journey was arduous, devoid of any basic human luxury, and fraught with its own particular peril. At every port, passengers embarked and disembarked. Tropical diseases came and went. On some mornings, the crew could be seen rolling deceased passengers over the rails and into the ocean. It was a journey that Sarah's daughters, Edna and Eileen, would remember all their years. Even into her seventies, eighties, and nineties, whenever someone in the family would complain about one trouble or another, Edna would invariably reply, "Just be glad you're not on a West African steamer."

Back in Belfast, Sarah was faced with a life that consumed her with bone-weary drudgery, soul-crushing servitude, and life-threatening infirmity. In the early 1900s, Belfast was the linen capital of the world. And it was the fate of women like Sarah—young, widowed, and with fatherless children to support—to work as a spinner in an Irish linen mill.

Linen had its deep roots in Ireland stretching back to the introduction of flax to the isles by the Phoenicians and Romans. By the Middle Ages, the production of linen became established as a true cottage industry. Families grew flax in the fields, harvested the long, fibrous stalks, and soaked them in ponds for days until the plant's soft sheaths rotted away in wet, dark clumps that cloaked the countryside with an inescapable stench. The rotted stalks were then dried, bundled, beaten with a mallet, and combed into yarn suitable for spinning and then weaving.

A confluence of global events then pushed women to the Belfast linen mills in droves. Following the potato famine, the production of linen in home looms virtually ceased. Shortly thereafter, the American Civil War caused a plunge in cotton production, and linen was left to fill the gap. Concurrently, the introduction of technology and machinery into the linen production process concentrated nearly the whole of Irish linen production into large textile factories and warehouses throughout

Belfast. As it happened, those factories were magnets for all the women left fatherless, brotherless, and husbandless by the Great Famine and ensuing diaspora. Thus, Belfast doubled in size. Then it doubled again. And again. Belfast grew, in a few short decades, into the largest city in Ireland.

Sarah would awake every morning at 4:00 a.m., clean her small room, make a modest breakfast, drape herself with a heavy woolen shawl, and trudge to the linen mill, a large, four-story brick edifice that was as imposing as a prison on the outside and a clattering cacophony of industrial production and resultant human misery on the inside.

Her workday would begin at 6:00 a.m. in the spinning room, standing barefoot in water and muck that typically covered the concrete floor up to several inches deep, a residue from the process of soaking the bobbins of yarn after they'd been spun from the rough flaxen fibers. Spinners like Sarah were often encouraged to wear clogs while working, but the women found such footwear completely unsuitable for the conditions. It was simpler to just go barefoot. Sarah would get a half-hour break for lunch. And twice a day she was allowed three minutes to go to the "wee room." She would finish, bone tired, at 6:00 p.m. Her hair and skin would be covered with a fine, blond flax dust. She worried incessantly about tuberculosis. Each day, someone she knew would fall ill from the disease, which ruthlessly stalked the linen mills and thrived in the damp and dust. Sometimes a woman would fall ill from the disease at the spinning station next to Sarah's. A new girl would be plucked from the crowd of waiting women outside the mill and placed within minutes at the station previously occupied by the unfortunate tubercular worker. Spinners were often required to pull yarn taut using their teeth. And spinning stations were rarely, if ever, sanitized. Thus, tuberculosis continued its march through the mill, unchecked. Before leaving for the day, Sarah would remove her shawl from its rack and shake it vigorously to remove the "clocks," small golden beetles that crawled throughout the workshop. She would arrive home, clean herself, make dinner, and drop into bed at 8:00 p.m. She worked a half-day—6:00 a.m. to noon—on Saturday before spending the rest of the day shopping for provisions that would get her through another week. She spent Sunday mornings in church before enjoying her only free time of the week on Sunday afternoon.

Day in, day out. Week in, week out. Year in, year out. Such was her lot in life.

So when she met William Harten, a widowed neighbor who had a decent-paying job as a ship's carpenter, she said, without hesitation, "Yes," as soon as he'd asked her to marry him.

William was dashing, handsome, intelligent, witty, and musically gifted. He was universally loved and admired seemingly by anyone he came in contact with. Sarah worried that he drank to excess. But nearly all Irishwomen shared this worry. Being the wife of a drinker was simply another burden to be borne in silence. It was a condition as ubiquitous and inescapable as the stench and noise of the linen mill. Furthermore, women in Ireland vastly outnumbered men, who'd not only disappeared in great numbers due to emigration but also due to death from drink, disease, and famine.

In spite of William's shortcomings and Sarah's misgivings about them, she didn't feel she had much of a choice. Though she didn't particularly love William, the decision to marry was easy.

Likewise, after the *Titanic* had sunk, the decision to leave for America was just as easy.

And so Sarah found herself walking home from church or grocery shopping in Preston, Idaho, a small town near the Utah border, populated by earnest but dull Mormon ranchers and farmers. She felt more out of place in Preston than in Africa. Most of Preston's streets were still unpaved in 1914. And after the snows from the bitterly cold winters had melted, the hems of her long, elegant Irish dresses—which had already traveled halfway around the world and halfway yet again—would drag in the mud and the muck. This left Sarah infuriated. She muttered incessantly about the crude Americans who didn't yet have the sense to pave their city roads.

That an Irish couple would end up in a small town at the edge of civilization in the vastness of the American West is strange enough. Stranger still is the story of how the Mormons, driven to attract ever more converts to their budding theocracy in the American frontier, would send missionaries fanning across the globe, seeking new believers, settlers, and young women ripe for marriage.

One of their most fruitful hunting grounds was Ireland. In and around the Belfast linen mills, it was easy to convince Irishwomen to abandon their lives of cramped, brutal servitude for the big skies, open ranges, clean air, and majestic mountains of Utah. They could come, marry a Mormon farmer, live in a spacious house on spacious land, and never go hungry. Some might marry into polygamy. Most not. Either way, it was an easy decision. Irishwomen came in droves. Two of those women were William's surviving daughters, rescued, in their opinions, by Mormons from the horror of the Belfast linen mills. They'd both married prosperous (and nonpolygamous) Mormon farmers in the 1890s. And compared to their previous lives, working as teenage linen spinsters, the life of a Mormon farmer's wife was idyllic.

William was quickly hired on to a work crew that kept busy on projects to dam the great wild rivers of the American West. It was the golden age of hydroelectric power, and William traveled to construction camps along the Snake and the Columbia as well as their many tributaries.

After only a few years, William and Sarah, yearning for metropolitan familiarity, moved north from one-horse Preston to Pocatello, a major rail hub for the Union Pacific. With a population of forty thousand, it passed for what was a big city in the West.

There, William landed a job with Union Pacific, built a house, and raised his family. He and Sarah had two sons, the eldest of whom was Kenneth, Don Harten's father.

William reveled in Pocatello. It was certainly no Belfast, but, unlike Preston, there were bars aplenty. In the evenings, he traveled from saloon to saloon, playing his Irish fiddle and singing Irish ballads for tips and drinks.

By the time Don was a child, William was a shell of his younger self. He'd descended fully into alcoholism. Quite simply, he'd become the town drunk.

We are all haunted by our past. We are all the confluence of personal histories that cascade from generation to generation down through the ages. Triumphs and tragedies, missteps and mistakes, drama and despair. Whether we are aware of them or not, we are all a cauldron of our ancestors' deeds and misdeeds.

And Don Harten was likely more of a captive of his past than most. It may have been the primary reason he excelled at flying combat jets.

Psychologists describe narcissism as a defense against core shame. Such shame is produced by a sense of inadequacy and internal damage. It is a condition that most often festers and takes root at a very early age, nudged into full blossom by an alcoholic parent or relative. A child who develops beneath the yoke of core shame often works diligently to create an alternate, idealized reality—a false self-image in which the child possesses superior, admirable, and heroic qualities. These self-ingrained personality traits are, of course, at odds with the deep internal self-loathing the child endures daily. In order to survive, such children put on a brave face and play out a daily drama in which they are the heroes of their own story. They create a parallel narrative for friends, family, and strangers in which they are smarter, faster, stronger, funnier, better in all things than all others. It's a defensive maneuver to prove to the world that they are— contrary to their often ugly and shameful upbringing—a winner. And as they grow into adulthood, this core shame never leaves. It's a behavior that individuals spend their entire lives trying to disprove and counteract. Such individuals strive tirelessly each day to garner the admiration and adulation of those around them. They often become perfectionists, striving relentlessly and tirelessly to become the kind of superhumans worthy of the adulation of hundreds, thousands, or millions.

Such core shame can often be compounded by the so-called warrior gene. Carriers of this genetic feature are said to be drawn to adventure and adrenaline-fueled experiences. Further, they are able to process information under extreme duress with the type of quick clarity that others simply can't match. They often don't experience fear and are thus able to dance on the edge of death. These people become in disproportionate numbers billionaires. Corporate titans. Ruthless politicians. Celebrities. Generals. And, perhaps, combat pilots. Their private inner stew of perfectionism and core shame drives them to heights to which most people would never aspire in the first place.

Don was such a person. Addicted to adrenaline. Obsessed with perfection. Consumed by inner shame. Nonchalant about death. Dedicated to building his own legend. Smooth under pressure.

⁓

The Chinook winds sometimes visit Pocatello in the winter, providing a sudden, unexpected respite from subzero temperatures. Driven by warm, heavy air blowing counterclockwise and first drawing from the warmer southern waters of the Pacific, Chinooks will barrel into the frozen ranges and narrow valleys of the Pacific Northwest in January, February, or March. Always a surprise, the winds can shove away the hard cold that typically settles in winter valleys, driving temperatures from minus ten degrees Fahrenheit to as high as fifty or sixty degrees Fahrenheit in a matter of hours or minutes.

On this evening, a Chinook rolled into the Bannock Range west of Pocatello, compressing and warming as it rose in waves over the nine-thousand-foot peaks. It raced down snow-packed slopes and funneled into the frigid Portneuf River valley. Soon it was whistling between buildings in Pocatello, rattling windows and reducing snowdrifts and snowbanks to melted mush.

William Harten stumbled out of the Gem Bar across from the Yellowstone Hotel and leaned into the warm, stiff wind. He had the gaunt look, tottering gait, and wan grin of an aging alcoholic. As a young man, he could "hold his liquor." Many who encountered him might not even know he were drunk. Back then, his supervisors usually couldn't tell he'd put in a full day on the job after an evening of drunken debauchery and little sleep. But now that he was in his sixties, his alcoholism was obvious to anyone who'd cast even a casual glance.

William tossed his head back, pointed his nose skyward, closed his eyes, and breathed deeply. He clutched the handle of his fiddle case tightly, as though to give himself some support. Nevertheless, he swayed with the uncertainty of a stack of teacups about to topple. He drew another deep breath and another. Gone was the usual dry, bitter-cold air of an Idaho winter night—the kind that if inhaled quickly would scour one's nostrils and induce a sharp cough. No, the air on this night was different—warm, damp, and soft. It harbored the incongruous, yet tantalizing, aroma of spring here in the depth of winter. Pungent aromas swirled around the still-swaying William. With each breath, he could detect hints of wet leaves, chimney smoke, lakes, mud, and damp sidewalks. It jostled his memory. It stirred a deep longing. He breathed again the air that was warm, damp, and soft. He smelled the ocean. He smelled Belfast.

William opened his eyes and teetered forward, stumbling and splashing through large puddles of just-melted snow and ice, pools brought to sudden life by the Chinook and whose surfaces now rippled beneath the warm winds. William grinned and broke into song, his lilting words and ringing melody carried aloft by the breezes.

> Ah, Tim Finnegan lived in Walkin Street
> A gentleman Irish mighty odd
> Well, he had a tongue both rich and sweet
> An' to rise in the world he carried a hod
> Ah, but Tim had a sort of tipplin' way
> With the love of the liquor he was born
> An' to send him on his way each day
> He'd a drop of the craythur every morn.

William stumbled and sang, sang and stumbled. He tottered home through Pocatello's orderly grid of elm-lined streets. All the presidents—Garfield, Hayes, Arthur, Harrison, Grant, Johnson, Lincoln—were arranged north-south. All the frontiersmen—Fremont, Bridger, Lewis, Clark, Carson, Custer—were laid out east-west.

> One morning Tim got rather full,
> His head felt heavy which made him shake
> Fell from a ladder and he broke his skull,
> And they carried him home his corpse to wake
> Rolled him up in a nice clean sheet,
> And laid him out upon the bed
> A bottle of whiskey at his feet
> And a barrel of porter at his head.

As the lyrics swirled through the late-night dark, some residents inside the tidy houses along the way would awake, enchanted by William's lilting voice. But most would simply roll over and curse, "Here comes that damn drunk Irishman again."

As a small boy, Don could always hear his grandfather coming home after the bars had closed from several blocks away.

> Whack fol the dah now dance to yer partner
> Around the flure yer trotters shake
> Wasn't it the truth I told you?
> Lots of fun at Finnegan's Wake.

Don would tread softly down the stairs and watch his father, Kenneth, standing like a dutiful sentry on the front porch as William's song grew closer and louder, closer and louder. Kenneth, wrapped in his robe and swaddled in shame, would step out to the sidewalk to greet his father. And though he knew the entire neighborhood was listening, he would kindly take the fiddle case from his father's grip, put an arm around him, and steady him for his journey up the front porch steps. Kenneth would step across the threshold and hand the fiddle case to Don, who clutched it with a sense of grave responsibility. Kenneth would then half-hoist and half-guide his father up the steep stairs to his bedroom, prodding him to keep quiet so as not to wake Sarah, his wife. But William rarely paid heed.

> Whack fol the dah now dance to yer partner
> Around the flure yer trotters shake
> Wasn't it the truth I told you?
> Lots of fun at Finnegan's Wake.

Don marched silently behind the pair, clutching the handle of the fiddle case, three generations of Harten men, shame cascading freely from each to each to each.

Outside the Chinook winds blew. Windows rattled and the surfaces of large puddles from just-melted snow rippled. The air outside was warm, damp, soft, smelling of wet leaves and chimney smoke. Smelling of the ocean. Smelling of Belfast.

Chapter Twenty-Five

The F-105 Thunderchief was derisively called the "Thud" by servicemen in Vietnam. Pilots had originally given the jet its moniker as a play on Chief Thunderthud, a character from the *Howdy Doody* TV show. However, as the Vietnam conflict mushroomed into all-out war, the name became eponymous with the sound of the supersonic jet nose-diving into a jungle hillside, which happened with alarming frequency. Of the roughly eight hundred F-105s produced, nearly four hundred were lost in combat. It has the dubious distinction of being the only American warplane pulled from duty due to a high loss rate. But that would come late in the war, after much of the damage had already been done. For the bulk of the war, the F-105 was America's workhorse in the skies.

The first Thunderchief had rolled off the assembly lines in 1955, yet another Cold Warrior designed not for conventional combat but rather as a nuclear attack jet, able to fly low and fast into the heart of the Soviet Union and drop a single nuclear bomb on its target.

When the Vietnam War erupted ten years later, the F-105 was retrofitted for a very different mission. It would be molded into an all-purpose attack fighter and bomber, thus making it for the remainder of its operational days a square peg in a round hole. For a fighter jet, it was large, fast, and more than a bit unwieldy. At fifty thousand pounds, it was by far the heaviest single-pilot jet ever produced. At sea level, it could fly much faster than the speed of sound; at higher elevations, it could double the sound barrier. It bristled with weaponry and could carry fourteen thousand pounds of bombs and missiles.

Pilots often complained that the F-105 flew like a cumbersome sled and lacked the aerial agility of the smaller American F-4 and Russian

MiG. But Don always believed that the F-105 was a brilliant war machine, and it suffered from being misunderstood and underrated by most pilots and war strategists.

And few understood the F-105 as intimately as Don. He had studied assembly diagrams and had memorized every part of the aircraft. He understood the physics of how and why the plane performed as it did. He knew its strengths, its weaknesses, and its limits. He also knew that recommended protocols for flight were often conservative and didn't match the plane's full capabilities in combat. When it came to flying the F-105, Don was one of the few pilots who knew when to push, how far to push, and where to push.

By January 1967, Don had completed his second tour of duty as a B-52 pilot and had logged over one hundred combat bombing missions. As a result, he was free to check out of the war and return stateside. Air force policy was to never force a pilot to fly more than one hundred combat missions. The choice was completely Don's to make.

In Don's mind, it wasn't much of a choice. He'd never once considered checking out of the war. Not so much because he loved war, but because he couldn't imagine life without it—without the jets, the bullets, the bombs, the adrenaline, the camaraderie, the flying, the combat high. It was all as addictive as heroin. Furthermore, he'd forged himself into one of the best pilots on the planet and was certain he could improve still. He had no idea what he might do after the war. He was so busy with the business of war that he hadn't devoted more than a few minutes of thought to the business of peace. He doubted he'd ever be as good at anything as he was at combat flying. It was at once depressing and exhilarating. And he chose to think of it as only exhilarating.

Additionally, the air force was quickly running out of combat pilots. McNamara & Co. had planned for a war that would last a few months to maybe two years. But as the war entered its third year, pilots were opting to leave the combat zone in droves—especially F-105 pilots, whose survival rates were so dismal to begin with.

The air force then compounded the F-105 casualty rate by calling up pilots from the Air Defense Command—pilots who weren't trained for combat. They typically flew only stateside in interceptor jets like the F-102 Delta Dagger. Their mission had always been to protect the United States from any Russian bomber attack. They'd been trained on defense, not offense. In flight school, the most skilled pilots were sent to fly combat jets, and the rest were sent to fly for the ADC.

Of their lack of experience, Don said, "ADC pukes didn't know anything about combat tactics or maneuvers. They were completely unprepared for Vietnam."

Unprepared or not, they were thrust into battle, and the F-105 casualty rates soared. Gone were the veteran pilots who possessed hard-earned combat experience from World War II and Korea. Going forward, the air force flight crews would be burdened with greenhorns and ADC pukes.

So it was that Don signed up for another tour of combat duty, deciding to switch from the mostly monotonous task of piloting B-52 bombers to the high-voltage thrill of flying supersonic fighter jets.

Don was assigned to the 354th Tactical Fighter Squadron, flying out of Takhli Royal Thai Air Force Base in Thailand.

The first time he walked out to the tarmac to inspect his jet, he was as overwhelmingly thrilled as the first time he'd ever seen a jet plane flying above Pocatello during an air show as a young boy. As was the custom in the air force, he was able to select a name for his jet that would be painted on the fuselage beneath the cockpit canopy. Don, at the time, loved the subversive and wickedly funny Pink Panther movies with Peter Sellers, as well as the Pink Panther Saturday-morning cartoon that featured a large, pink animated cat.

Thus, he dubbed his F-105 the *Pink Pussycat*, and he paid the aircraft maintenance crew an extra fifty dollars to paint a bright pink cartoon cat next to the name.

He then sidled up to two of the most experienced pilots in the squadron: Capt. George "Toby" Tobin and Capt. Ed Cleveland.

"They were great, great pilots," Don would recall, "and I followed them everywhere. I ate what they ate. I did what they did. I slept when they slept. I was like a human sponge. They taught me everything."

Prior to his first combat mission aboard the F-105, Tobin and Cleveland took Don to dinner at Cabaret Kays, a restaurant just off base that doubled as a Thai massage and bathhouse. Don wanted to be sure to get enough sleep, so he left the two veteran pilots just after dinner and decided to walk back to his barracks. As he strode along a path that led back to the base's main gate, he opted to take a diagonal shortcut across a dark field. After a few steps through waist-high grass, Don plunged into a black morass and sank to his neck. It was an open-sewage canal, and by the time Don was able to hoist himself back to land, he was covered in feces and muck. He squished and sloshed his way to his barracks, careful to avoid close encounters with any of his fellow pilots. And as he peeled away his befouled uniform, he hoped this mishap wasn't an omen of things to come.

The following morning, Don prepared for combat. He'd pushed his inauspicious encounter with the sewage canal far from his mind as he strutted across the tarmac, confident in his flight suit, with his helmet cradled in his right arm. As he approached his plane, he could see that some letters were missing from its customized moniker. Some of his fellow pilots, most likely, had pooled their funds to pay the air crew to scrape off part of the name they'd recently painted on. The name beneath the canopy now read: *Pink Pussy*.

Normally, Don would've been furious. But all combat missions were life-or-death endeavors. There was no time to become distracted. So he ignored it for this flight. And the next. And the next. By the time he thought to change it, the name, ironic and salacious as it was, began to grow on him and became a source of subversive pride. He would thus pilot the *Pink Pussy* in the skies over Vietnam for a remarkable 151 missions.

But on this first mission, Don's inexperience as a fighter-jet pilot showed. He had much to learn and little time to learn it. Either that, or perish. There wasn't much of an alternative.

Don flew off the right wing of Tobin as they streaked above a green expanse of jungle somewhere over North Vietnam.

As they overflew their target, Tobin, who'd just released his ordnance, calmly radioed Don, "OK, just put yours ten meters north of my smoke."

"Roger," Don replied as he released his bombs.

The squadron pulled up and began circling back to base. Don could see fire and smoke billowing from where Cleveland's and Tobin's bombs had exacted their damage. But there was no third column of smoke to be seen anywhere.

The radio crackled.

"Uh, you'll need to work on that," said Tobin. "By my calculation, you dropped about three kilometers north and east of target."

Don seethed in his cockpit—angry at himself for being such a rookie. First the fall into raw sewage, then the jet name prank, and now this. He couldn't wait to get back to base to begin studying for his next mission, vowing to be better prepared.

Chapter Twenty-Six

[Sports are] a ritualization of war and tribalism. There's a reason why teams on the field of battle excite such powerful emotions in us. In Darwinian terms they have acquired prestige and rank and power relative to the other competing teams.

This is the profound identity we feel with a group as it competes with another group. It's a sort of a communion that transcends our individual selves. There is an ecstasy that is almost religious. In fact, I believe that religion has its roots right here in this sense of this profound communion we can feel in these situations of collective euphoria. Being lifted out of ourselves. That sense of collective belief. Of bonding in the service of a greater cause. Religion is the highest expression of our tribal longings to be part of a greater whole. [It's] a celebration of the collective communion that [Darwinian] group selection has predisposed us to.

—*OF ANTS AND MEN*, E. O. WILSON

<hr>

Time and time again we see ants, humans and other eusocial creatures giving up their lives for the good of the group. . . . The idea [of group selection] is simple. It's not just about the survival of the fittest individual, but the fittest group, too. . . . Within groups, selfish individuals win; however, groups of altruistic individuals always beat groups of selfish individuals.

—*OF ANTS AND MEN*, E. O. WILSON

DON LOVED TO FLY. HE LOVED COMBAT. AND HE HAD NO FEAR OF death. None whatsoever.

"I always just assumed I would die in Vietnam," he often said. "It never occurred to me that I wouldn't."

With his first combat mission resulting in a horrific crash in which he cheated death by beating astronomical odds, for the rest of his time in Vietnam, he always just figured he was playing with house money—he had absolutely nothing to lose. Today they might call that kind of mentality survivor's guilt or maybe posttraumatic stress. But back then, they just called Don one helluva pilot.

And one helluva pilot he was. He was also a perfectionist of the highest order. After each combat mission, most pilots were simply thankful to be alive. Not Don. He rarely gave it a thought. Rather, his entire mind, body, and spirit were devoted to becoming a great fighter pilot—not a merely good one, but a great one. He didn't want to be the best in just his squadron, but in the world. It's all he thought about, nearly all day, every day. Other pilots, when they landed after a combat mission, would tremble as their feet touched the tarmac. They would bow their heads to God and give thanks for another few hours on earth. Then they would slap each other's backs and spend the night raising shot glasses, making toasts to dead comrades, and drinking themselves into oblivion—anything to escape, if only temporarily, the horror and terror of war.

But not Don. He would shower, change, and spend the rest of the day and much of the night—stone-cold sober—in the squadron war room with the military planners and strategists. There he would study the statistical results of that day's mission. He would review airspeed, bomb patterns, enemy aircraft activity, plane damage, troop movement, successes, failures, antiaircraft patterns—anything and everything that would increase his knowledge, that would make him a better pilot, that would increase his odds, thus helping him to continue cheating death. It wasn't so much an exercise in survival and self-preservation but rather a game, an intellectual challenge—a tantalizing puzzle to be solved.

In 1967 alone, American forces had lost an astonishing number of aircraft in combat—318. An F-105 pilot could expect a one-in-four chance of dying before his single tour of duty—typically fifty combat missions—was up. He had better odds simply putting a single bullet in his service revolver, spinning the chamber, pointing the barrel at his temple, and pulling the trigger. The survival odds for two tours of duty was a coin flip. Anything over three tours was considered a death sentence—not likely survivable.

By 1967, the whole of North Vietnam bristled with antiaircraft installations, courtesy of the Russians and Chinese. An F-105 pilot on a single mission could expect to get shot at over ten thousand times. The North Vietnamese and their allies threw everything they had at the American jets. There were surface-to-air missiles (SAMs); fixed, large-caliber antiaircraft guns; small-caliber guns; flack; and, of course, MiGs—the feared Russian-made fighter jets.

To compound the problem, the American air campaign labored under an unwieldy and bureaucratic command and control structure. Since its inception, the air force had always operated under a single air manager who was responsible for all aircraft activity within the theater of combat. In Vietnam, however, the war had been highly political from the outset. Politicians in Washington, DC, rather than experienced combat pilots and planners, managed the war with a heavy hand. Air strike requests originated with air divisions in Vietnam. They were then sent up the chain of command to the military's chief of Pacific operations. He then submitted the request to the Joint Chiefs of Staff at the Pentagon in Washington. They submitted the requests for review by the State Department and the CIA. Only after the request had cleared all hurdles and obstacles could it be submitted to the president and his Tuesday cabinet for a final thumbs-up or thumbs-down. It was certainly no way to manage a war, and hundreds of pilots died unnecessarily as a result.

Likewise, pilot flight protocols were developed in Washington for implementation in Vietnam. Each pilot was told precisely how to fly each mission. Everything from altitude and air speed to targets, angles of attack, and evasive maneuvers was printed in manuals and drilled into the pilots' heads. Any deviation from these tactics was highly discouraged and punishable.

Don was not impressed. This was plain-Jane tactical flying. And it differed vastly from combat flying. It was something that any veteran pilot from World War II or Korea would tell you. Unfortunately, there were few veteran combat pilots in the higher-up chain of command.

Whenever Don reviewed such flight manuals, he cringed. It was all paint by numbers. There was no artistry. No cunning. No aggression. No warrior spirit. No surprise. No killer instinct. Instead, it was a simplistic diagram for a quick death.

By his eighth mission in the F-105, Don realized that he wouldn't survive until his tenth unless he seized control of his own fate rather than allow that yoke to be steered by a distant politician who had likely never flown in combat or had never whiffed the acrid scent of the battlefield.

Don had already solved the puzzle and was surprised no one else had. It was all there for anyone to see. Hidden in the complexity of the numbers and data from hundreds of combat missions was a pattern—a clear path for survival. He told anyone who would listen his plan for keeping American jets out of harm's way. They told him not to make waves and to stick to the flight manual.

So on his ninth mission, Don was forced to choose between near-certain death and survival. Without hesitation, he chose the latter.

Don's F-105 roared from the tarmac of Takhli Royal Thai Air Force Base and rose into the sticky haze that blanketed the lowlands of Indochina. A gray-green world of rice paddies and muddy rivers fell away. The sun brightened. Once a pale disk lording over a thick layer of tropical swelter, it was now its more familiar self—a blaze of bright yellow radiating against a deep blue sky. The Mekong River snaked broad and brown on the horizon. Don studied its mesmerizing features as it drifted beneath and away. A series of ever-higher plateaus stepped up toward a rolling mist that broke in places to reveal a canopy of deep, wet green.

Now streaking above the Laotian highlands, Don cruised at fifteen thousand feet. It was his ninth F-105 mission. On his previous eight missions, he'd been forced to follow the bureaucratic tactical flight manual that had been developed in the bowels of the Pentagon. He was convinced that his demise would be imminent if he stuck to that predictable, unimaginative playbook that was heavy on a data-driven concept, evangelized by McNamara's Whiz Kids, called statistical process control. It was a way to build predictability, and thus quality, into a system. And while it worked wonders for American manufacturing, Don was certain it was a disaster when applied to combat flying. As a combat pilot who was up against a cunning and deadly enemy, predictability was not his friend.

The F-105 flight manuals dictated that pilots approach their targets from an altitude of twelve thousand feet and then descend at a thirty-degree angle. They were to pull out of their dives at altitudes of 1,500 to 3,000 feet above ground level and pop their air brakes so that they could fly over their targets at the rather pedestrian speed of 500 knots (575 mph) before firing their guns and releasing their bombs. They were to then bank left before pulling up and circling back to base. Every pilot performed this maneuver every time. Thirty degrees. Fifteen hundred feet. Air brakes. Five hundred knots. Drop bombs. Bank left. Pull up. Circle back.

Don had studied thousands of mission reports and bombing pattern photos. He'd spent hundreds of hours speaking to World War II and Korean War fighter pilots and bombardiers. And he'd concluded that the American tactical manual for the F-105 was nothing more than a death trap. It minimized the plane's advantages—speed and accuracy—while maximizing the enemy's advantage—cookie-cutter predictability.

Don knew that the F-105 was designed to fly beneath radar, hugging the contour of the earth while flying faster than the speed of sound— all to deliver a nuclear bomb deep into the heart of Russia before ever being detected. It was a plane whose very essence was to fly very low and extremely fast. But McNamara & Co. had decreed that the jet be flown high and slow over bomb targets. It made no sense to Don.

The Annamite Range now jutted just ahead. Don could see waterfalls cascading in thin streams down narrow, jungle-clad canyons. Pockets of clouds clung to mountainsides. Pinnacles, some as high as eight thousand feet, pierced into the sunlight.

"Uh, Bison Two," Don called out to his wingman over the radio. "We're going in steep, low, and fast. Just stay tight, and we'll get everyone back to base before lunch."

Don spoke with calm authority, like he'd done this a hundred times before. There wasn't a doubt in his mind or a hint in his voice of uncertainty. If there had been, his fellow pilot might've at least pointed out that he was taking them well out of the bounds of regulations. But he didn't.

They simply flew in synchronization. He knew that Don had already flown over a hundred B-52 bombing missions. And while that was much different from flying a fighter jet, at least he'd had more than a taste of war. The young wingman hadn't. Don was his only tether. He had his life in Don's hands. And so he trusted him.

"Uh, Roger, Bison One," came the affirmative response over the radio.

The Annamites had drifted past their view. Laos was behind them, Vietnam now below them. The jungle highlands had dropped into the humid haze. A small string of hills, the Tam Dao, lay just ahead and ran from the northwest to the southeast. F-105 pilots famously referred to the spine of this range as Thud Ridge. Most pilots would swoop low and try to use the Tam Dao as a shield before making a final dive into the broad, flat valley of the Red River, which ran through Hanoi.

But Don stayed high.

Just prior to this mission he'd determined that the F-105 could perform at much higher tolerances than the flight protocol manual writers in Washington had ever considered. From this point on, Don had decided he would always come into an attack high—at fifteen thousand feet rather than the recommended twelve thousand feet. At the last possible moment, he would throw his plane into a dive—not at the recommended thirty-degree slope, but rather at a sixty-degree angle. As a point of comparison, most commercial jetliners approach their runways at about a five- to eight-degree slope. The steepest mountain peaks rarely drop at a steeper pitch than forty-five degrees. The backside of Half Dome in Yosemite at its most precipitous has a slope of less than forty-five degrees. If you were in the cockpit of a jet diving at such an angle, you'd have the sensation of going straight toward the ground.

Additionally, Don would enter his bombing run fast. And he'd stay fast. Instead of popping his air brakes and slowing to the recommended five hundred knots, he would forgo the air brakes completely and scream through the sky just under the sound barrier, flying at 600 knots (690 mph). The F-105 could easily handle that speed. It's what it was built for.

Of course, the high speed and steep attack angle would mean extra g-forces when he leveled off just prior to his target approach. It meant five g's instead of the recommended three. This was a fairly trivial matter by Don's calculations for both man and machine. The F-105s could handle fifteen g's, and pilots could do fine up to about nine g's.

As far as accuracy, Don had charted his higher-speed theory on numerous test bombing runs. It was simply a matter of math and physics. Once the speed was adjusted for, it was only an issue of releasing bombs a split-second earlier. Don found that bombing accuracy was virtually unchanged.

As a final flourish, Don would bank whatever way the situation warranted after releasing his munitions. Sometimes left, sometimes right. The enemy had calibrated all their weapons to planes that banked left. They rarely saw an American plane bank right—especially a plane flying at nearly seven hundred miles per hour. By the time they'd swung their weapons around, Don would be already completing his S-maneuver—rocketing steep toward the sky and out of range of enemy fire.

Don and his squadron screamed high over Thud Ridge. The jungle erupted with silent puffs of smoke and bright sparks from large-caliber artillery. But by the time the enemy had fired at Don, he and his squadron were already several hundred yards, if not a full mile or two, beyond. A thunderous sheet of bullets and flack and missiles tore through the sky. But Don was only vaguely aware of it. For most pilots, getting shot at felt like an exercise in controlled terror. It often meant stomach nausea, back spasms, trembling hands, and sweat dripping down your forehead and into your eyes. But to Don it was simply a game of chess. He'd outsmarted his opponent and he knew it. He was confident and alert. Adrenaline flooded his brain. He was aware of every sensation—visual, tactile, auditory, smell, taste. His mind processed every thought clearly in rapid procession. Even though he was traveling at nearly the speed of sound, he felt as though he were passing through the world in slow motion. He felt he could do anything—almost like a god.

In the high plateau of China's Yunnan Province, the Himalayas begin their sharp, steady rise toward the northwest. Yunnan Province is bordered by Tibet to the northwest and Laos and Vietnam to the southeast. In the steep valleys of these highlands, fed by both monsoonal rains as well as snowmelt from mountain peaks, the Red River begins its journey southwest toward the South China Sea. By the time it reaches the lowlands of Vietnam, where it flows wide, slow, and muddy, it is faintly tinged with the red soil of Yunnan.

In 1899, the French colonial government in Indochina began work on a one-and-a-half-mile span across the Red River. When it opened in 1903, it became one of the longest bridges in Asia, a cantilevered marvel that provided Hanoi with an economic railroad lifeline to Haiphong's harbor and the shipping lanes of the South China Sea. The project was spearheaded by Paul Doumer, the French colonial governor who would be elected president of France only to be gunned down in 1932 by a deranged Russian émigré. Doumer was a former math professor who possessed a love for intricate architecture. As such, the Paul Doumer Bridge, as it was named, was renowned for its bold engineering and dramatic iron latticework. It resembled something of a horizontal Eiffel Tower. It had been famously bombed three months previously by squadrons of F-105s, and its once-elegant spans now appeared like a mangled erector set. But the North Vietnamese had busily replaced the collapsed spans with pontoons and were close to getting the bridge operational. Don's mission was to take out a railyard and North Vietnamese rolling stock on the far riverbank near the bridge.

Don entered the valley, banked right, and followed high above the Red River toward Hanoi, which he could see sprawling flat and gray beneath the tropical haze. There were no skyscrapers, landmarks, or any signs of modernity. The tallest building was maybe four stories. The only striking feature was the Paul Doumer Bridge, which stretched long and dark and still elegant in places against the plain, muddy waters of the Red River.

Don pushed forward on his yoke and threw his jet into a dive. The flat valley floor rushed toward his cockpit. The reddish-brown river grew broad. Don could see the left bank begin to spark with antiaircraft fire. And again, because of Don's speed and steep slope, the bullets traced harmlessly behind him. Don carefully watched his altimeter as it spun counterclockwise, lower and lower. The river loomed, and a seeming lake of muddy water flowed beneath him, its banks nearly a mile away on either side. At two thousand feet, Don pulled back hard on the yoke. He tensed his body to absorb the g-forces, grimacing and grunting to counteract their effects. The plane seemingly hesitated before grabbing the air with its broad, flat underbelly and whooshing forward, snapping Don's helmeted head back into his seat. The jet leveled at 150 feet above the river. Don accelerated. He could see the Paul Doumer Bridge downriver on the horizon and banked toward his target near the far base of the bridge. An array of Russian-made 37mm and 57mm antiaircraft cannons sat atop a barge about a mile in front of the bridge, exactly as depicted in the aerial photos Don had studied before the mission. The artillerymen never heard Don coming. He was flying much lower and faster than any American jet they'd ever shot at. Don put the barge in his sights and squeezed a trigger, firing his nose-mounted 20mm machine gun. The bullets made a metallic twang as they raced toward their target. A row of water splashed in the river before stitching through the barge. More antiaircraft fire erupted from each side of the river, but the bullets remained high and far behind Don and his wingman. Don acquired the railyard in his bomb sight. As he released both bombs, the top span of the bridge passed maybe fifty feet beneath him in a blur. He was certain he'd scored a direct hit. Don banked hard right. His wingman followed in a tight pattern. The g-forces pressed him into his seat as he raced toward the opposite riverbank just south of Hanoi. The moment his plane leveled off, he jerked the yoke left and accelerated nearly straight up into the tropical sky.

Don flew 165 such missions in Vietnam. Air Force statisticians had calculated that an F-105 on a typical mission drew the fire of over ten thousand enemy projectiles. That meant more than 1.6 million shots were fired at his aircraft. His plane was hit three times. Twice in the tail by a small-caliber rifle and once by a piece of shrapnel that caused a barely perceptible leak in his fuel tank.

Fifteen thousand feet. Dive at a sixty-degree angle. Level at three hundred feet. Drop bombs. Bank hard right, pull up, bank hard left, and then circle back home. It was a stroke of genius. He was only sad that it was considered a rogue maneuver and didn't become protocol for other pilots.

Don's plane leveled out at twenty thousand feet, far away from enemy fire. The Annamite Range drifted back into view, and he once again admired the green-clad pinnacles.

"That was a direct hit, I believe," he called out over the radio to his wingman. "Back before lunch, just like I told you."

Chapter Twenty-Seven

Show me a hero and I'll write you a tragedy.
—F. Scott Fitzgerald, *Notebook E*

Don was descended from a witch. On his mother's side. A real, bona fide American witch. One who'd been hanged in Salem. On July 19, 1692. For the crime of witchcraft and sorcery. Her name was Susannah Martin.

And in the reading of her trial transcripts, Susannah comes across as dignified, rational, and fearless. Amid the mayhem and lunacy of a seventeenth-century Puritan witch trial, she keeps her composure, and fears death not a whit.

> As soon as [Martin] came [into the courtroom] many had fits.
>
> Magistrate: Do you know this woman?
>
> Abigial Williams saith it is Goody Martin, she hath hurt me often. Others by fits were hindered from speaking. Mercy Lewis pointed to [Martin] and fell into a little fit. Ann Putnam threw her glove in a fit at her.
>
> [Martin] laughed.
>
> Magistrate: What! Do you laugh at it?
>
> Martin: Well I may at such folly.
>
> Magistrate: Is this folly, the hurt of these persons?
>
> Martin: I never hurt man or woman or child.
>
> Mercy Lewis cried out, she hath hurt me a great many times and pulls me down. Then Martin laughed again. Mary Walcott saith this woman hath hurt me a great many times.

Magistrate: What do you say to this?

Martin: I have no hand in witchcraft.

Magistrate: What did you do? Did not you give your consent?

Martin: No, never in my life.

Magistrate: Pray, what ails these people?

Martin: I don't know.

Magistrate: But what do you think ails them?

Martin: I do not desire to spend my judgment upon it.

Magistrate: Do not you think they are bewitched?

Martin: No, I do not think they are.

Magistrate: Tell us your thought about them then.

Martin: No. My thoughts are my own when they are in, but when they are out they are another's. Their master.

Magistrate: Do you believe these do not say true?

Martin: They may lie for aught I know.

Magistrate: May not you lie?

Martin: I dare not tell a lie if it would save my life.

Magistrate: Then you will speak the Truth.

Martin: I have spoke nothing else. I would do them any good.

Then Mercy Lewis and all many of the rest were afflicted. John Indian fell into a violent fit and said it was that woman, she bites, she bites, and then she was biting her lips.

Magistrate: Have you not compassion for these afflicted?

Martin: No, I have none.

Magistrate: Do not you see how God evidently discovers you?

Martin: No. Not a bit for that.

Magistrate: All the congregation think so.

Martin: Let them think what they will.

The story of Susannah Martin had been handed down, generation to generation, in Don's family. She was celebrated, especially around Halloween, for her resolute stand against the malignant mania that had swept through her New England community. She was pointed, funny, and wicked smart. And even in the face of certain death, she was absolute in her refusal to suffer fools.

But the story that is missed by many who study or read about the Salem witch trials is that Susannah was killed not so much because she was perceived to be a witch but because she was a woman. And old. And alone. And once wealthy.

From the time of her husband George's death a few years earlier, several of her neighbors had actively and aggressively coveted her goods—so much so that they'd begun fabricating fantasies as soon as Susannah's inheritance had come into play. One neighbor proclaimed that he'd visited George, who happened to be one of the largest private landowners in the region, on his deathbed, and only minutes before he'd expired, George had muttered that he wished for his neighbor, not his wife, to receive all his worldly possessions, even though his written will stipulated otherwise. The neighbor went to court and was somehow successful in getting George's imaginary mumblings validated as a contract. Susannah sued, and the fight was on—until it ended, conveniently, with Susannah hanged for the practice of witchcraft.

Susannah had come to America as something of royalty—descended directly from Baron Roger North and Baron Richard Rich, two of England's most infamous sociopaths, who were also henchmen for perhaps England's greatest sociopath, King Henry VIII.

Of Baron Rich, little good could be said. He was given the task by Henry VIII of looting, plundering, and destroying Catholic churches, monasteries, and holdings throughout the land. It was a job he performed with a rapacious zeal, and it made him fabulously wealthy. His false testimony ultimately caused Sir Thomas More, a lifelong friend, to lose his head. Literally. The only woman ever to be tortured in the Tower of London was a poet named Anne Askew, whose crimes were to secretly harbor Protestant beliefs and to loudly advocate a woman's right to divorce. For this, she was stretched out on the rack. And when even the constable of the Tower grew squeamish of the task at hand and left to seek the king's pardon, Rich was undeterred and turned the wheel himself, dislocating most of the joints in her body and sending her horrific screams echoing off the nearby stone walls and cobblestone streets for all Londoners in proximity to hear. He later finished the job by having her burned, ever so slowly, at the stake. The *Oxford Dictionary of National Biography* proclaimed that Rich had earned "a reputation for amorality and treachery with few parallels in English history." Given the country's imperialistic tendencies, its global conquest of people and places over the course of centuries, that's an honor not bestowed lightly nor earned without great effort and amid fierce competition.

Yes, it's a long journey from London to Plymouth Rock. As it is from Plymouth to Pocatello. And from Pocatello to Vietnam.

But much can be learned from these sweeps of history, the travels through time and place of those who came before.

One of the lessons is that we can never fully escape who we are. We are driven by forces seen and unseen. By our genetic code. By world events. By experience. By friends. By family.

Another is that a surprising proportion of world history has been impelled by sociopaths who, through a lust for power, an unflinching willingness to do anything to attain it, and an unquenchable addiction to the thrill of adventure, danger, and death, are ever in motion, ever seeking the next horizon, ever fearless in the face of their own demise.

Don's mother, Lucille, was much like her ancestor Susannah Martin—whip-smart, reserved, observant, and matter-of-fact. She had a sense of humor that sneaked up on most people; she always seemed a step or two ahead, and there was frequently a delay in recognition among others. She was down-to-earth and often blunt—able to offer a pithy comment that always seemed to get to the heart of the matter at hand, no matter how impolitic or cutting. Lucille was a masterful pianist who practiced relentlessly and could get lost in her music for hours at a time. She had an understated beauty and Donna Reed good looks. And she was surrounded by male relatives, most of whom could likely have been classified as suffering from—by at least some degree or another—sociopathy or narcissistic personality disorder.

The two-centuries-long road from the Salem witch trials to Pocatello was a bumpy one for Lucille's family, as it was for the United States. It's a history that was cleaved by the Civil War, an event that traumatized most families who lived through that time and place. And Lucille's was no exception.

Both her grandfathers were officers in Indiana regiments, volunteering at the outbreak of the war and fighting in blood-soaked battles in Nashville, Yellow Bayou, Vicksburg, and Parkers Crossroads. A great-uncle served as a colonel under Gen. Ulysses Grant. And a great-grandfather was killed during Grant's siege and capture of Fort Donelson, a Confederate stronghold in Tennessee.

But war is never a short-lived event. It's something that can traumatize a person, a family, a nation. And it's often a trauma that can cascade from generation to generation to generation. The Civil War achieved this effect perhaps as no American war had done before or has since.

William Boyatt took up arms and marched south as an eager, clear-eyed boy of seventeen. He returned three years later as a lieutenant with a mysterious intestinal disorder (two-thirds of the 620,000 Civil War dead succumbed to disease rather than battle wounds) as well as a newfound penchant for whiskey spiced with ginger. Both afflictions would haunt him for the rest of his days.

He would go on to practice law with his war-hero brother in their small southern Indiana town. Calamity was his constant companion, and despite repeated interventions, he was never able to abstain from his whiskey and died an inveterate drunk. But not before raising a family.

Lucille's father, and William's son, was one Edwin "Red" Boyatt. He was by all accounts restless, rambunctious, and ever hungry for adventure. The sleepy Indiana burg of Brownstown was in no way big enough to hold his dreams, aspirations, and lust for all things grand. He grew into his teens as a talented musician and a star baseball player. He considered either as a possible ticket out of the stifling plainness of the agrarian American heartland. Baseball had already taken him barnstorming throughout the Midwest—to farm-belt crossroads like Vincennes, Paducah, and Terre Haute—and to bigger centers like Lexington, Cincinnati, and Indianapolis. But he yearned for the likes of Chicago, New York, Philadelphia, and Washington, DC, and hoped that perhaps Major League Baseball might afford him the possibility. He played catcher with such grit, determination, and grace that scouts from the St. Louis Browns and Cincinnati Reds gave Boyatt tryouts, but he was never able to make the step up to the big leagues.

In 1899 he married Lucille's grandmother, Orpha Martin, a school-teacher who hailed from a prominent Brownstown family of doctors, landowners, and breeders of regal Kentucky thoroughbred horses and much-sought-after shorthorn cattle. What he and Orpha did next surely verged on lunacy in the eyes of friends, family, and neighbors, shocking their sturdy midwestern mores. They joined the circus. Or rather they purchased one. Or won it in a card game, as Red used to like to say. It was something of a traveling vaudeville show, complete with blackfaced minstrels, musicians, dancing bears, and horses jumping off high dives.

As implausible as it seemed, the rag-tag production served as a vehicle for adventure and exploration. For two years, the couple toured the country, playing in small, medium, and large towns throughout Georgia, Florida, Texas, Arizona, and California. On a swing through the West, they played to increasingly sparse crowds in Reno and Boise before going bust in Pocatello and becoming marooned in a place they'd probably never heard of before. So they stayed, settled down, and started a family, with Orpha taking a job as a teacher in a one-room schoolhouse, while William, who like his father had taken to drink, was able to catch on as a baggage handler with the Union Pacific railroad.

There Lucille was raised. And in contrast to her calm demeanor and stately air, her three older brothers were hellions. Sociopaths, probably. Alcoholics, definitely.

Each was charming, brilliant, educated, loquacious, and dashing. All were bound to tragedy in one form or another. None lived past the age of fifty-two.

The oldest, Paul, killed a man. Shot him twice in the chest with a .38 revolver. Had it coming, Paul would say. These things tend to happen when you own a brothel/dance hall/beer garden and your wife is the madam.

In 1936, Averell Harriman, chairman of the Union Pacific Railroad, capped his dream of ferrying tens of thousands of well-to-do passengers to central Idaho by rail when he opened the Sun Valley Resort, America's first destination ski area featuring the world's first chair lift. Anchored by the Sun Valley Lodge, the resort aspired to be a sort of St. Moritz in the Idaho Rockies. And though Harriman hewed it from a rough-and-tumble, slightly downtrodden gold and silver mining town that had seen better days, he invested heavily in publicity and spent a small fortune cajoling and paying Hollywood's A-list to suddenly take up skiing and agree to be photographed cavorting in the snow. Celebrities like Gary Cooper, Carole Lombard, Clark Gable, Errol Flynn, and Ernest Hemingway were regulars in the early days.

Harriman added to Sun Valley's cachet by helping to bankroll movies that agreed to be filmed in and around the resort. The first was the screwball comedy *I Met Him in Paris*, starring Claudette Colbert, Melvyn Douglas, and Robert Young. That was followed by *Sun Valley Serenade*, with Sonja Henie, Milton Berle, and Glenn Miller.

With the influx of tourists, Hollywood production crews, and big-city spenders who would ride the train in from Chicago, Seattle, San Francisco, and Los Angeles, Paul Boyatt sensed an opportunity to capitalize on the vice that often accompanied such money.

He and his new wife, Barbara, purchased a dilapidated apartment building just off Highway 75 in Hailey, a shabby hamlet that had sprung up on the east bank of the Big Wood River just a few miles from Ketchum, Hailey's comparatively glamorous neighbor to the north. Paul and Barbara erected a big red sign, announcing to all travelers in and out of the Wood River Valley: "Bobby's Place."

In the winter of 1936, the sign caught the eye of one Bert Slater, a set director for Paramount Studios in Los Angeles, who'd been sent into the wilds of Idaho to help scout filming locations and construct sets for *I Met Him in Paris*, a vehicle for Claudette Colbert, Hollywood's biggest female star at the time, that centered largely on her character's romantic wintertime escapades through the French and Swiss Alps—a movie of tenuous quality that would later bomb at the box office.

Slater, a married father of four, was fond of Bobby's Place and fonder still of the proprietor's wife. During the two months of Idaho filming, Slater was a regular. Though he returned to Los Angeles as soon as the movie wrapped, he was smitten with Paul's wife and returned the following summer, taking up house with Barbara, while Paul was away in

Pocatello, picking up some extra work during the slow summer season. Slater spent his time impressing Barbara with his Hollywood money and tales of Los Angeles glamour, whispering, as such men are inclined to do, that he would soon take her away from all of this, though it was an empty promise, as they both knew.

Word had gotten back to Paul that he was being cuckolded; he sped back to Hailey. But not before stopping at a Bellevue, Idaho, bar, at the southern mouth of the Wood River Valley, sopping up beer for courage and borrowing a pistol from a friend.

"I might need a little authority," he would later explain in court, "and I may want to run a little bluff on a fellow."

He purchased a box of bullets from Campbell's Drug Store and arrived at Bobby's Place with a loaded gun, a booze-addled mind, and an anger-crazed disposition.

The story Barbara first told to authorities—and the one that is certainly most plausible, as well as the one prosecutors put forth in court—was that she and Slater were in bed drinking whiskey when Paul burst in, gun drawn. Slater ran to the kitchen, where Paul shot him twice in the chest, severing his aorta and killing him instantly.

However, Paul had the good fortune of being the older brother of one Clyde Vernon Boyatt, a bright, up-and-coming attorney with a burgeoning law practice in Pocatello. C. V., as he was called, recruited the former Idaho attorney general, and together they took on the case to defend C. V.'s rakish brother against a capital murder offense that under Idaho law could mean hanging by the neck until dead.

By the time the court case rolled around later that fall, Barbara had changed her tune. She told of how Paul had arrived home to find Bert and her having a drink. A conversation ensued. Paul calmly asked the Hollywood big shot to leave. Bert refused. Paul demanded. Bert became violent, pulling a gun. He pointed the gun and tried to pull the trigger, but the safety was on. He lunged at Paul. Paul grabbed Bert's wrist, but not before Bert had clubbed him on the head with the butt of the gun. Paul's weapon fell to the floor. The two wrestled in what was described as a death struggle. Paul was able to twist the barrel of Bert's gun away. Gripped by both men, the gun somehow fired twice. Bert was hit, but hardly fazed, and the fight rambled on. The pair tumbled into the kitchen, where Bert resumed clubbing Paul on the head, this time with an iron stove poker. By now, both guns had fallen to the floor. Paul bled profusely, his face and clothes covered in his own blood. Bert punched him in the nose, and Paul dropped, dazed, to his knees. He groped on the floor desperately before his hand found a gun. Just as Bert was lifting the stove poker and preparing to finish off his adversary, Paul wheeled up, clocked the murderous interloper on the head with the gun, and got him in a clinch. The pair fell onto the floor, still in a clinch, wrestling for about thirty seconds more before the mortally wounded Bert finally succumbed, declaring, "I got enough. I'll leave." To which Paul calmly replied, "Okay."

Paul would later tell the court that he left his home with a bloody face, bloody hands, and a blood-soaked shirt. This is in spite of a police officer's testimony of how he'd pulled Paul over on the highway just south of town only minutes after the killing but had decided to let him continue on his way because his car didn't quite match the description the officer had been given and Paul didn't seem like he'd just shot someone at all—he was cool and calm, with hair that was perfectly parted and a white dress shirt that was neatly pressed and spotless. No blood whatsoever.

At the end of the trial, Paul was convicted only of second-degree murder and received a twenty-year sentence, which was reduced to ten years on appeal. The Idaho jury apparently didn't believe that the death penalty should apply to a love-scorned husband for shooting a big-city adulterer. Further, without the help of his lawyer brother, he would've surely received a first-degree murder conviction with either the death penalty or life in prison.

Paul would serve eight years of his sentence in the Idaho State Penitentiary, after which he moved to Reno, Nevada, landing a job in a casino, dealing blackjack and seeking a fresh start. But fresh starts seldom arrive for individuals of Paul's disposition and alcoholic tendencies. Shortly after his release, he was found dead from an overdose of pills and alcohol.

His brother C. V. would enjoy a rapid rise in the legal profession. He was renowned for his keen mind and deft handling of cases—abilities that earned him an appointment as district attorney. But his career, too, would soon hit a wall, dragged down by his relentless and ongoing battle with alcoholism. His bosses, at their wits' end about what to do with their brilliant but beleaguered colleague, ordered him to a sanitarium after one particularly onerous bender. C. V. was given an injection meant to curb his alcoholic cravings. The drug sent him into cardiac arrest, from which he died instantly.

In the mountains southwest of Reno, Galena Creek tumbles cold, clear, and fast down the eastern escarpment of Mt. Rose, which rises prominently above the city to an elevation of over ten thousand feet. Just south of town, the Mt. Rose highway branches west from Highway 395 as it begins its bold ascent into the High Sierra. The narrow ribbon of asphalt follows Galena Creek to near its source at the mountain divide along the northwestern rim of Lake Tahoe. It climbs, serpentine, through stands of ponderosa pine, which cling to near-vertical slopes that fall away from the guardrail for a thousand feet at a time. Cars creep up and down the mountain in low gear, wending tediously from switchback to switchback. Everywhere there are rocky chutes and narrow canyons choked with flattened trees, gray and dead from season upon season of winter avalanches. Near the summit, boulders as big as buses bulge above signs warning motorists to watch for falling rocks. In the summer, the air is dry and cool with the mountain scent of pine and manzanita.

On July 20, 1956, Bill Boyatt, the most dissolute of Lucille's brothers, took a late-afternoon break from his long, hot drive from Fresno, California, back to his current home in Reno, Nevada. Now forty-seven, his life a long-running shambles, Bill stood beneath a stand of ponderosa, anchored in the sand, only a few yards from where two-foot-high waves curled and crashed, curled and crashed, curled and crashed onto the coarse granite sand of Lake Tahoe's shore. A breeze blew stiff and steady across the surface of the expansive mountain lake, as it did on most summer afternoons. Bill breathed deeply. The air, heated by the sun, cooled by the water, was fresh, bracing, and a joy for the senses. The lake sparkled, an impossible shade of high-altitude blue, stretching for miles, ringed by distant gray, granite peaks, which in turn were flanked by blue-green carpets of pine. To Bill, this was heaven.

He stared out at the water, mesmerized, and grew ever more tired. He walked to a tall, thin boulder that jutted like a headstone just above the narrow beach. He sat atop a layer of pine needles, leaned back against the smooth, hard granite, and again breathed deeply the warm but cool air. Behind him, in a dirt clearing, Bill's black Hudson shimmered with heat beneath the summer sun. Its engine was off, but having just powered nonstop up the western slope of the Sierra, it still hissed and crinkled from beneath the hood, as though urgently reminding the driver of a journey not yet complete. In front of Bill, the waves continued to curl and crash, curl and crash, curl and crash. Lulled by the hypnotic hush of the lake, the drowsy warmth of thin mountain air, and the narcotic scent of pine, Bill closed his eyes and slipped into the kind of bone-weary sleep from which one might jolt awake an hour or two hence, startled, lost in space and time, wondering, after a bewildering number of seconds, how and when a person came to be sitting by a boulder, near a lake, in the mountains, alone.

Though Bill was whip-smart just like his brothers, he couldn't seem to stick with anything for too long—school, jobs, friends, wives—and he thus rambled throughout the West—spending a year in Boise, two in Salt Lake, six months in Sacramento, a year and a half in Logan, and so on. No one was quite sure how many wives he had. Definitely one in Utah. Another in Idaho. Still a third in Nevada, and yet a fourth in California. There was certainly a girlfriend in every port—sometimes two and maybe three. His devastating charm and wholesome good looks made sure of that. He seemed like the kind of guy a girl would want to bring home to her mother. But he wasn't. Far from it. He drank, gambled, dried out, worked odd jobs, and traveled incessantly. Growing up, his teachers fretted over his lost potential and his sharp but undisciplined mind. They said he could've been a fine doctor, a notable attorney, or a renowned politician. If only he could focus, sit still, and direct his energies toward productive things like academics. But he wouldn't. Couldn't.

Don and his siblings would often notice the strange goings on of their uncle—things like how it came to be that several of their cousins had different mothers yet were only two or three months apart in age.

"Are some of our cousins illegitimate?" they would ask their mother, Lucille.

"No," she would reply, stern and indignant. "There are no illegitimate children in this family. Your uncle Bill married all their mothers."

As if that made everything okay.

In 1954, he'd hitched on as a cook at Stone's Truck Stop and Diner in Truckee, California, near Donner Pass. For an entire year, Bill was punctual, hard-working, resourceful, and sober. He labored diligently to become Bob Stone's most trusted and valued employee. Toward this end, he was so effective that when Bob left on a three-week overseas vacation, he put Bill in charge of the whole operation.

Bill beamed at the prospect. He then quickly forged a power-of-attorney document and proceeded to sell the entire business for cash to an unsuspecting Sacramento businessman before slipping out of town. Calamity, of course, ensued when Bob returned to find a new sign flashing above the business he'd spent most of his life building from the ground up.

Whenever this story made the rounds at Thanksgiving gatherings for years afterward, the adults would guffaw before Lucille would glare and say in her calm, low voice, "That's perhaps the most un-Christian thing one person could do to another."

Chastised, the adults would grow momentarily quiet before one would plead their case, "Yes, Lucille. But even you have to admit, in hindsight, it's pretty damned funny. I mean, the thought of the owner driving up and seeing his truck stop under new management."

The adults would resume laughing. Lucille would drop her head and fight back a wan smile.

—◆—

As Bill slept, a warm, humid mass of air pushed into California from the Pacific and blew steamily across the Central Valley, which baked beneath a hot summer sun. The air piled into the Sierra foothills before climbing higher, higher, higher—heavy, moisture-laden molecules wrung ever tighter by the increasing altitude.

On the Nevada side of the range, temperatures soared beneath cloudless skies, and the treeless, sage-covered flats shimmered beneath waves of heat, which sent columns of hot, dry air racing up the mountain escarpment to the east and into the stratosphere.

High above Lake Tahoe, a band of clouds—puffy, white, innocuous—dotted the horizon. And as the western moist air collided with the eastern dry air, the clouds ballooned with restless fury, roiling ever upward, shouldering aside the sky's pristine blue and leaving the lake to brood beneath darkening shadows and hastening winds.

Lightning flickered bright against the purple, gray backdrop of anvil-shaped clouds. Thunder rolled across the lake upon a gathering wind. Waves crested higher and crashed louder. Prickling specks of sand were plucked from the beach by bursts of wind. Tops of ponderosas swayed in unison, wind whistling through needles, blanketing the forest with an ominous "Shhhhhhhh."

Bill jolted awake. He blinked at the scene before him, confused. Sand stung his arms and face, forcing him to his feet. Thunder cracked, rumbled, and was swallowed by the loudly whispering trees.

The impending storm was indeed enough to make a man wonder how he came to be by a boulder, near a lake, in the mountains, alone. Most men would've scrambled by now for their cars and sought shelter. But Bill was not most men. He, for better or worse, was undaunted by things, even a force as great as nature's wrath.

He stood his ground and thought about the past. About a woman he'd met during a long-ago trip to San Francisco. She was young, soft, and beautiful—her hair brown, shiny, and silken. He dazzled her with talk of his travels and his bold plans for the future. He was the most handsome, charming, interesting man she'd ever met. After only a week, he'd asked her to marry him, and they spent the next month in a small apartment near the Embarcadero, oblivious to the outside world—the war, money for rent, what they would tell friends and relatives.

They lived in bliss, making incessant love, until, unexpectedly, the woman told Bill she was pregnant and that some of their grandiose plans should maybe find anchor in reality in deference to a coming baby.

Bill nodded, agreed, wiped her tears, held her tight, and assured her everything would be okay. She trusted his strength and confidence, burying her head into his shoulder, sobbing happily as he stroked her long, silken hair.

That afternoon, he walked to the US Navy recruiting center, enlisted, and spent the next three years as a cook aboard a battleship in the South Pacific.

He never saw that wife again, nor did he meet his child, a boy. Never, that is, until he received a call from the woman, against all her better sense and judgment, in July 1956, apologizing for having tracked him down but letting him know that her son—their son—for years had always wanted to meet his father. And she had always promised him that when he was old enough—maybe a teen—she would make such arrangements. She would secretly hope that her boy would forget or that time would assuage the wound of a fatherless son. But he never did; it never did.

And so she called Bill and asked him to come to Fresno. That is how, as he stood pondering these events, he'd come to be by a boulder, near a lake, in the mountains, alone.

The rain first came with the intermittent splatter of big, cold drops. This was followed in rapid sequence by a cool rush of wind, the unmistakable scent of a summer storm, and the sudden deluge of a full-throated downpour.

Bill gave ground, ran to his car, and drove back along a sandy, rutted road through the pines to the highway, his windshield wipers slapping uselessly against the ferocity of the pelting rain.

A prudent man might've ducked into a restaurant in Incline Village, waiting out the storm over a quiet meal of steak, potatoes, and coffee. But, again, that was not Bill.

He turned east onto the Mt. Rose Highway, and as he crested the nearly nine-thousand-foot pass, the storm, chasing just behind, had roused to the height of its fury.

Bill was forced to turn on his headlights even though sunset was more than an hour away. Sheets of rain rippled in curtains across the highway, which plunged in a series of switchbacks toward Reno, which lay in the Truckee Meadows, more than a mile below.

And Galena Creek—it hissed and frothed white in the headlights each time Bill crossed over via switchback. He worked his brake, clutch, and gearshift in unison, deftly creeping down the slope, only occasionally forcing the Hudson to accept a lower gear with a metallic *chunk-chunk*. Farther down the switchback, the creek, which had been only a summer trickle just minutes before, had begun to stream across the pavement in places, clattering small rocks onto the asphalt.

Bill made note, but continued on.

Two turns later, his headlights were thrown onto a crowd of maybe a dozen drivers and passengers who'd pulled over their cars, gotten out, huddled in the rain, and were now pointing to a dangerous dilemma up ahead.

Bill stopped momentarily and studied the scene. A car coming up the grade had stalled in the rising torrent, which now rushed maybe two feet deep across the highway. A family of five—a man, his wife, their young daughter, and two young sons—crouched on the front hood of a sedan, waving frantically and eerily in the headlights that beamed upon them from other cars that had halted in each direction.

Most men might've turned off their engine, gotten out, and begun conferring in the rain with the other men—pointing, talking, worrying, and ultimately concluding that there was nothing to be done but to wait and hope.

But Bill, of course, was not most men. It wasn't so much that he was preternaturally brave; rather, it was likely that, possibly due to genetics, he simply lacked a healthy sense of fear.

Bill stomped his clutch, shoved the gearshift forward, and rolled slowly past the crowd. He nosed the Hudson carefully into the rushing water, deeper, deeper, deeper. He could feel the car becoming buoyant, his tires losing traction, scuffing toward the guardrail to his left. The force of the swelling creek slammed broadside into the car, and he could hear rocks, carried by turbulent waters, pinging beneath his floorboard.

Bill stopped a couple feet from the stalled car, opened the driver's door, and left the engine running. Water surged beneath him. He glanced at the frantic family and stepped cautiously into the flood. The soles of his leather shoes connected with solid pavement, but a firm balance eluded him; the current tugged at his wool pants and yanked hard at his ankles. Bill shuffled, unsteady, toward the stranded family.

The father first handed Bill his ten-year-old son, who, trembling, eyes terror filled, wrapped both arms tight around Bill's torso. Bill shuffled back to his car, stowed the boy inside, returned for the wife, and brought her back to safety, too.

The father, impatient and fearful of the relentlessly rising water, tucked his four-year-old daughter and six-year-old son beneath each arm. He slid off the hood and into the flood, the water now as high as his waist.

The force of the current had grown so great that Bill could only move by steadying himself, hand over hand, along the guardrail. The father took a tentative step toward Bill. Then another. And another. He wobbled in the torrent, both hands occupied with children, his balance compromised. Bill gripped the guardrail tight with his left and stretched toward the father with his right. The man shuffled, precarious, almost there.

It was then that Galena Creek attacked from below, pulling each ankle quick and hard. The man, still gripping his children tight, toppled beneath the surface and vanished in an instant. The water hissed foamy and white. And even though Bill knew that all had been lost, he lunged to where the man had just stood, plunging his right hand deep into the torrent—groping, groping, groping—his left hand still clutching the guardrail for support.

Bill stopped, stood erect, and looked at his empty hand in disbelief.

A woman shrieked, the piercing sound rising above even the roar of the storm and the flood. The wife, wailing, stepped from Bill's car to atop a guardrail post. Bill waded toward her, frantically waving her back.

She jumped.

Bill watched her head bob downstream in the frothy current, which was bathed white from car headlights. The woman slowed, swirled amid the aspen, and was able to latch onto a low-hanging branch.

Bill paused for only a second before he, too, stepped atop a guardrail post and leapt. The water sucked him fast down the mountainside. He held his breath and struggled pointlessly to keep his head above water. The main current shot him into the pool beneath the aspen grove, pinballing him among the tree trunks before he was able to wrap one tight with both arms. The woman was only a few feet away, still clinging to her branch, but Bill could do nothing now except try to save himself.

Exhausted, cut, bruised, and near hypothermic, he'd done all he could. He pulled himself as high into the tree as he was able, just above the violent waters, where he thought he had a chance to wait out the flood.

The air then cracked with a mountainous roar. A ten-foot-high wall of water, churning with boulders and tree trunks, slammed into the two cars on the highway above, lifting them like so much flotsam and jetsam and hurtling them downslope with apocalyptic fury.

Bill looked up and in an instant knew it was time. The big aspen, which had gamely provided refuge until now, was pulled by its roots like a common weed and sent rocketing down the mountainside.

Sometimes death comes in a flash, like a strike of lightning in a summer storm. Sometimes death comes slowly—lingering, lingering, lingering—setting up an immovable camp for days, weeks, months, years. Sometimes death comes peacefully—a mist in the night—revealing its presence only later, wet blades of grass sparkling beneath a morning sun. Sometimes death comes ferociously—fangs fearsome, sharp, and bared. And sometimes death just swallows you whole, like Jonah's whale, dragging you to the ocean deep before suddenly, inexplicably, coughing you back up to life's shore, perhaps for one last shot at redemption. Or perhaps just because. There's no accounting for it. But come death will. And come for us all it must.

The Associated Press distributed this account of the incident:

RENO, Nev. (AP)—Search for the bodies of three flash flood victims was to be resumed today along the ravaged watercourse of Galena Creek 20 miles south of here where four persons died Friday.

*Searchers yesterday found the body of 4-year-old Vicki Wacho-
wicz two miles from the spot where a roaring wall of mud, water,
trees and boulders swept away her mother, brother, and another
motorist, William Boyatt of Reno.*

*The girl's father, Matt Wachowicz still was confined to Washoe
Medical Center where his condition was described as satisfactory. He
was found five miles downstream from the highway.*

Matt Wachowicz was indeed swept away by death, sluiced for miles
by a raging, foaming, churning river of boulders, trees, and mud, plunging through granite canyons, over cliffs, between massive ponderosa tree
trunks—any which thing might've, should've killed him—before he was
improbably, impossibly belched back onto life's shore.

Reprieved, Matt would eventually remarry, start a new family, and
stand a patriarch among dozens of grandchildren, great-grandchildren,
and great-great-grandchildren. Death wouldn't return to him for decades.
And when it did, it would come peaceably, softly, expectedly. He would
be ninety-seven.

Fred Wachowicz, aboard Bill's Hudson, tumbled one hundred yards
downslope before the vehicle wedged between a pair of ponderosa pines.
The trees, tall and sturdy, had seen plenty of such floods over the centuries
and barely wavered. Fred climbed out the car window and took refuge in
a pine branch.

He would go on to live a life that was by all accounts as upstand-
ing and resolute as Bill Boyatt's was wanton and shiftless. He would
develop into a leader, quarterbacking his high school football team and
becoming something of a star in his hometown of Sacramento. He
would earn a congressional appointment to the US Naval Academy
before serving for years with distinction as a naval officer. He would
leave the military and take an executive position in the San Francisco
Bay area with one of the world's first biotechnology firms that would
pioneer a vaccine for AIDS.

Perhaps it was a right and just trade—Bill's life for Fred's. Or perhaps
it just was. And nothing more.

At the age of forty-five, shortly after giving birth to the last of her six children, Lucille decided to do something for herself: She went to college. This was not something most middle-aged women ever considered at the time. But she persisted. She proved to be a superb student and earned a bachelor's degree in anthropology and a master's in paleontology.

In quiet moments, she sometimes shared her thoughts that the Bible was merely an interesting collection of tribal tales, thus calling into question the whole of Christianity. On the matter of faith, most suspected her as a nonbeliever.

So why bring the entire family to church every Sunday without fail?

"Oh," she would explain, "I never wanted any of my children to end up like my brothers, and I knew that given the family background, they could all use as much training in ethics and morality as possible."

In addition to Uncle Bill's truck-stop caper, another favorite family discussion was the dilemma of St. Peter and what he might do with a man whose life was so barren of good but whose last moments were so brave, heroic, selfless. He'd literally sacrificed his own life, around which had been strewn so much carnage, so that another could live. Might a person's whole journey through life be redeemed in an instant?

But whenever this philosophical discussion came up—and there were few things her family loved more than discussions of deep, philosophical, almost unanswerable questions—Lucille always said she had such a hard time getting around the notion that a benevolent god would sweep a wife and two of her children to their horrific deaths that it made the question of St. Peter's dilemma rather moot.

No, Uncle Bill was a Boyatt, likely a full-fledged sociopath, whose mind craved adventure, calamity, and excitement. Such traits caused mostly trouble in everyday life, but sometimes, in extraordinary circumstances, they were traits that served a genuine purpose. In narcissism, there can be selflessness.

Lucille preferred to just leave it at that.

—◆—

Galena Creek spills from the eastern slope of the Sierra onto the Great Basin floor in a sage-covered valley just south of Reno. There it flows slowly and languidly before its waters sink deep into the decomposed granite soil, feeding an underground reservoir that is in turn heated by geothermal forces, bubbling to the surface in the form of foul-smelling fumaroles and mudpots. The water is brackish, the stench of sulfur fills the air, and the ground is covered with a white alkali crust. The area is known as Steamboat. And it was into this hellish landscape that Galena Creek finally disgorged Bill's body, some twenty miles from the guardrail from which he'd first leapt. It took a full week before searchers finally found him—lifeless, putrid, bloated by the summer heat, and tangled beneath a mass of shattered trees.

In the decades since, a number of Bill's nieces and nephews, as well as grandnieces and grandnephews, had attended the University of Nevada, Reno. Avid skiers, they'd had occasion to drive the Mt. Rose Highway dozens of times. It was always family tradition to "wave to Uncle Bill," his wrecked Hudson still visible—now just a twisted frame of dark, rusted metal—still lodged between a pair of ponderosas along the banks of Galena Creek, an eternal reminder of one man's redemption.

Chapter Twenty-Eight

Juliette Laurent was an exotic dream. Half French, half Vietnamese, her eyes were a golden green, her body lithe, her skin smooth. Her rich brown hair was long with a slight wave. She often flashed a smile that was broad and inviting, her white teeth made striking against the contrast of light tan skin. She dressed brightly and stylishly and was fond of wearing fragrances that relatives regularly sent from Paris.

She resided in a small, elegant third-floor apartment in the embassy sector of Bangkok, where she taught French to the children of British and American diplomats and English to the children of French diplomats.

She disliked Americans as a general rule and avoided servicemen at all costs.

How she came to be Don's lover was simply an accident of time and place—something that couldn't be avoided. Not in 1968. Not in Bangkok. Not with a war raging to the north and to the east. Not with a combat pilot as smart, handsome, and dashing as Don. Not with a woman as stunning, worldly, and witty as Juliette. It was an unavoidable collision. And it served them both well for that time and that place.

"Who's that?" asked Juliette of a friend about the American officer who looked heroically irresistible in his crisp khaki uniform from across the room in a Bangkok restaurant.

"Who's that?" asked Don of a colleague about the woman with the runway model looks, Western flair, and silk Hermès scarf seated at the bar.

Two hours later, he stood outside her apartment door, having walked her a short distance home in the dark swelter of a Bangkok night.

They stood face to face, he only slightly taller than she. Sweat trickled down each of his temples and beaded on his forehead. The skin on both her delicate forearms glistened beneath the dim hallway light. The air hung thick, heavy, hot, and still. Amid the stifle, she spoke—ever so soft and in her half-French, half-Vietnamese accent:

"You're a presumptuous man."

"Yes, I am."

"And you don't ever take pause?"

"Not when I know I'm right."

"And you think you're right about me? About us?"

"Oh, I know."

She flashed her broad smile with her striking white teeth.

"Come back tomorrow."

"I'll be dead tomorrow. Probably."

"The day after then. If you're still alive."

She turned, paused, entered her apartment, and began to slowly close the door in Don's face—right before she stopped, whispering, "Just this once."

In 529 AD, on a strategically important mountaintop above the ancient Roman city of Casinum, St. Benedict built one of the first and most important monasteries in all of Catholicism. His first act was to topple a statue of Apollo, ending nearly a millennium of worship at the majestic Roman temple that had stood atop Monte Cassino previously, before constructing his sprawling abbey that would house in the coming centuries a trove of Catholic treasures overseen by a communal order of monks who lived by St. Benedict's Rule: *pax, ora et labora.*

"Peace, pray, and work."

The abbey at Monte Cassino had survived incursions by the Ostrogoths, Lombards, and even Napoleon. But in the winter and spring of 1944, a force of 140,000 Germans had encamped in and around the great historic edifice in an effort to form a choke point through which a force of 240,000 Allied troops would be unable to pass on their march to Rome, which lay some eighty gentle miles to the north.

Stalled for five months in the shadow of Monte Cassino and with casualties mounting into the tens of thousands, several dozen Allied commanders and their lieutenants began clamoring to unleash squadrons of American bombers upon the abbey, which was internationally renowned as one of the most important and sacred archaeological sites in the Western world.

Lt. Gen. Mark Clark of the US Fifth Army scoffed at the military necessity of leveling the abbey, arguing that none of his intelligence reports showed there were any Germans at all in the abbey itself.

Gen. Clark pressed the issue with the commander-in-chief of the Allied armies in Italy, Gen. Sir Harold Alexander.

Exasperated, he finally said to Gen. Alexander, "You give me a direct order, and we'll do it."

Gen. Alexander gave him the order. Gen. Clark carried it out.

On the morning of February 15, 1944, 142 B-17s, 47 B-25s, and 40 B-26s unleashed their maximum fury—over one thousand tons of explosives and incendiary bombs—upon the millennia-old monastery, which, in spite of having already been evacuated of truckloads of antiquities, still housed thousands of paintings, statues, mosaics, bound histories, and handscribed works of literature gathered from the far corners of the ancient world. By February 16, the entire mountaintop was reduced to rubble.

There were no German soldiers in the abbey. Only 230 civilian refugees, who were all killed.

Peace, pray, and work.

John Boyatt, Don's uncle and his mother Lucille's younger brother, learned to play poker amid the ruins of Monte Cassino. As a Boyatt, he'd always known how to play poker, of course, but there he honed his skills to that of a razor-edged cardsharp.

John had dropped out of college and enlisted in the army just after Pearl Harbor, with the hopes of escaping the boredom of northern Utah, seeing the world, and perhaps killing some Germans or Japanese. In that order.

He registered off the charts on his military aptitude tests, and the army estimated his IQ at over 140. In their wisdom, they made him an ordnance supply officer, responsible for shipping and loading explosives as well as keeping bombs at the ready for the advancing armies ahead of him.

He and his supply unit trailed behind the US Fifth Army as it raced across North Africa and into Italy's midsection before stalling near Monte Cassino. After the fall of Monte Cassino, the collapse of the Gustav Line, and the modern sacking of Rome by Allied forces, John and his crew were inadvertently left behind in Cassino. They awaited orders but had been, apparently, lost in the fog of war. So at Cassino they stayed. For weeks. Then months.

To their unit's relief and glee, a number of subterranean wine cellars in the region had withstood the relentless above-ground bombings. John and his men worked tirelessly to remove rubble from above the cellars and provide the Benedictine monks with renewed access to their stores of wine. The monks repaid the Americans during their stay with exquisite nightly meals of Italian cuisine as well as all the wine they could drink. Which was a lot.

In between the food and drink, the Americans played poker.

Every day, all day.

Every night, all night.

John expertly counted cards. He had the kind of mind and the discipline to memorize every card that had been played in each deck up to that point as well as the ability to calculate the probabilities of each upcoming hand.

During his three-month "lost deployment" at Monte Cassino, John amassed winnings, which he sent home to his parents, of over ten thousand dollars, a small fortune then for a twenty-two-year-old. He won much of the money from his American comrades, some of whom put up decent resistance at the poker table, along with a collection of New Zealand and Polish troops, most of whom had poker skills ranging from suspect to nonexistent.

Peace, pray, and work.

—•—

Poker was life for the American pilots of Vietnam.

Between moments of white-knuckle, adrenaline-filled, Russian-roulette terror that was the average combat mission, there lay vast expanses of boredom—boredom that was partially assuaged by poker.

The men played poker in the Officers' Club. They played poker on base. They played poker off base. They played poker in the backrooms of bars and clubs in Bangkok.

Poker was a way to maintain camaraderie. To talk to each other candidly—man to man, emotionally even—with the macho buffer of a card table between them. To sustain a certain mental acuity. To compete. To win. To dominate.

Not lost on any of the men was how the game put the vagaries of chance on full display. Just as each of their lives was now fully subjected to the great spinning wheels of Fortune and Fate, so was each hand of poker. An ace of spades here. An inside straight there. All so random. All so essential to the game.

And, of course, poker was something in which Don reveled.

Like his uncle John Boyatt, it was a game at which he excelled.

Don had played cards—mostly family favorites like pinochle and bridge—from a young age and had an exceptional mind for calculating probabilities and tracking the remaining cards in each deck.

At the age of sixteen, Don was scheduled to spend the weekend at a church camp near Pocatello. His uncle instead took him on a road trip to a country club in Sandpoint in the state's far northern panhandle. It was ostensibly a golf outing but instead turned into a marathon game of poker with a group of well-to-do club members. Don and his uncle drove back to Pocatello with more money than Don could've earned in an entire summer of working at his father's business.

Don would later recall, "On that trip to Sandpoint, Uncle John told me, 'It's great that you can count cards and that you have a wonderful technical grasp of poker. But here's ten thousand dollars' worth of advice that I learned the hard way in World War II: if you got 'em, bet 'em. If you don't got 'em, fold. It's really that simple. Don't try to overthink.'"

It was advice Don would take to heart and later live by.

"I maybe bluffed three times in all the poker games I ever played in Vietnam. And when I returned stateside, I had enough from all my winnings—of which I saved every penny—to buy a brand new Corvette and a penthouse apartment."

Whenever Billy Sparks was hungover, which was often, his fellow pilots would yell out, "Hey, Sparky, let me see that aerial map of Hanoi."

Sparks would then oblige. He had the ability to pull down on one of his lower eyelids, flex a combination of facial muscles, and force his eyeball to bulge gruesomely from its socket. Though Billy's bulging, bloodshot eye the morning after a long night at Takhli's Stag Bar was unnerving, pilots viewed it as something of a good-luck talisman. And its resemblance to the air force's bombing maps of Hanoi was so uncanny as to be satirically hilarious.

In 1967, President Lyndon Johnson crowed, "They can't even bomb an outhouse without my approval."

Which, sadly, was true.

And it was clearly no way to run a war.

But that was the reality the pilots of Takhli found themselves in. And as good soldiers, they flew the missions they were told to fly, even though the strategy was so clearly unsound.

The F-105 pilots were all familiar with the aerial map of Hanoi. They'd all spent hours studying every statute mile, river, tributary, road, bridge, building, and landmark. Their lives depended on it. The map featured a solid red circle, five miles in diameter, encompassing the city center. No target within this circle could be engaged without direct approval from the Joint Chiefs of Staff. And of the approved targets, most likely were handed down from President Johnson himself. The pilots were essentially left to peck at their enemy, all at the whim of politicians and bureaucrats over eight thousand miles away.

Radiating from the solid red blotch encircling downtown Hanoi were thin, red, jagged lines representing railways, roads, and supply lines, essential for keeping the North Vietnamese war machine humming. These extended to the edge of another circle, extending ten miles from Hanoi's city center.

Viewed from a few feet back, the map, with its blood-red pupil and surrounding web of throbbing red veins, was indeed an eerie likeness of Sparky's eye.

Further complicating the map of Hanoi and the pilots' missions was the fact that the North Vietnamese had so readily adapted to the

US playbook and highly predictable aerial intrusions. It would be akin to a football team running the exact same play over and over again and expecting success.

By 1967, downtown Hanoi bristled with the most sophisticated, jam-packed aerial defense system on the planet, courtesy of the Soviet Union. "Going downtown," for an F-105 pilot, meant flying directly into the blood-red circle of Sparky's eye. More than seventeen thousand Soviet missile men had been dispatched to Hanoi to operate more than 7,600 SA-2 electronically guided surface-to-air missiles. One particularly skilled Soviet SAM operator was Lt. Vadim Petrovich Shcherbakov, who by himself downed twelve American fighter jets over Hanoi. By the end of the war, some 205 US aircraft had succumbed to Soviet-made and mostly Soviet-launched guided missiles.

The missiles were typically fired in a series of three at an incoming jet. The amount of physical and mental energy required of each targeted pilot to avoid each missile was nearly overwhelming. If the pilot were able to jink away from the first missile, he then had split seconds to locate and jink away from the second. And if the second missile could somehow be avoided, the third missile almost always proved to be the deadliest. The slightest mistake, inattention, or fatigue would result in a fireball of death. If a SAM operator had successfully locked onto your plane, it was fairly similar to three pulls of the trigger in a game of Russian roulette.

Don's first encounter with a SAM came on February 22, 1968, during his sixth mission in an F-105 and on his first "downtown" run. He was tense in flight, and the sensation of fear—a sensation that clouded judgment and slowed reaction time—began to creep over him. He rarely flew while scared, but this time was different. He was flying into the maw of Sparky's eye, and it was inevitable that he'd encounter a SAM launch.

Don's squadron, dubbed Bison for this mission, was tasked with bombing a MiG airfield, called Hòa Lạc, on Hanoi's western outskirts. Flying in a four-plane finger formation, the Bison pilots streaked through clear skies at eighteen thousand feet as they approached Hanoi, which was shrouded beneath a thick undercast at ten thousand feet. This added to the pilots' unease. Should any SAM be fired at them, they would have only an eight-thousand-foot buffer in which they could visually locate the missile—which by then would be flying at nearly Mach 3—and attempt an evasive maneuver.

As the squadron prepared to dive toward their target, predictably, Don's radio crackled: "Valid launch at one o'clock."

It crackled again: "Valid at ten o'clock."

And again: "Valid at twelve o'clock."

Don hesitated. His mind froze. He could think only of incoming missiles. He checked his E-scope, but for whatever reason, it wasn't registering the SAMs.

Don's mind reflexively began to count.

"Seventeen seconds to die."

"Twelve seconds to die."

Don was unsure of what to do. Drop in elevation? Jink right? Jink left? Dive?

He was the number four plane in the formation, so he just stayed close to his wingman, Lt. Col. Larry Pickett, and continued to count.

"Ten seconds to die."

"Five."

"Three."

There is no sound other than radio chatter in the cockpit of a fighter jet. It's not like the movies with lush flourishes of audience-gratifying special effects: supersonic whooshes, thunderous explosions, and rat-a-tat machine-gun fire. If death were to come, it would come in a silent burst. The pilot would almost never live to hear it.

Don's cockpit lit up as though someone had flashed a camera bulb in his face. The SA-2 sliced between his wingman and him, only a few feet from taking down either of the planes, traveling at three-and-a-half times the speed of sound—over 2,600 miles per hour. The flame from its solid-fuel rocket motor lit the daytime sky. A trailing squadron reported that the missile had exploded about one thousand feet above the pair of jets, its timing off by only a split second.

Anticipating the second oncoming missile, Lt. Jim Butler swooped beneath the squadron, deploying a rudimentary radar-jamming device and using his plane as a decoy. The maneuver worked. The missile curved slightly before detonating to the left of squadron leader Capt. Erik Lunde, peppering the side of his plane with shrapnel and debris.

None of the pilots had an answer for the third missile other than to hope and pray.

Don spotted it as soon as it burst from the undercast, slicing brilliant yellow against the gray backdrop, streaking laser-like from the clouds below, flying directly toward his jet.

Don braced for impact. There was another camera-bulb flash. And then it was over. Film from an automated camera mounted near the nose of Don's plane showed that the missile had skimmed just a few feet beneath his fuselage before detonating some yards past his tail. Don was well within the missile's "kill zone" as it exploded, leaving mission analysts wondering how he and his aircraft had escaped unscathed.

Don's hands shook uncontrollably as he followed his wingman into an attack dive. The Bison squadron flew into bursts of antiaircraft fire above Hòa Lạc; Don strained to push his fear aside and to focus only on acquiring his target and dropping his bombs. The squadron swooped above the airfield and dropped its bombs, leaving the tarmac and MiG hangars devastated beneath the fearsome rumble of ordnance.

Don pulled up and shot skyward. Though his hands still trembled from his SAM encounter, he was nearly overwhelmed with relief.

As the squadron reassembled for the flight south, Don's radio again crackled.

It was Capt. Lunde: "Bison One. Seems Three hasn't come up with us. I've got him still flying north. Four, can you go get him? I think those SAMs messed with his head."

"Uh, Roger," replied Don, who banked hard, turned on his plane's afterburners, and raced north in search of Lt. Col. Pickett, a highly experienced combat pilot on his second F-105 tour.

━━━━

Humans, like nearly all mammals, have evolved sophisticated mental and physiological responses to life-threatening danger. In simple terms, this is known as the fight, flight, or freeze response. The process, which can be entirely involuntary, begins with a huge surge of adrenaline triggered by a perceived threat. As it flushes through the body, adrenaline works almost instantly to increase heart rate and cardiac output as well as respiratory rate and blood pressure. This is designed to prepare muscles for a maximum burst of energy. Adrenaline also causes pupils to widen and the digestive system to shut down.

A person fleeing imminent danger will be primed by an adrenaline surge to run faster, jump higher, and be more cognitively attuned to the threat at hand than a person whose nervous system hasn't been sparked by fear.

In fight mode, however, an almost converse physiological reaction occurs. The body's vascular system contracts, especially at the extremities (arms, legs, hands, feet). This is nature's way of reducing the potential danger from cuts, bruises, or abrasions suffered from a fight. If blood vessels are constricted and an arm gets slashed, blood loss from the wound will be significantly diminished, and chances of survival will be increased. Of course, there is a tax from this process on other bodily functions. Fine motor skills will be impaired as the body places its bet on large muscle groups more useful for fighting. And subtle cognitive tasks will be difficult as the mind shoves away all sensations, sights, sounds, and thoughts that might distract from winning or surviving the battle.

Fighter pilots are trained to manage their heart and respiratory rates in an effort to maintain optimal use of their mental and physical abilities during flight. However, unlike combatants on the ground, pilots are strapped to their seats and confined to their cockpits. They can't run, jump, box, wrestle. Their large muscle groups can't be used to expend excess energy in order to shunt the effects of an adrenaline rush. And because of the nature of their work, pilots are required to maintain a high level of mental acuity and fine motor skill.

And for all those reasons, Don's mind thrived in an adrenaline-soaked environment. He'd learned to carefully manage and balance the multitude of mental and physiological inputs demanded of a fighter pilot.

Some pilots, no matter how experienced or skilled, however, are susceptible to a flood of adrenaline so intense that they ultimately "freeze." This typically occurs when the body shifts to fight mode, thus constricting vascular systems at the extremities. In the meantime, the heart begins to race, sometimes beating at over 185 beats per minute—as fast as or faster than a sprinter or distance runner at full exertion. But a fighter pilot is sitting still in the cockpit. This contrast between a racing heart and constricted blood vessels can lead to a catastrophic mental and physical breakdown. Muscles become starved for oxygen and stiffen. Cognitive abilities plunge and the ability to think rationally is lost. Respiratory rates soar, and hyperventilation occurs. Control of some bodily functions becomes impossible; bowels and bladders release. Simple tasks become exceedingly difficult. Complex tasks such as flying a plane become nearly impossible.

A SAM missile sizzling just past one's cockpit is certainly an event that can trigger such an involuntary adrenaline surge. Which is exactly the condition Lt. Col. Pickett found himself in.

———

Don caught up with Pickett's jet as it cruised at three thousand feet, now well north of Hanoi. He was nervous about MiGs, more SAM missiles, and a flight path that would soon take them dangerously close to Chinese air space. However, he put all those considerations out of his mind and focused on getting Pickett's attention.

"Uh, Bison Three, this is Bison Four," Don radioed to the stricken pilot. "Do you read, Bison Three?

"Uh, Three, do you read?

"Three?"

It was clear that radio contact wasn't going to be sufficient to get Pickett's attention. So Don attempted a maneuver he'd read about but had never had been required to use. He had his doubts it would even work.

Don swung wide of Pickett's plane and began swerving back and forth in front of him like a highway patrolman running a traffic break on a freeway. On the third swerve, Don swooped so close he thought the two planes were in danger of colliding. Pickett was finally able to track Don's plane and put his jet into a bank just off Don's right wing. Don carefully banked east toward the ocean. He and Pickett followed the coast south, away from enemy territory, and eventually back to Takhli.

Of the incident, Don would later say, "Pickett was in such bad shape that I'm pretty sure he would've flown until he ran out of gas before finally crashing somewhere in central China."

~

Schlitz, according to its motto, was "The Beer That Made Milwaukee Famous."

But Milwaukee's international renown was of little concern to the pilots at Takhli, even though the US Air Force provided them with all the free Schlitz they could stomach.

Following his close encounters with the SA-2, Don, back on base, rushed through the doors of the Stag Bar like a gunslinger, striding straight to the bar, hopping on a stool, and promptly ordering a can of Schlitz, which was served to him cold, with rivulets of condensation dripping down its aluminum sides due to the perpetually thick tropical air.

He tipped the can back, took three big gulps, set the beer on the bar, and belched.

"Schlitz does taste like piss water," he thought.

It was something every pilot agreed on. But it was free.

He sat alone, staring at the word "Schlitz," written on the can in a white, florid script against a brick-red background.

Piss water or not, Don prayed into his beer.

He thought of all the men he'd known who'd died. Good men, smart men, most better pilots than he was right now.

Slowly and solemnly, he bowed his head and spoke to the Schlitz can: "Dear Lord, I need your help. I need to get better as a pilot. I can't afford fear. Not now. Not ever. If you don't help me, I'm not going to make it. Amen."

With a few more quick swigs, he finished his beer, setting the empty can, which he began to study intently, back on the bar in front of him.

"Jos. Schlitz Brewing Co."

"Contents 12 Fluid Oz."

The bartender walked near, nodded in assumption that Don wanted another, and reached to take away the empty. Don gripped the can with both hands, waving the bartender off with a quick shake of his head.

Don resumed his silent study. He traced with his finger the word "Schlitz," which scrolled up at an angle across the can. He lifted the can a couple of inches off the bar to gauge its weight, swinging it back and forth like a dinner bell and detecting that there was still a half swig sloshing at its bottom. He threw his head back, drained the remnants fully into his mouth, set the can back on the bar, and proceeded to stare in vacant meditation for a full fifteen minutes. This time, the bartender knew not to come near.

Don would later explain, "I stared at that empty can and stuffed all my fear inside it. I vowed never again to be afraid when I flew. And I never was. From that point on in the war, flying was fun. I made it so. I vowed I would never again become unnerved by the death of a fellow pilot. And I never was. I simply pledged that I would save all my grief until after the war was done. Which I did. And, finally, I came to terms with all the killing I'd done and was about to do. I simply and plainly told myself that every single person I'd killed would have gladly killed me in a second, given the chance. It was my job to never give them that chance. It's something I still believe, something I still tell myself to this day."

———

"Hey, Weeze," Maj. Jim Metz called out to Don as the two prepared to walk out to the tarmac and go on their separate missions.

Don's call sign was Weeze, as in Wild Weasel. Don liked to think he'd earned the name because he was renowned as a cunning, agile killer. But perhaps it had more to do with the fact that most of the men at Takhli had lost money to him at poker. Either way, it had become a term of endearment, such as it is among men in combat.

Don walked over to Metz.

"What time you got, Weeze?"

Don lifted his left wrist.

"Just about oh-nine-hundred on the dot."

A childish fraternity-like prank had broken out among the men on the base. They'd taken to breaking each other's crystal watch faces. No one was sure how it had started, but Don was one of the few men remaining with an unblemished wristwatch.

Like a viper, Metz snapped his right fist onto Don's watch, his bulky college class ring cracking the crystal face like an eggshell.

"Oh, you bastard," said Don. "You fucked up my watch."

Metz laughed. "Man, I've been planning this for a week. I figured the only time you'd fall for it was right before a mission. Welcome to the club of pilots with fucked-up watches."

"Okay," laughed Don. "This just means I'm going to go extra hard on you in poker tonight."

"Roger that, Weeze," laughed Metz. "But I'm feeling lucky, so you best come with some extra cash."

They slapped each other's backs—a nonverbal "be safe out there"—and strode toward their jets.

———

The odds of being dealt a royal flush in five-card draw poker are about 650,000 to 1. Putting that in perspective, if a person played twenty hands of poker every day, that person could expect to be dealt only one royal flush in eighty-nine years. The odds of being dealt a four-card royal flush, discarding the unmatched fifth card and drawing the necessary card to complete the royal, are about 130,000 to 1. It would take a person playing twenty hands of poker per day about eighteen years to behold such a hand. For in poker, a royal flush is near mythical—a unicorn.

Having returned from his mission that day with nothing more severe than a broken watch face, Don sat with his fellow pilots at the Officers' Club to play poker. About an hour into the game, he was dealt a ten, jack, king, and ace of hearts, as well as an ace of spades. It was tempting and probably wise to keep the two aces and try for two pair or three of a kind. But Don had a feeling about this hand. Plus, the cards in the deck were getting low, and he was pretty sure the queen of hearts was still there to be had.

He tossed a dime chip in the pot, not too confident of his hoped-for outcome, and the three other players followed. The dealer spun a card, face down, toward Don. As he lifted it, a glow washed over him. Don fanned the four cards in his hand, tucked the newly acquired queen of hearts between his jack and his king, and paused to admire the symmetrical beauty. Ten, jack, queen, king, and ace of hearts. All in a row. Maybe a once-in-a-lifetime hand. Don's face remained vapid, his hands steady. But the import of Fate's smile wasn't lost on him in the least.

"That's a quarter to anyone who wants to see whether the one card I drew was any good or not," said Don in a flat tone, kicking off that round of betting by tossing a blue poker chip into the pot at the center of the table.

"Fold," said the pilot to his left.

"I'm in," said the next pilot, tossing his chip into the small pile.

"In, too," chimed the next.

"Alright, Weeze, let's see 'em," said one of the pilots who hadn't folded.

Don chuckled, laid his cards elegantly in the center of the table, let out a gleeful laugh, and rubbed his hands quick together.

"Holy shit," said his poker mates in awe and near-unison.

The table then erupted with laughter as each man leaned close to inspect the regal hand. A crowd gathered, and soon more than a dozen men were slapping Don on the back, admiring his work.

Don reached with both hands across the table and scooped the chips in the pot toward him. After stacking his winnings, he announced: "One dollar, on the nose."

He added, "You'd think with a hand like that it'd be worthy of a king's ransom, but not with you cheap bastards at the table."

As the crowd laughed, Don had become fully aware of Maj. Metz's absence.

He lifted his left wrist to check the time, saw his cracked watch face, and knew.

———

Earlier, Maj. Metz flew his F-105 into a heavy barrage of flak and caught fire above a heavily populated area of Quảng Bình Province just north of the coastal provincial capital of Đếng Hới.

Metz banked his wounded plane, flames and smoke streaking behind it, toward open water in hopes of an ejection and safe rescue in the South China Sea.

Capt. Dick Rutan, who would later become the first pilot to fly an aircraft, the Voyager, nonstop around the globe without refueling, was aboard a nearby F-100 when he saw Metz and his flaming jet, first mistaking it for an SA-2 missile.

Rutan observed Metz ejecting just short of the beach and parachuting into a tree, where he was swarmed by enemy troops. Aerial recovery teams later came under heavy fire and were forced to abandon the search after they'd seen the North Vietnamese removing Metz's parachute.

In 1973, 591 Americans were released from Vietcong prisons. Maj. Metz was not among them. The North Vietnamese denied that Metz had ever been a POW, holding that ruse until his remains were finally shipped home in 1977.

＿＿

Back at the Officers' Club, Don looked again at his watch and made note that the hour was growing late.

In war, sometimes it's your lucky day. Until it's not.

There was nothing to do now but deal another hand.

Chapter Twenty-Nine

A FAVORITE AXIOM OF HISTORIANS IS THAT THE PAST WILL ALMOST always find a way to come back to haunt you.

Sometimes it's from a distance.

Sometimes it's at your doorstep.

Sometimes you will have to work hard to connect the dots to discover the past's mischief.

Sometimes the cause and effect will be obvious.

Sometimes a person or a society can build systems and precautions to insulate themselves from historical transgressions.

Other times the past will just reach out—suddenly, unexpectedly—and snatch you from the sky.

This is such a story.

In the nineteenth century, adjacent to Hanoi's French Quarter, rose a shamble of shops and a scrum of merchants, most of whom sold a variety of coal- and wood-fired stoves for either cooking or heating. Dubbed the Hỏa Lò, it was a district whose translation roughly means "stove" or "fiery furnace" (or, colloquially, "hell's hole").

The French were famous administrators, planners, and bureaucrats. From their punctiliously planned cities to their arrow-straight streets and their meticulously coiffed gardens, the French, for the most part, craved order. And when it came to their empire, which was far-flung throughout the globe's tropics, they were especially attentive to the task of hewing precision from jungle chaos.

Such linear thought and logic extended to their judicial and political systems. For what was a colony without order? What was order without laws? What were laws without justice? And what was justice without jail?

Indeed.

And so the French built a network of prisons and penal colonies that stretched from North Africa to South America, the South Pacific, and Indochina. Begun as a logical extension of the French rule of law, of an embodiment of the national motto of "*Liberté, égalité, fraternité*," and of a lust for creating order from chaos, the French delivered with zeal the gift of incarceration to their colonies. But those facilities, which had begun with such high-minded intention, soon metastasized into some of the most brutal and inhuman—physically and psychologically—on the planet.

In the 1880s, an elegant edifice rose in Hanoi. Wrapped in the clean lines and right angles of expert masonry, its exterior walls were painted a delightful canary. The double doors of its solid-iron main gate, above which bent a graceful keystone arch, were painted a matte black, which popped as an imposing, if not stylish, counterpoint to the surrounding yellow.

The French called the building Maison Centrale, an innocuous name for the types of jails typically built next to courthouses in city squares in towns, big and small, throughout France.

At first, the French populated the facility with a smattering of riff-raff and small-time criminals. But as colonial resistance in Indochina ebbed and surged, the prison population at Maison Centrale began to swell with those who would dare to speak out against their European overlords, those who would foment rebellion, those who would carry out sabotage.

Soon the prison population grew to double its intended size. Then triple. Then quadruple. There was simply not enough room to house all those who harbored festering hatred for their colonial masters. In the early twentieth century, the French had begun implementing programs of political reeducation. Programs that involved intensive propaganda. Programs that employed all means of torture and execution.

By the 1920s and 1930s, Maison Centrale housed amid its subhuman conditions a simmering cauldron of malcontent. In time, its yellow and black facade fooled no one. The Vietnamese came to call it Hỏa Lò Prison, a derisive jab at their high-minded French masters, as well as a universal acknowledgment of the hell hole it had become.

By the 1940s, the prison's exterior walls were enveloped by a crush of street peddlers, revolutionaries, and spies. Food, contraband, political treatises, and anti-imperial directives were tossed back and forth over the prison walls. Many of the political leaders and military generals who would come to fight the Americans two decades later were first indoctrinated in their anti-Western hatred amid the slow-cooked stew that was Hỏa Lò Prison.

As soon as the French had vacated Vietnam in 1954, they turned the keys of the prison over to their subjects, who in turn proved to be apt pupils. The Vietnamese transformed the Hỏa Lò into a political re-education center, employing all manner of torture and execution, most of which had been learned from their former colonial masters.

And so it goes.

On February 11, 1965, Lt. Cmdr. Robert Shumaker was snatched from the sky.

The naval aviator had launched from the USS *Coral Sea* with the directive to strafe and bomb a North Vietnamese military barracks at Chánh Hòa in Quảng Bình Province. The raid was ordered by President Lyndon Johnson as retaliation for a North Vietnamese attack that had killed and wounded dozens of American military advisers at Pleiku four days earlier. As Shumaker dropped low for his attack on the compound, his F-8 Crusader flew into a fusillade of machine-gun fire. He ejected, injured his back, and was captured.

And so Lt. Cmdr. Shumaker found himself in Hanoi, looking at the exterior of Hỏa Lò Prison for what would be the only time in eight long years. Beneath the elegant keystone arch, the prison's solid-iron gates were still painted a matte black that contrasted nicely with the still-canary walls.

As only the second American pilot captured in the Vietnam War, Shumaker could've devoted ample time to contemplating the random nature of getting plucked from the sky or the collision of Eastern and Western cultures—centuries in the making—that led to the construction and establishment of the hellhole of a prison that was now his home. Instead, he devoted all his attention and energy toward the fight for survival.

The torture was savage and relentless. It involved all manner of isolation, psychological terror, binding, beating, near-drowning, starvation, forced standing, forced sitting, hanging by thumbs, by wrists, by elbows, ankles, feet, toes. It was a place where the guards often told the prisoners, "Dying is easy; living is hard."

Lt. Tom Moe was snatched from the sky in the most improbable of manners. He and other pilots in his squadron had complained to higher-ups that faulty bomb fuses were causing early detonations of ordnance—detonations that in some instances, they believed, had caused the accidental downing and deaths of several US pilots. At first, their complaints were ignored. Then the pilots began refusing orders—going on strike, as it were—refusing to fly until all the faulty fuses were replaced. After a cursory investigation, safety officers advised Lt. Moe and others that all fuses had been given a clean slate, and it was once again safe to fly. And since he'd brought the issue to the fore, Lt. Moe was ordered out on a guinea pig mission over North Vietnam. As they approached their target, Lt. Moe's wingman released his bombs. Predictably, one of the Honeywell FMU-35/B fuses sparked almost instantly upon release. A shock wave rocked both planes, and shrapnel shredded their tail assemblies. All four pilots ejected, parachuting into the jungle behind enemy lines. Three were rescued, but Moe, who at one point was only a couple of hundred yards from an American rescue expedition, was captured and marched north to Hanoi. Some twenty-five years later, he would describe a snippet of his five years in captivity thus:

They pounded me for six or eight hours. By then I was getting pretty shaky. Then they got serious. I was introduced to a bowl of water, some filthy rags and a steel rod. The guards stuffed a rag in my mouth with the rod, then, after putting another rag over my face, they slowly poured the water on it until all I was breathing was water vapor. I could feel my lungs going tight with fluid and felt like I was drowning. I thrashed in panic as darkness took over. As I passed out, thinking I was dying, I remember thanking God that we had made a stand against this kind of society.

When my senses returned I discovered I had been blindfolded and trussed into the "pretzel" position. Thick leg irons shackled my ankles, my wrists were tied behind me, and a rope bound my elbows just above the joints. The guards tightened the bindings by putting their feet against my arms and pulling the ropes until they couldn't pull any harder. Then they tied my wrists to my ankles and jammed a 10-foot pole between my back and elbows. After a few hours the leg irons began to press heavily on my shins and feet like a vise. The ropes strangled my flesh, causing searing pain and making my arms go numb and slowly turn black.

Living was indeed hard at the Hỏa Lò, which had become populated by hundreds of downed pilots, all of whom had been snatched from the sky, randomly tapped by fate.

On May 31, 1965, Air Force Lt. Robert Peel was on a bombing run over Thanh Hóa Province when an antiaircraft projectile tore into the fuselage of his F-105. He ejected, was captured, and marched north.

Upon entering the gates of Hỏa Lò Prison, Peel was tossed into a small, isolated cell and handed a bucket upon whose handle Lt. Cmdr. Shumaker had forever condemned the prison to worldwide infamy by surreptitiously inscribing: "Welcome to the Hanoi Hilton."

—❧—

Word of torture at the Hanoi Hilton spread like a conflagration through the ranks of American airmen. Fear of capture, imprisonment, and torture outweighed the fear of death—for the pilots and their crew knew, as did the Hanoi Hilton guards, that death was easy.

In April 1968, a squadron of F-105s screeched up the coast of South Vietnam, just north of Da Nang. The pilots flew less than a mile inland, careful to keep the coastline within sight. The sky was jolted alive with the buzz of tracer bullets, which whizzed around the lead jet before connecting with an ominous thump-thump-thump. The pilot banked hard right toward the ocean, riding his crippled plane as long as he could before ejecting a few hundred yards out to sea, where he was quickly rescued.

The following day, mission planners at the Bien Hoa Air Base north of Saigon dispatched another F-105 squadron to take out what they believed was a single Russian-made 100mm KS-19 antiaircraft cannon. Developed just after World War II, the KS-19 was a conventional weapon that, with the guidance of an expert operator, could send a barrage of tracer bullets and fragmentation shells in front of an oncoming jet, knocking it out of the sky.

Another squadron was launched from Bien Hoa with the sole mission of taking out the Russian cannon. Like their predecessors, the F-105s followed the coastline north before swooping inland and then west to east before being riddled with cannon fire and forced to ditch their aircraft at sea.

Three successive squadrons were sent out to silence the Russian gun, and three successive planes were lost, though each pilot was able to maneuver his wounded aircraft east so that he could eject just off the coast and be rescued.

The American mission commanders at Bien Hoa were nearly apoplectic. They cursed the KS-19 and mused among themselves that the cannon was very likely manned by a real Russian—probably an old-timer on loan who'd earned his chops shooting down Messerschmitts during the siege of Stalingrad in World War II. They plotted ways to take him out. To do something the Germans hadn't been able to do. To prove that modern American technology and know-how still trumped conventional weapons from the 1940s. To mete out revenge.

All the while, Don was pretty sure he knew the reason for the Russian cannon's success and the American pilots' repeated failures. It boiled down to the lethal combination of fear and predictability. Pilots had begun talking—gossiping, really—about the horrors of the Hanoi Hilton. As a result, the fear of capture haunted them more than the fear of death. And by 1968, it began affecting pilot behavior. Don had studied enough mission reports and had talked to enough pilots to know that it had become almost gospel: If your plane was ever hit, head east toward the ocean. And whenever you were on a bombing run, sweep over your target from west to east. That way, if you happened to pick up any stray bullets or shrapnel like so many roadside nails, you could always streak toward the ocean—ride your wounded bird as far as it would carry you, and, god willing, gently parachute into the clear blue waters that were devoid of any enemy presence. But a north-south or east-west run meant the potential of being downed in the jungle. Of being culled from the herd. Of being hunted like an animal. Of being captured and marched to the Hanoi Hilton.

During a subsequent mission review, Don stood up and proclaimed with cocksure certainty that he could take out the antiaircraft cannon along the coast. In what may have sounded like braggadocio to others but seemed like simple fact to Don, he said that the Russian artilleryman may have survived the Luftwaffe, but he hadn't yet seen the likes of an F-105 flown by Lt. Harten, and, thus, his days on earth were numbered.

———

Don climbed into the cockpit of the *Pink Pussy* and, after running through his preflight checklists, reached into a small breast pocket on his flight suit and pulled out a lone bullet. It was the same .38-caliber round from his service revolver that he'd saved after his B-52 crash—the one that was only to have been used in case of a shark attack. On this and other missions, Don had kept the bullet, not so much as a talisman or good luck charm—he didn't believe in luck—but rather as a safety net. By having already made up his mind to die rather than be captured by the North Vietnamese or to be torn apart by a shark—he'd removed fear from the equation. While most pilots might have held disdain for his private decision, it all seemed highly logical to him. Maybe it was a coward's way out. Perhaps he should just suck it up and endure his multiyear dose of torture like a man. Perhaps. But in Don's mind, there was no point to getting captured alive. First, the chances of surviving more than a year or two in the Hanoi Hilton were less than a coin flip. Second, he was no use to anyone sitting in a prison cell. Third, he'd never see combat again after doing a stint as a POW. Fourth, the fear of capture made pilots do stupid things, and Don hated doing stupid things—it often got you and others killed. Though he respected the hell out of anyone who'd survived as a POW, it just wasn't for him. A bullet to the brain right before capture just seemed more rational.

Don hoisted the bullet up toward the canopy, its brass casing glinting in the sunlight as he rolled it between his thumb and index finger. Don lowered it to his lips, gave it a kiss, and tucked it back into his flight suit pocket.

—— ——

Don scorched off the tarmac at Takhli with nothing but killing on his mind.

"Okay, you Russian SOB," he muttered.

He streaked with his four-plane unit in a finger formation—Don in the lead with a wingman to his left and two to his right. They followed the place where the jungle hills tumbled to the flatlands and into a quilt of rice paddies and villages. About an hour northeast of Takhli, the formation made a wide sweep toward the east. They dropped to seven thousand feet and accelerated to seven hundred miles per hour, which was low enough to draw fire from the Russian cannon but high and fast enough to outrun any projectiles.

"Three, take the lead," Don radioed to the number three plane in his formation. "I'm going to circle and see if I can spot any muzzle flashes below so we can lock the gunner's coordinates."

The ocean broke blue on the horizon, its dark hue sandwiched between the hazy green of land and light blue haze of sky.

"C'mon, you SOB," Don said to himself. "I know you're down there."

The ocean grew from a sliver and began to fill the horizon with its blue vastness, now only two or three miles away.

Don banked hard away from his formation, tilting his plane so that it was nearly inverted. As he circled solo, Don peered upside down through his cockpit, studying the terrain below intently.

Tracer rounds flashed orange and yellow, slashing skyward just behind the formation of three F-105s as they raced toward the sea. Don now knew the gunner was down there, but he still couldn't spot the muzzle flashes because of the likely camouflage netting that hung above it. Don continued to circle and continued to plead.

"C'mon, you stupid Russian SOB. Be stupid just one more time."

Rounds began to trace toward Don, flashing behind the tail of his jet. The gunner had spotted him and had begun firing. Don looked down and finally located a series of silent muzzle flashes coming from the one angle in which the gunner's cannon was exposed and could be seen beneath the camouflage. As he watched puffs of smoke billowing from some trees bunched between rice paddies, Don locked the coordinates and smiled.

Outside his cockpit, the sky crackled with artillery bursts and buzzed with bullets, all erupting harmlessly out of range.

Don leveled, accelerated, and bolted east toward the water, where the horizon was split with two shades of blue.

He calmly settled into his seat and prepared to execute an attack roll. He pulled back on his stick. The world turned hazy blue and the g-forces pressed him back as the F-105 shot skyward. He gently coaxed the plane into a roll. The horizon spun, and now the dark blue of the ocean was up and the light haze of the sky was down. The plane corkscrewed and Don became weightless. As he pulled the aircraft into a dive, he could feel the wings grabbing the air and gravity pulling the entire heft of the F-105 toward the ocean. His view turned dark blue, and the whole of the South China Sea rushed toward his cockpit. The wings gripped harder, Don grunted against the intense g-forces, and the plane felt mushy in the air—like it was plowing its way through the sky. The horizon spun again. Don grimaced and squinted hard against the ever-strengthening centrifugal pull. He felt the tail sink down and the nose tilt up just as the wings clutched the air tight like they were on rails. The F-105 leveled and shot west, back toward the green on the horizon, back toward the Russian gunner.

Don dropped to three hundred feet and thundered over the water at nearly the speed of sound. A narrow strip of sandy beach flashed beneath him as he streaked west with the green of rice paddies spreading before him and blue haze above him.

The Russian lit a cigarette amid the acrid fog of spent gunpowder. He spat on the ground and cursed this formation of American pilots for flying higher and faster than he'd expected. With a crumpled, unfiltered cigarette hanging from his mouth, he spun the gun's seventeen-foot-long barrel toward the west in anticipation of more American jets, which always came in from the west and flew out to sea.

"Fucking cowards," thought the Russian, who knew exactly why the Americans had a tendency to fly toward open water every chance they'd get.

Don streaked low above the rice paddies and checked his coordinates. He could see the copse of trees straight ahead.

The Russian waved his hand as though to shoo away the thick artillery smoke that seemed to stick low to the ground with the humidity.

Don released a five-hundred-pound bomb from beneath his left wing, accelerated, and pulled hard skyward.

The Russian looked out over the rice paddies and took a deep drag from his cigarette, the tip of which glowed bright red amid the sticky smoke.

The shriek of a near-supersonic jet just overhead tore the sky. Ensconced in the roar was the dull whine of the five-hundred-pound bomb, which spun through the air before plowing into the levee just a few feet behind the Russian.

The trees, the dirt, the cannon, the Russian were at once flattened, incinerated, and sucked skyward into a small fiery mushroom of dust and fire and smoke.

Don leveled off, preparing to regroup with his formation and fly back to base.

"Stupid Russian SOB," Don muttered. "Never saw me coming."

Chapter Thirty

Billy Sparks flew the last of his 145 F-105 combat missions over North Vietnam on November 5, 1967. He'd come to Takhli with the stated goal of becoming the first American pilot to complete two hundred F-105 missions, but on this day, he would fall short.

His directive was to take out the last remaining aircraft hangar on the Phúc Yên air base about twenty miles north of Hanoi—a mission complicated by the fact that Phúc Yên was fortified by over one thousand antiaircraft cannons, flak guns, sixteen SAM launch batteries, and MiG-21s. He was assigned the unenviable Tail-End-Charlie position, meaning he'd be the last plane in on the raid. Consequently, all the antiaircraft systems would be locked, loaded, and firing by the time his plane made its pass.

But Sparks was not daunted—he of two Silver Stars, seven Distinguished Flying Crosses, and fifteen Air Medals.

He and his squadron flew over Laos, Thud Ridge, and across the Red River without incident. However, they came into Phúc Yên too high and had to roll into their attack at a bad angle. The flak and cannon fire came up so heavily that Sparks couldn't see the airfield and had to resort to manual bombing mode. In spite of that, the squadron placed eighteen of its twenty-four 750-pound bombs through the hangar roof.

After releasing his ordnance, Sparks pulled up hard and rolled left, pulling over five g's. Unfortunately, he was now headed straight for Hanoi, right into Sparky's Eye.

Three SA-2 missiles were fired at the tail of his plane from six o'clock. Sparks now had three options, none of them good: fly back over Phúc Yên through increasingly worse flak, antiaircraft fire, and more missiles;

fly over the northern rail line, where he would also certainly encounter flak, antiaircraft fire, and missiles; or drop low and fly at a supersonic speed over rice paddies at an elevation of no more than fifty feet. The pilots called this maneuver "mowing grass."

Sparks chose the latter.

He dove into the weeds, skimming over paddies at 860 miles per hour, with the first missile closing fast. He jerked his plane left just in time to see the first missile dive parallel to him into the ground.

His wingman radioed that he'd just seen the second missile lose guidance and spiral harmlessly skyward.

The third missile closed in on the planes, but at such a low altitude, it too lost guidance, dove into some houses, and exploded into a giant fireball, setting a neighborhood aflame.

Sparks heard on the radio that one of the planes ahead of him, Red Dog Four, had taken fire from a 57mm optically fired gun and was aflame.

Col. Dick Dutton and Lt. Col. Glenn Cobeil bailed out and parachuted into a village. Dutton was stripped down, blindfolded, tied at the wrists, and led down the rocky streets barefoot with a noose around his neck. Villagers lined the route and beat him with bamboo poles, fists, and clods of dirt as he passed. Both men were shipped to the Hanoi Hilton. Dutton would be released in 1973. Cobeil, however, would die at the hands of Fidel the Torturer, a Cuban torture expert brought to Hanoi by the North Vietnamese expressly for the purpose of teaching them innovative methods for extracting information.

Sparks rocketed up out of the rice paddies at a steep angle and was promptly hit by the same 57mm gun that had downed Red Dog Four.

One round hit near his afterburner, one went through the bomb bay just under his feet, and the third hit the air turbine motor compartment just in front of his right knee.

Sparks maintained his steep climb and gunned the jet as fast as it could travel. But the plane caught fire and the cockpit filled with smoke.

Determined to stay with his plane as long as possible or die trying, Sparks pulled a manual release lever, and his canopy flew into the air. The cockpit was now largely smoke free, but he was flying what was essentially a supersonic convertible at over eight hundred miles per hour.

Sparks climbed toward Thud Ridge, egging on his mortally wounded jet. The only system operating was his plane's compass, which he could read only by shielding it with his hand, which he had to keep low and out of the slipstream, lest his arm get ripped off by a blast of supersonic wind.

Sparks knew that American rescue crews weren't allowed to cross the Red River for pilot extractions due to the ease that the North Vietnamese would have in shooting down the Sikorsky HH-3E Jolly Green Giant rescue helicopters.

Sparks crossed Thud Ridge and banked toward the Red River. At this point, he was either going to die in his plane or get rescued. There was no third option.

Sparks reached forward and could feel that his air turbine motor compartment was on fire and melting. Flames had devoured his right front panel, melted his right windscreen, and raced out across his right wing. The tire beneath the wing had caught fire and exploded. His bomb bay doors had blown off, and his landing struts now dangled, useless. His right rudder pedal collapsed and hung from its cables. Flames began to lick at his left foot, and he had to now hold his foot high and out of the fire.

But he calculated that he was only two minutes away from the Red River, if he could hang on that long. That's when his controls seized and the plane shuddered and began to pitch into an inverted spin. Sparks performed three sharp successive pull-up maneuvers to keep the plane from inverting. It had been over seven minutes since he'd been hit, and he was amazed that he was still airborne. Just as the plane began to invert for the final time, Sparks pulled up his ejection handles and squeezed the triggers.

He was slammed into the sky at 24,000 feet and saw his wingman streak past. Sparks had indeed made it south of the Red River but was floating toward a village, none of whose occupants would likely have been friendly. He guided his chute over two ridges, opting to land in an expanse of elephant grass. As he fell close to earth, though, he discovered the elephant grass was instead a patch of seventy-foot-high stalks of bamboo.

Sparks crashed into the bamboo and splintered his way toward the ground before his parachute hung in the bamboo, forcing him to free fall the final forty feet to the ground, where he sustained fractures in both feet, a broken patella, a dislocated shoulder, and a chipped bone near his elbow.

After a tense two hours of wondering who would arrive first, a North Vietnamese patrol or an American rescue unit, Sparks heard the thump, thump, thump of a Jolly Green Giant, and he was plucked from his dilemma, the second-farthest-north rescue of a pilot during the war.

For his troubles, he was awarded yet another Silver Star and sent home for the duration of the war.

Chapter Thirty-One

Tết Nguyên Đán means "feast of the first morning of the first day" and is the Vietnamese culture's most important celebration. It is held on the first day of the Vietnamese New Year, typically in late January or early February, depending upon the phase of the moon in Vietnam's lunar-dependent calendar. It is a time of family reunions, homage to ancestors, holiday foods, paying off debts, and facing the coming year with a fresh slate. It is a time of hope and renewal, harkening the arrival of spring.

In 1968, Tết arrived on January 30. And that's when the North Vietnamese, in a surprise offensive, launched massive coordinated attacks on American positions throughout South Vietnam. With eighty-four thousand ground troops, they struck some 150 American military outposts, airfields, and provincial capitals as well as key targets within Saigon, including the newly built US embassy, central military command headquarters, and the national radio station.

The North Vietnamese assault, known as the Tết Offensive, was quickly beaten back by the Americans and South Vietnamese, often in only hours in most places. The Vietcong sustained massive casualties that soared to over one hundred thousand by the time all three phases of the offensive were complete. Generally regarded by military historians as a brash, ill-advised operation, Tết was ultimately a disaster for the Vietcong, draining the country of valuable personnel and supplies.

And while Tết may have been unwise from a military perspective, it was a bold propaganda play that helped sway public opinion in a distant land. Before the Tết Offensive, the American people had been assured that the country's military and politicians had a firm grasp of the goings-on in Vietnam and that decisive victory was at hand. But the returning body bags told another story. And Tết simply provided an exclamation point upon the dark doubts that had begun enveloping the United States from coast to coast.

The American people, at home watching the world's first televised war, were stunned to see Vietcong troops occupying the US embassy in Saigon, located over four hundred miles from the Demilitarized Zone that separated North and South Vietnam. Never mind that the two dozen intruders were quickly mowed down by American military police, the fact that they could penetrate so deeply into the heart of American defenses was unnerving—as was their eerie, kamikaze-like devotion to their cause.

"What the hell is going on in Southeast Asia?" became the cry, floating like a malaise across the land.

In February 1968, the "most trusted man in America" went to find out. He returned home and presented his fellow citizens with an hour-long *CBS News Special Report* that rocked American public opinion about the war.

He ended his report with an anguished flourish. This is what he said:

"Tonight, back in more familiar surroundings in New York, we'd like to sum up our findings in Vietnam, an analysis that must be speculative, personal, subjective. Who won and who lost in the great Tết Offensive against the cities? I'm not sure. The Vietcong did not win by a knockout, but neither did we.

"Then, with as much restraint as I could, I turned to our own leaders whose idea of negotiation seemed frozen in memories of General MacArthur's encounter with the Japanese aboard the battleship *Missouri*.

"We've been too often disappointed by the optimism of the American leaders both in Vietnam and Washington to have faith any longer in the silver linings they find in the darkest clouds. For it seems now more certain than ever that the bloody experience of Vietnam is to end in a stalemate. To say that we are closer to victory today is to believe in the face of the evidence, the optimists who have been wrong in the past.

"To say that we are mired in stalemate seems the only realistic, if unsatisfactory conclusion. On the off chance that military and political analysts are right, in the next few months we must test the enemy's intentions, in case this is indeed his last big gasp before negotiations.

"But it is increasingly clear to this reporter that the only rational way out then will be to negotiate, not as victors, but as an honorable people who lived up to their pledge to defend democracy, and did the best they could.

"This is Walter Cronkite. Good night."

On March 31, 1968, the conflict in Vietnam claimed another victim, President Lyndon Johnson, who, in a nationally televised speech, said this:

"Good evening, my fellow Americans.

"Tonight I want to speak to you of peace in Vietnam and Southeast Asia.

"No other question so preoccupies our people. No other dream so absorbs the 250 million human beings who live in that part of the world. No other goal motivates American policy in Southeast Asia."

He went on to deliver a long assessment of American military and political strategy in Vietnam before ending his speech with this stunner:

"Accordingly, I shall not seek, and I will not accept, the nomination of my party for another term as your president."

It was into this political and military stew that Don flew for the whole of 1968. With Johnson's lame-duck status, the American political will to win the war had wilted. Don and the pilots with whom he flew knew it. And the North Vietnamese certainly knew it.

In Don's opinion, the most telling line in Johnson's speech was this: "Our objective in South Vietnam has never been the annihilation of the enemy."

Said Don for years following the conflict: "The key to victory in Vietnam never changed an iota from that February day in 1965 when we sat in the briefing room at Mather Air Base with a plan to level Hanoi with thirty B-52s. The key to that war was always Hanoi. It was so in 1965,

'68, and '72. It never changed. But our political leaders were always too unwilling or too incompetent to face that reality.

"And the army? They loved the B-52, which was a problem. They would call in BUFF strikes to support ground troops. They thought that the BUFF should be used to scare the hell out of the Vietcong militia. Which was wrong. It was a gross waste and misuse of valuable American prowess. The only thing the B-52 should've been used for was to pound Hanoi into submission. That's the sort of thing it was designed for—not for lighting up the countryside."

And so America careened, directionless, through Southeast Asia and would continue to do so through the whole of 1968, which was an election year. There would be no decisive action in Vietnam until after the January 1969 inauguration of a new president, and maybe not even then.

While pro-war and antiwar sentiments ripped asunder America's social fabric back home, the war from the sky—from Don's perspective—appeared very different in 1968.

"We won the Tết Offensive," he would later say. "It wasn't a stalemate. It wasn't a draw. We flat-out steamrolled the North Vietnamese. That's a misconception that's gnawed at me every day since. By the end of 1968, the North Vietnamese capacity to make war had been decimated. We'd bombed pretty much everything worth bombing. They were out of materiel. They had no air cover. They were out of soldiers. They were reduced to running bicycle brigades down the Ho Chi Minh Trail. Bicycles loaded with three hundred pounds each of supplies would be pedaled from Hanoi practically to Saigon. Hell, I saw them. Hell, I bombed and strafed them. Bicycles. It was the damnedest thing. And, yet, we only went after Hanoi piecemeal. That was the damnedest thing, too."

Chapter Thirty-Two

After having prayed to his can of Schlitz, after having eliminated all fear from his mind, Don learned how to love flying combat. He
learned how to love war.

"I would fly combat. I would spend hour after hour studying maps,
reconnaissance photos, and mission strategy in order to become the best
fighter pilot in the world. I would play poker. I would make love with my
beautiful girlfriend in Bangkok. Once you submitted to the fact you were
destined to die—and soon—it was rather fun.

"I got so that I really liked bombing and strafing Vietcong military
and supply line convoys on the Ho Chi Minh Trail, which we did a lot
of in 1968. The Vietcong moved jillions of tons of materiel down those
jungle trails that cut through the mountains of Laos and Cambodia. We'd
calculated that for every supply truck we eliminated, we'd save ten South
Vietnamese soldier lives and five American soldier lives. So there was sort
of a point system."

—◆—

In the fall of 1968 and into 1969, Don had become one with his jet. He
understood fully the lay of the land, the weather, geographic landmarks,
hilltops, rivers, streams, rice paddies, villages, foliage, truck paths. He
understood which antiaircraft batteries were where, and how the electronic guidance systems of an SA-2 worked. The complex radio banter
between squadrons of fighter pilots was almost inscrutable when he first
arrived, and his inability to decipher it without thinking almost cost him
his life on a number of occasions, but now it sounded like a symphony.
He could tell where to go and which way to turn just by the ebb and flow

of the language, not necessarily even by what was being said. He could fly now by instinct, by rhythm, without fear. To young pilots, he was viewed almost as a savior, a lifeline that might help them survive the war. To the enemy, he was an absolute terror—devastation from above.

In October 1968, he prowled the skies above Laos with his wingman, searching out Vietcong supply convoys that lurked surreptitiously beneath the jungle canopy as they moved men and materiel south along the scattered labyrinth, much like an ant path, that the Ho Chi Minh Trail comprised.

The rumpled hills floated beneath Don's F-105—green, mist shrouded, serene. He was under strict orders not to go beneath seven thousand feet. Rarely would the pilots get a clean look at a VC convoy. Rather, they would receive coordinates from spotters and often had to guesstimate where the convoys might be along the trail.

Just ahead, Don spotted three supply trucks out the open, traveling on a road that clung to the base of a two-thousand-foot-high cliff. They were in a difficult spot to reach, for sure. It would be sort of like trying to squash a spider hunkered deep in a crevice between the baseboard molding and a hardwood floor. Further, if he wanted the kill, he'd have to violate his order not to descend below seven thousand feet. But the target was too tempting. And by his calculations, forty-five lives depended upon his courage and skill.

"Stay high, I'm going low," he told his wingman.

Don rolled left and dropped into his dive. He screamed into the mountain valley, the cliff on his left a blur. He was coming in "faster than heat"—as the fighter pilots liked to say—too close and too fast to drop a bomb and at too awkward an angle to get a clear shot. He leveled off, maybe twenty-five feet from the ground, banked hard, and started firing his 20mm Gatling cannon at the cliff wall, hoping the ricochets might cause damage. As he skimmed over the convoy with an air-splitting roar, he glanced at his controls to see that he was coming out of his dive at over 980 knots or 1,127 mph—1.5 times the speed of sound.

Don pulled up hard, circled around to view his handiwork, and could see the convoy immolated beneath three fireballs mushrooming up the cliff walls. Don wasn't sure whether it was his gun or his afterburners that had set off the ordnance-filled trucks. Either way, by Don's count, the bad guys were dead and forty-five lives were saved.

By the spring of 1969, Don's missions had begun to pile up. He was at 140 and counting. His commanding officer told him on several occasions to go home. But Don couldn't, wouldn't. He had no idea what to do once he got there and was pretty certain it wouldn't be anything he was as skilled and expert at as flying combat. He had a toddler son in Sacramento, but war and his overseas deployment had doomed his marriage a couple of years earlier, and he didn't even have that as a magnet to pull him back. It got to the point where he started fudging his counts. Every time a pilot flew over Laos or Cambodia, the flight didn't "count." Every time a pilot flew over North Vietnam, it counted as a combat mission. To this day, he's not really sure how many official combat missions he actually flew.

Another thing Don had stopped counting was the number of fellow pilots who'd died. There were far too many, and Don had promised himself and the can of Schlitz that he'd save all that for after the war.

That day wouldn't come for another two decades.

The Vietnam Veterans Memorial is the most unusual of shrines, designed and built under the most unusual of circumstances—by a female Asian American university student with absolutely no professional architectural experience. Located on the National Mall in Washington, DC, between the Lincoln Memorial and the Washington Monument, the memorial stands as a series of black granite slabs, polished to an obsidian sheen and joined side to side in a series of *V*s like a stretched-out accordion. On it are listed the names, chronologically, of more than fifty-eight thousand American servicemen and servicewomen who gave their lives in Vietnam.

The monument was erected in 1982, its design selected from a competition of over 1,100 entries. Were it not for a format of blind submissions, however, it's a near certainty that the memorial wouldn't stand today in its current configuration. The political furor and posturing would have simply overwhelmed the clean lines, simplicity, and existential elegance that make up the memorial today. Politics and art make for poor bedfellows.

Maya Lin was a twenty-one-year-old undergraduate architectural student at Yale University when she submitted her design for the memorial in 1981. The structure, with its polished black stone, is configured to represent a dark gash in the earth, a symbol of loss and a reminder of the gravity of war. Like an abstract talisman, the memorial perfectly evokes the kind of grief and raw emotion for which it was designed—which the Vietnam War delivered. Today the memorial receives over three million visitors annually and is ranked by the American Institute of Architects as one of the most revered architectural sites in the United States.

In the spring of 1988, Don made his pilgrimage to the memorial. A breeze blew, soft and warm, and Don made sure to arrive just after sunrise to avoid the crowds. He'd made a list of every pilot he'd served with who'd died in Vietnam. He began on panel 2E with the eight crew members who'd perished in his B-52 collision in 1965, tracing his fingers over each name: JAMES A. MARSHALL, JAMES M. GEHRIG, TYRELL G. LOWRY, ROBERT L. ARMOND, HAROLD J. ROBERTS, JR., FRANK P. WATSON, JOE C. ROBERTSON, and WILLIAM E. NEVILLE. He spent over two hours at the wall, careful not to miss anyone on his list, careful to trace his fingers over each engraved letter, careful to remember, careful to say a prayer. It was the least he could do, given that he'd done his best to ignore the death and carnage during his time in Vietnam. By the time he'd gotten to JAMES H. METZ on panel 50E—exhausted by grief and overwhelmed by sobs—he'd traced his fingers over eighty-four names.

⌐⌐

"Why are you here?" Juliette Laurent whispered into Don's ear as the monsoon rains thrummed on her apartment roof early on a March morning in 1969.

"Because there's no place I'd rather be than in bed here with you. It's what I sometimes think about when I fly. 'Dear Lord, let me live just one more day so I can make it back and be naked in bed just one more time with Juliette.'" He laughed.

She gave his shoulder a punch with the heel of her palm.

"No, really, why are you here?"

"Seriously? To kill communists. If it weren't for me, millions would die. The communists are great at genocide. Did you know that Joseph Stalin and Mao Zedong killed more than forty million of their own people? Forty million. Look it up. It's true."

"Yeah, but you're not going to stop Mao Zedong in a single jet."

"You never know, I might."

"No, I'm serious," she whispered, gently kissing his forehead, her hair soft on his face. "I worry about you. When are you going home, and what will you do when you get there?"

"I don't know. It doesn't really pay to think that far ahead. But whatever happens, I want to thank you."

"For what?"

"For being here. For being beautiful. For spending time with me. I really did think about you every time I took off on a mission and every time I touched back down on the tarmac. It made a difference. You were good luck."

"I was good luck?" She laughed. "I thought you didn't believe in luck. How do you know I was good luck?"

"Well, I'm still alive, aren't I? Now, be quiet and make love to me."

He kissed her deeply and held his naked body close to hers.

The rain fell, hard and steady on the roof above, and they both moaned.

———

A week later, Don completed his 165th F-105 combat mission. His time was up. His commanding officer gave him orders to leave Vietnam for redeployment at Nellis Air Force Base near Las Vegas. The new F-111 fighter jet was having technical problems, inexplicably flying into hillsides and killing its own crews. The air force needed experienced fighter pilots to help get its F-111 program back on track. Don would now be assigned as a test pilot and F-111 safety officer in the United States. He'd never see Juliette again.

Chapter Thirty-Three

"Son," bellowed four-star general and commander of the Seventh Air Force John W. Vogt, while standing nose to nose with Maj. Don Harten in a nondescript training room at Takhli Air Base, Thailand, in 1972, "I have been summoned here before you by direct personal order of the president of the United States, your commander in chief—my commander in chief—Richard M. Nixon. And, son, I can tell you without equivocation that one of two things is happening right here, right now, in this very room: You are quite possibly in the biggest shitstorm of trouble that an officer could conceivably imagine finding himself in within this US Air Force—and, I might add, I will be the individual who personally sees to it that you will never find your way out of the nine circles of hell I'm about to shitcan you into—or—and this is a very thin thread of an "or" that your entire future is hanging by—OR!—what you have written in this report has even some semblance of verifiable truth to it. Now, sit down and explain to me why you think there's a defect in the F-111's pencil-beam radar system and why you, of all people, found this potential defect so compelling that you would personally circumvent the entire chain of command of the US Air Force and send your sniveling-ass aircraft loss report all the way up to the president of the United Fucking States of America, who, I might add, has better things to do than send my sorry ass halfway around the world to some shithole air base in Thailand to talk to a shitstain of a fighter pilot like you."

The F-111 was the last of America's Cold War aircraft.

And perhaps because of that, its birth was mangled, protracted, and painful.

In the late 1950s, military strategists dreamed of a nuclear-armed supersonic jet that could fly faster, farther, and deeper into the Soviet Union without detection than anything else in the American fleet.

In those days, all the Pentagon had to do was whisper to Congress apocalyptic tales of nuclear Armageddon at the hands of godless Soviet communists, and such pet projects would get funded.

Here's one of the tales they whispered: as reliable as the B-52 had proved to be, Soviet air defenses had developed new technology in the form of advanced surface-to-air missiles and MiG fighter jets that could shoot down incoming American bombers with relative ease. As fast as the F-105 was, it could still be detected far enough in advance by Soviet radar, thus succumbing to the same fate as its B-52 brethren. No, what America needed was a new breed of nuclear-armed fighter jet. One that could fly blazingly fast. One that could fly attack missions in any weather due to sophisticated avionics. One that could fire weapons at and drop bombs on targets beyond the view of human pilots. One that could use terrain-following systems enabling it to fly *under* enemy radar. One that could use computerized flight controls to hug the contour of the earth, maintaining an altitude of only two hundred feet above ground level, whether flying over hills, valleys, oceans, mountains, or plains. One that could, in any kind of weather, scream above the steppes, Urals, Black Sea, Caucasus, Siberian taiga, or frozen Arctic at a mind-blurring speed of Mach 1.3—one and one-third times the speed of sound, or roughly 1,000 mph. One that might barely skim treetops in supersonic fashion. One whose ground-contour pilot would be a computer rather than a human, whose comparatively slow reflexes would put such a plane at such an altitude at such a speed into the ground in under 0.25 seconds. One that could fly from a NATO base in Germany or Turkey and be over Moscow in less than an hour.

Of course, Congress, which controlled the Defense Department purse strings, loved this particular tale, which was first whispered to it in 1957. It was a tale that spoke of American excellence and ingenuity. Of scientific and technical prowess. Of military and economic superiority. Of, perhaps even, religious apocalyptic fervor.

Development of this cutting-edge jet was in full swing in 1961 as the Eisenhower administration bowed out of Washington, making room for Kennedy and his meticulous defense secretary, Robert McNamara, who soon grabbed hold of the project with both hands. He dictated that the jet should serve not only the air force but also the navy. Turf battles ensued. Several feet of length needed to be shaved from the original design so that the plane could fit onto aircraft carrier elevators. The air force preferred two-pilot, tandem (front-and-back) seating, while the Navy argued for side-by-side, single-cockpit seating. Because the jet would have to be able to take off with heavy payloads from short runways while also being able to fly at supersonic speeds, engineers would have to develop the world's first delta-wing jet; its wings would extend out for maximum lift at takeoff before tucking in narrowly toward the fuselage during high-speed flight.

The first F-111 off the General Dynamics assembly line completed its maiden flight in December 1964, at the dawn of McNamara's massively escalating war in Vietnam. By then, the men who'd dreamed up the F-111 were no longer thinking so much about the Soviets as they were about the jungle quagmire they'd just been plunged into. None could wait to see how their marvelous creation might perform over the skies of Southeast Asia.

But the F-111 had a timeline of its own. As perhaps the most technologically complex plane ever built, it was ever so finicky and beset by a swarm of glitches. Thus, it had a propensity to crash. A lot. And for reasons flight engineers found difficult to decipher.

As the Vietnam conflict mushroomed into all-out war in 1965, 1966, and 1967, and as F-111s began rolling off the production lines by the dozens, the plane remained stateside, mired in tedious and seemingly endless rounds of test flights, fixes, and technological patches.

By the spring of 1968, the generals and Pentagon planners could wait no more. Like a football coach whose star player had been marooned on the sideline with a series of nagging injuries, the frustrated generals— engineers be damned—rushed their player, the F-111, onto the field of battle.

The results were predictable. Three of the eight jets sent to Vietnam immediately crashed. Four pilots were killed. Nearly all the planes, at some point, inexplicably and intermittently lost control midflight. By the fall, the F-111 was deemed unreliable for battle and was shipped back to the States for further testing and repairs.

A firestorm broke out in Congress. Budgets were slashed. Accusations were hurled. Fingers were pointed. The navy canceled its order. Only the air force stood by its much-maligned prodigy, even as the plane had been draped with the ignominious moniker of McNamara's Flying Edsel.

Over the following three years, flight crews and engineers continued testing, fixing, and improving the F-111. Pilots began giving it respect. Begrudgingly at first. But eventually, that sliver of respect blossomed into full-blown admiration. The plane could be flown solo with high stealth at great distances without protective convoys of refueling tankers and anti-aircraft, antimissile defenders. It could be flown at night or in heavy rain or in dense cloud cover—conditions that would ground conventional jets of the time—and still accurately find and strike targets. It was impervious to the air defenses of the day and nearly impossible to shoot down by either enemy jets, missiles, or ground fire.

Pilots began calling it the Aardvark, after the specialized hunter of ants and termites. Equipped with a long, pointed snout and powerful claws, the aardvark roamed the veldt of South Africa. It hunted solo and at night, traveling great distances and using its tremendous sense of smell to home in on its prey. As a predator, the aardvark was underestimated, underappreciated, and largely unloved.

And so it was that from 1968 to 1972, the F-111 Aardvark streaked across the skies above Texas, New Mexico, and Nevada—underestimated, underappreciated, and unloved—biding its time, waiting for technology to catch up with its abilities, being continuously improved, and awaiting another chance to prove its worth in battle.

―⁓―

By the spring of 1970, after having flown two tours of duty and 124 combat missions aboard the B-52 as well as two tours of duty and 151 combat missions aboard the F-105 (not counting the two or three dozen additional missions he'd surreptitiously kept "off the books"), Don now found himself flying as a test pilot out of Nellis Air Force Base near Las Vegas aboard the inexplicably finicky and wholly lethal (to its own pilots) F-111. It was a job that only the adventurous, the highly skilled, and the adrenaline starved would think of volunteering for.

To Don, it was an honor and a challenge, both physically and intellectually.

Following its disastrous combat debut in 1968, the F-111 was temporarily grounded while air force flight specialists and General Dynamics aeronautical engineers scrambled to fix whatever they surmised to be the problem *du jour*.

Assured that the F-111 was finally, definitely flight and combat worthy, the air force once again cleared the plane for Vietnam combat duty in the spring of 1969.

By the late fall of 1969, the spate of F-111 crashes continued unabated. Some fifteen of the planes had now been lost for reasons that were difficult to pinpoint. Because the plane was designed to be flown solo and not as part of a formation, almost none of the crashes had any witnesses. Additionally, because the planes flew so low and so fast, their crashes were particularly deadly. Pilots often didn't have time to eject, usually riding their supersonic charges right into a mountainside crater. And because the planes were almost always flown deep into enemy territory, as they were designed, the few pilots who did manage to eject from a wounded or unstable aircraft were left to parachute into North Vietnam, where they were either swiftly pitchforked by the enemy or marched off to the Hanoi Hilton, not to be heard from for years, if ever.

Wreckage from these crashes was difficult, if not impossible, to recover. Frequently, the planes were lost beneath the dense jungle canopy, never to be found, or they were wrecked well behind enemy lines, making recovery equally impossible.

Theories abounded. Some crashes were attributed to mechanical failure—perhaps an engine or structural defect. Some were attributed to pilot error—perhaps pilots weren't used to the high-performance autopilot capabilities of the plane. And some were attributed to the enemy—perhaps the North Vietnamese had figured out how to shoot the F-111 easily and frequently from the sky.

None of these theories sat easy with Don. An engine or structural defect would have been fairly easy to replicate and pinpoint by the hordes of aerospace engineers who'd been assigned to help resolve this problem over the past half decade.

Pilot error was also a cop-out in Don's opinion. It's always easy to blame a pilot. Maybe once. Maybe twice. But a couple of dozen times or more? No. The men who'd met their demise in the F-111 were among the most skilled and highly trained aviators in the world. It was doubtful that all had made similar fatal errors.

Enemy fire was also a stretch, Don thought. The plane flew way too low and way too fast to even trigger a response from a surface-to-air missile. Those were worthless against the F-111, as were traditional antiaircraft guns and cannons. Further, the planes flew one by one. There were no advance planes or multiple-plane formation to alert enemy gunners to oncoming aircraft. Rather, by the time a North Vietnamese gunner had discovered an F-111 was within range, that plane was long gone. Those in the enemy-fire camp were left only with the "golden BB theory"—that is, the planes must've been shot down by a lucky soldier firing a lucky gun from the ground, striking each supersonic jet with a lucky shot in maybe the one or two vulnerable places that would bring such an aircraft down.

Don had pored over each of the F-111 accident reports and had concluded that neither the air force nor the plane's manufacturer had any idea what was bringing down their multimillion-dollar technological marvels. And so he approached his new job as an F-111 test pilot with both trepidation and excitement. While he loved a good puzzle, a challenging game of chess, and a long game of poker, he felt he'd come to this task already down a queen and a rook, or maybe holding only a pair of deuces. As such, he felt compelled to solve the riddle quickly and definitively before he, too, would join the others—aboard a supersonic plane making a split-second dive into the side of a mountain.

Don loved flying over northern Nevada in the spring. The valleys were green and flowered from winter snowmelt. The north-south ranges stood tall, blue, and snowcapped in the distance. Wilderness stretched from horizon to horizon. Signs of civilization were sparse, and it was a thrill to be alive.

On this particular flight in early May 1970, Don streaked supersonic, his autopilot set at one thousand feet above the ground. The springtime sage blurred a dusty green below, and parallel ten-thousand-foot ranges rushed past like twin walls only a few miles to his left and to his right. The clear, crisp, dry conditions were in stark contrast to Vietnam.

"The F-111 was flat out the best fighter jet ever made," he would surmise years later in retirement. "It had more technological breakthroughs than any aircraft before or since. You could release a bomb miles before you could even see the target, and its systems were so accurate that it was rare a pilot would ever miss by a foot or more. On top of all that, it was as fast as a son of a bitch and an absolute joy to fly."

The jet could be easily identified by its distinctive long, black nose cone that housed its forward radar systems, which enabled its terrain-following capabilities. The plane sent out a wide radar beam that scanned ahead ten miles or more. In conjunction, two narrow pencil-beam radar systems were used to scan more immediate terrain. One of the beams scanned back and forth vertically, while the other scanned quickly left to right and right to left. The data would be gathered instantly and cross-hatched by an onboard computer, which would display the upcoming terrain in an echoscope within the cockpit. The continual split-second information would control the plane's altitude, enabling the aircraft to fly extremely fast and extremely low—sometimes only one hundred feet above the ground if necessary.

As Don scorched north through the sky, he could see the bright, desolate salt flats of western Utah to his right and the Ruby Mountains rising blue and majestic in the distance to his left.

Don banked hard and headed low toward a saddle in the Rubies between Tipton Peak and Pearl Peak. The Ruby Marshes, in the lowlands just east of the range, sprawled blue amid miles of green meadows and rushes, the vast expanse fed by abundant snowmelt. As Don's F-111 raced toward the clear, cold marshes, he could see the afternoon sun glinting golden off the water. His plane then dropped unexpectedly before seeming to catch itself. The echoscope tied to the terrain-following radar system blinked, and the plane steadied briefly before dropping and catching yet again.

The Ruby Marshes glided quickly beneath him, and ahead the most imposing mountain range in northeastern Nevada rose, sudden and solitary before him. His plane shot upward, following the angle of the mountain slope skyward. A patch of snow, maybe a half-mile across, was all that was left of a deep winter snowpack. It had retreated to a gentle saddle-shaped pass between two peaks, where it now lay exposed beneath the warm May sun. The high-altitude scrub sage grew low here, hunkering as close to the earth as possible for protection against relentless, year-round battering from wind, snow, rain, and sun. The soil beneath the sage was a rich, ruddy brown, still damp from snowmelt but dark enough to gather solar heat and nip at the snowbank's edges, accelerating its daily retreat.

The contrast between the dull-dark earth and the bright-white snow was striking to Don, even at a speed of nearly one thousand knots and with his helmet visor's glare-reducing glass.

The plane had almost reached its apex, and like a cart atop a roller coaster, Don lifted, weightless, beneath his seat harness. As the F-111 leveled and shot between the mountain notch, Don could feel the jet almost stutter. He glanced at the echoscope, noticing that it had gone completely blank as the plane flew past the snowfield and dropped roughly down the Ruby Range's western slope.

As Don's plane stabilized and he banked south toward Nellis, he made note of his echoscope's seeming quirk. On the way back to his home base, he surveyed the empty majesty of the Great Basin, with the sun sinking low in a cloudless sky toward the western horizon. Everywhere the landscape glinted and gleamed, reflecting sunlight as though someone had scattered pennies and dimes across the mountains and valleys. High patches of snow shone in the bright salmon shade of the approaching sunset. Flat granite faces of barren peaks caught the sunlight just right and gleamed a leaden silver. Small ponds dotted the high desert valleys, appearing almost metallic from above, like rounded beads of mercury. Farther south as Don neared Nellis, great sand dunes rose from the desert floor and reflected sunlight with nearly the intensity of the snowfields in the north.

A notion began to take shape in Don's mind—a notion that would soon creep and grow before finally blossoming into a full-blown, morning-noon-and-night obsession that would not be assuaged until the puzzle was solved and the problem fixed.

Over the next three months, Don meticulously reviewed every accident report of every wrecked F-111. He checked the coordinates of each incident, both stateside and in Vietnam, poring over maps and corresponding satellite photos. In most instances, there was the nearby presence of a highly reflective natural surface—a snowfield, dry lake bed, river, ocean, sand dune, exposed rock.

He investigated his theory on numerous test flights and came to discover that when he flew the plane over a reflective surface like water, sand, or snow, the twin pencil-beam radar systems—one of which swept side to side and the other, front and back—would sometimes fall out of sync. And when that phenomenon happened, the plane's computer would essentially be temporarily blinded. With data streaming from only one radar beam at a time, the computer would paint upcoming terrain in two dimensions, not three. Thus, it would sometimes be fooled whenever flying over a lake or a snowbank into calculating that the aircraft was perhaps ten thousand or twenty thousand feet high, not one thousand or two thousand feet. And when that happened, the computer would initiate a dive maneuver within milliseconds. At a cruising velocity of one thousand miles per hour or more, the pilot would be helpless to counter, and death would be instantaneous.

Don was much relieved when he'd solved the riddle. He was further excited because he suspected that the fix would be simple, involving only an inexpensive electronic device called a comparator, which would continually check the electric currents from each radar device and keep them perpetually in sync, no matter what terrain or reflective surface they were flying over.

Thrilled to tell the world, save lives, rescue a multibillion-dollar defense project, and provide the American military with the assurance of a highly reliable, highly advanced war machine, Don assumed that fixing the problem would involve the basic task of writing a report and sending it to a superior.

Which he did.

Then he waited. And waited. And waited.

Nothing.

Frustrated, he sent his report to a broader audience that included high-level officers and General Dynamics safety engineers.

Again he waited. And waited. And waited.

Exasperated, he sent his report to even higher-level officers as well as a smattering of congressmen.

Again, nothing.

It turns out that there is no such thing as simple when it comes to fixing mistakes within a bureaucracy as big and byzantine as the American military-industrial-political complex. Especially not during an unpopular war. Elected officials jockey for dollars that big aerospace contracts bring to their districts and constituents. Military contractors hate admitting mistakes that might harm current and future business and prefer to keep such things quiet. They also have a hard time believing that someone outside of their ring of highly skilled aerospace engineers could resolve a problem that had kept them stumped for years. Air force officers are conditioned to follow the chain of command and prefer to steer clear of any potential career-ending potholes. It makes for an ossified system in which solutions are brought to bear in years, not days or weeks. And none of the intertwined parties ever wants to admit to the public that a deadly, multibillion-dollar disaster struck because of a simple technical oversight that could be fixed with a gadget that could be purchased at a radio repair shop for twelve dollars.

And so the gears of change locked tight.

And the F-111s kept mysteriously, inexplicably crashing.

And pilots kept dying.

———

In the fall of 1972, the F-111 had once again been deemed combat worthy. Though Don had been scheduled for a plum assignment at Royal Air Field Lakenheath, England, he instead chose to return to Takhli Royal Thai Air Force Base, Thailand, both to fly combat missions in the waning days of the war and to serve as the chief safety officer for the squadron.

He continued to harbor extreme concerns about the F-111's balky radar system and felt he'd be of more use in Southeast Asia than in Europe.

The first pilots to trumpet the F-111's return to combat were Maj. Bill Coltman and Lt. Robert Brett, who rocketed off the tarmac at Takhli and into the tropical night on September 28, 1972. They'd only just arrived in Southeast Asia a few hours earlier. Their destination was a target north of Da Nang. They would never return, vanishing inexplicably from radar before ever reaching North Vietnam. Their crash site—in the mountainous jungles of Laos—wouldn't be located for over a quarter century, and their remains wouldn't be positively identified and returned home until 2001.

On October 16, 1972, Capt. James Hockridge and Lt. Allen Graham vanished following a bombing run over Phúc Yên Air Base near Hanoi.

On November 7, 1972, Don returned to his quarters after a night mission and fell into a deep sleep. He awoke in the morning to notice that the bunks of his roommates Maj. Robert Brown and Capt. Robert Morrissey were empty. Without knowing any details, Don rubbed his eyes, shook his head, and immediately knew. Radar coordinates had last placed their plane over the Laotian mountains. To this date, it has yet to be found.

On the evening of November 21, 1972, Don had dinner with Capt. Ron Stafford less than an hour before Stafford was scheduled to fly an F-111 mission to Hanoi with Capt. Charles Caffarelli.

Don awoke the next morning to find he'd been placed on yet another F-111 accident investigation detail. Stafford and Caffarelli were missing, and parts of their plane were washing ashore on a beach near Da Nang.

Don simmered. As mangled plane parts were recovered from the sand and shipped to Takhli for inspection, he could tell that Stafford's F-111 had hit the water unexpectedly and at a high velocity. Neither pilot's body was ever found. Each was presumed lost in the South China Sea.

Don dutifully wrote his portion of the accident report and, in the strongest language he could summon, beseeched the air force to investigate and deploy his recommended fix for synchronizing the plane's pencil-beam radar system.

The report was filed, placed in an official US Air Force manila envelope, and stamped for delivery and distribution to the usual suspects at the Seventh Air Force, the Pentagon, and General Dynamics.

Don went to dinner at the Officers' Club and thought about his colleagues who'd been lost in the F-111. He knew them all. Stafford was just the latest.

Following dinner, he walked over to the base mail room, retrieved the Stafford-Caffarelli crash report, and added to the distribution list: Richard M. Nixon, President, United States of America. He then added a brief personal note to the report, advising the president that though the problems with the F-111 had been buried under an oppressive layer of bureaucracy, they were eminently fixable. Additionally, Don pointed out that over the previous two years, he'd exhausted all traditional channels of command to effect such a fix and was now left in the awkward position of asking the president for help.

He thought for a moment about what he was about to do. But the war for Don had been long. He'd seen and done things most men shouldn't ever see or do. He walked back to the mail room with the newly addressed packet, stared at it once more, and muttered to himself, "Fuck it. Stafford, this is for you."

He tossed the envelope onto the outgoing stack of official correspondence, walked back to his quarters, and slept soundly.

———

Gen. Vogt leaned back in his chair, accident report papers strewn deep atop the desk before him.

"That's a helluva story, son. And I'm sure you believe it to be true. Hell, I even think it might be true. So we'll skip the court-martial. For now. I'm going back stateside, and I can assure you, I will get to the bottom of this, come hell or high water. If your theory proves out, you might just survive this without me having to skin you alive. You are dismissed."

Don snapped to attention, saluted, wheeled, and strode to the Officers' Club for a rare drink, where he smiled, held up a Schlitz, and muttered, "Stafford, this is for you."

Three months later, General Dynamics made modification number 996 to its F-111 aircraft, which was the addition of a comparator to the plane's pencil-beam radar system. The plane went on to become one of the safest and most reliable in the US Air Force. And the modification is now standard on virtually all American fighter and bomber jets.

CHAPTER THIRTY-FOUR

The first few times I experienced a B-52 attack, it seemed, as I strained to press myself into the bunker floor, that I had been caught in the Apocalypse. The terror was complete. One lost control of bodily functions as the mind screamed futile orders to get out.
—TRUONG NHU TANG, *NEW YORK TIMES MAGAZINE*

THE B-52 IS AN APOCALYPTIC WAR MACHINE.

It was never designed for bombing impenetrable jungles. Or supporting ground troops. Or "softening" the enemy.

Which is exactly how the US military deployed the B-52 all throughout its nearly decade-long war in Vietnam.

That is, until December 18, 1972.

That's when President Richard Nixon, frustrated by his North Vietnamese adversaries' foot dragging and overt efforts to run out the clock on a proposed peace treaty before a decidedly antiwar American Congress took office in January 1973, and determined to remove a bloody inherited albatross from around his and all Americans' collective necks, finally released the B-52 from its yoke.

That's when, for the first time since the initial and only planned B-52 raid on Hanoi was scrubbed—midmission—in February 1965, the Strategic Air Command was issued orders to deploy all 209 of its available B-52s in the Asian theater to the skies over the North Vietnamese capital, which served as the country's military, industrial, and political heart and brain.

That's when Nixon did what none of his other predecessors had the will to do. Not Eisenhower. Not Kennedy. Not Johnson.

That's when the president and the Joint Chiefs of Staff dusted off Gen. Curtis LeMay's eight-year-old combat plans and finally and decisively ended a war—over the course of only eleven days—that in all likelihood should have never been fought or most certainly should have been abruptly ended eight years earlier—by B-52s—before it had ever really started.

That's when Richard M. Nixon truly, viciously, and resolutely visited the apocalypse upon Hanoi.

—✦—

Every two weeks since arriving back at Takhli, Don would hear a new "the-war's-over, we're-going-home" rumor, especially in the days and weeks following the late October utterance by National Security Adviser Henry Kissinger that proved prematurely optimistic: "We believe peace is at hand."

Several air crews throughout Southeast Asia, Guam, and the Philippines had been slated to return home throughout November and early December, but those orders had been hastily rescinded at the eleventh hour each time.

So on December 16, 1972, when Don walked into a crowded briefing room at the air base, he, too, expected an announcement that perhaps the war was over and that they were all going home.

That notion was promptly quashed the moment the briefing officer lowered an aerial map of Hanoi.

Two days earlier, President Nixon had issued these orders to his military commanders: "You are to commence at approximately 1200 Zulu, 18 December 1972, a three-day maximum effort, repeat maximum effort, of B-52/Tacair strikes in the Hanoi/Haiphong areas. Object is maximum destruction of selected targets."

—✦—

A full moon rose into broken clouds that hovered just above the horizon east of Takhli, while a forlorn sun, appearing as a weak, orange disc, slipped beneath a haze of mist to the west. The coming night would be chilly, and though there appeared to be a break in the monsoon rains, forecasts called for Hanoi to be shrouded beneath a ground-hugging fog.

Don sat in the cockpit of his F-111 and rat-a-tatted crisply through his preflight checklist, a ritual he'd performed hundreds of times before. But this time was different, and he knew it. He wasn't so much astounded by the fact that he wouldn't be home for Christmas—he'd remarried, had a newborn daughter, and was making a concerted, honest effort to transform himself into a "family man"—rather, he could hardly believe that his commander in chief, the Joint Chiefs of Staff, and the whole of the US Air Force had finally landed on the combat plan Don had since 1965 believed to be the only plausible way to end a savage war that had sapped so much of America's blood, treasure, and prestige.

But once he completed his checklist, he shoved all those notions out of his mind. It now wasn't his job to be politician, husband, father, statesman, military strategist. He was a paid killer. A single-minded assassin. He had one duty on this night. And he was determined, as always, to perform it to perfection. He would fly forward support of the largest American bombing raid ever launched. He would fly over Thud Ridge, scream beneath the radar across the Red River, and then bomb a MiG airfield on the outskirts of Hanoi, thus helping to suppress any potential North Vietnamese aerial response to the coming onslaught.

Just behind him would be squadrons of low-flying F-4 jets, dropping radar-jamming chaff—a sort of metallic confetti—like a blanket over the whole of Hanoi and the nearby port city of Haiphong. F-105s would follow, armed with newly developed Shrike missiles that could detect radar signals emanating from mobile SAM missile sites. Once fired, the Shrikes would home toward the SAMs with deadly accuracy. Overhead, EB-66 aircraft would circle, emitting a cloak of electronic, radar-jamming mayhem, contributing to the air defense confusion and combat blindness on the ground.

The North Vietnamese knew the B-52s were coming. They just weren't quite sure how many the Americans would send. They also, after all these eight years of war without a single B-52 ever overflying Hanoi, had difficulty believing the Americans would actually, finally send the big, slow bombers into the heart of one of the most heavily defended cities in the world.

In the mountain passes of Laos, along the flight path traditionally followed by American fighter jets inbound for Hanoi, the screens of North Vietnamese radar outposts lit up with the unmistakable profile of high-flying B-52s. They excitedly contacted their commanders to the north. When asked how many, they replied that they weren't exactly sure, just that there were "waves and waves."

On the northern banks of the Red River, closer to Hanoi, a SAM radar crew inside a van about the size of a semi truck, became instantly overwhelmed and frantic. Screens flared bright white from the blizzard of chaff dropped by the F-4s. Electronic jamming pulses from the EB-66s further rendered the screens useless.

The first wave of B-52s numbered forty-nine in total. Twenty-one were from the American air base of U-Tapao, Thailand; the other twenty-eight were from Andersen Air Force Base, Guam. The crews attacking Hanoi were given "press-on rules," possibly the first issued to American pilots since World War II. Such rules dictated that each bomber maintain its course toward its target, regardless of any incoming SAMs, ground fire, flak, or MiGs. It was destroy or be destroyed.

—⁓—

Don slipped over Thud Ridge undetected, flying low and supersonic into the nighttime fog. He locked his target, released his bombs, and rocked a MiG airfield north of Hanoi. The American Joint Chiefs of Staff had tabbed ninety-six key military sites for destruction during Operation Linebacker II, the moniker the military had given to this, the largest American bombing campaign ever. Others would later dub it the Christmas Bombing. The MiG airfield was but one of the sites targeted for destruction. Don pulled up, broke through the overcast, and banked hard left and into the nighttime sky. Below, moonlight washed bright upon the low clouds blanketing Hanoi.

Then came the B-52s.

For over an hour, the city shook and rumbled and shattered. Bombs fell in clustered strings, pounding craters—some thirty feet in diameter and thirty feet deep—in and around the city. Rail lines were severed. Bridges obliterated. Airfields demolished. Command centers smashed. Munitions warehouses detonated. The military might of North Vietnam, such as it was, began to dissolve.

Deep within a Hanoi prison, surrounded by thick concrete walls, Maj. Norb Gotner, an American F-4 pilot who'd been shot down nearly two years earlier over Laos, immediately recognized the unmistakable thunder of a B-52 bombing. As the walls of his prison cell swayed and the ground beneath him jumped, Gotner said aloud, "The BUFFs are here and will bring an end to this damned war."

A second wave of several dozen B-52s streamed over Hanoi around midnight, followed by a third wave at around 4:00 a.m., local time.

For three successive nights, American airpower decimated the North Vietnamese nerve center in Hanoi as well as its supply lifeline in the port of Haiphong.

But the execution of Linebacker II was far from flawless. The aerial battle plan, developed at the Strategic Air Command's headquarters in Omaha, Nebraska, called for each B-52 to fly into Hanoi on identical tracks, single file, at the same altitude, airspeed, and heading. Each pilot was directed to execute a hard-right combat break immediately after bomb release, sending planes and their crews into stiff headwinds that served to slow the bombers' speed by nearly three hundred miles per hour, keeping them in the SAM kill zone longer.

This predictability enabled the radar operators on the ground to guesstimate some of the B-52 coordinates. Additionally, North Vietnamese technicians discovered that they could often lock onto a B-52 as soon as the jet made its postrelease bank, turning its radar-jamming strobe away from the deadly SAM site below and leaving the big bombers momentarily vulnerable to detection.

Over the course of the first three days of Linebacker II, the Americans were indeed inflicting "maximum destruction." However, they were also sustaining unacceptable loss rates. Three bombers were shot down during the first two nights of the offensive, with four more bombers irreparably damaged. On night three, the SAM operators had broken the code due to American predictability, shooting down six B-52s and damaging one.

A near-mutinous cacophony arose from the B-52 flight crews, reverberating all the way back to both Washington, DC, and Omaha. As a result, for the remainder of Operation Linebacker II, air tactics were drastically altered. B-52 cells would now be sent to Hanoi and Haiphong in swarms, each entering enemy airspace simultaneously at different altitudes, air speeds, and headings. Each wave would drop all its bombs within a fifteen-minute window before exiting quickly along a multitude of tracks. As a result, American losses plunged, while North Vietnamese resistance, beneath relentless pounding, wilted.

Christmas Eve came debauched to Takhli Royal Thai Air Force Base in 1972.

To a man, the pilots knew the war was over. Even though the Linebacker II bombings would continue for another five days, including a Christmas Day respite, air crews had destroyed all ninety-six critical targets in Hanoi and Haiphong as dictated by the Joint Chiefs of Staff. Further, Hanoi had been laid nearly defenseless, the city bereft of communication and depleted of SAMs.

The Officers' Club was jammed with celebrants, none reverent of the season. A small orchestra played big band tunes at a feverish pace. The loud rhythm of jazz horns and percussion throbbed above the clusters of men, all prodigiously drinking, smoking, hooting, laughing, and sweating. A troop of Thai dancers, some dressed as elves, swayed on stage in graceful rhythm to the music. But as the hour grew late, the night devolved. The men hurled catcalls and wadded bills upon the stage. The women responded by removing their tops, contributing further to the surreal nature of the event. Christmas decorations. Artie Shaw. Duke Ellington. Glenn Miller. Topless Thai elves. The end of the War That Wouldn't End.

Three of Don's fellow pilots suggested he sit in as a guest drummer and show off his chops. Don demurred. The pilots, none close to sober, forcefully insisted, carrying Don onto the stage, barreling past startled elves and wresting the drumsticks away from the band's regular drummer, who acquiesced in the face of the menacing odds.

Don sat before the drum set, deftly twirling a drumstick through the fingers on his right hand, then through the fingers on his left. He paced through a quick drum set warm-up exercise that he'd first learned as a youth before nodding toward the orchestra leader, who lifted his baton toward his horn section. A pair of trombonists and a trio of horn players stood, blaring in upbeat syncopation the opening of Benny Goodman's "Sing, Sing, Sing." Don had played the tune dozens of times with his father's band and jumped in with a determined tom-tom beat.

The crowd of officers responded with a drunken roar at one of their own, hip and skillful, banging on the drums. The topless elves gyrated in synchronized rhythm. The thick haze of cigarette smoke conspired with a stage spotlight to blind Don of anything farther away than the orchestra leader. Sweat dripped down his brow and into his eyes. For three minutes he followed the lead of the horns and trombones before the orchestra leader silenced them with a slash of his baton, signaling Don to launch into a solo. He obliged.

The men cheered louder, and Don played harder. For one minute. Two. Three. Five. Seven. Sweat cascaded down his face. His tan uniform became dark and wet throughout his chest and beneath his armpits. The orchestra leader rescued him by inviting the horn section to step in and finish the tune. As soon as the piece ended, Don, near collapse, tossed his drumsticks in the air, caught them, and stood to thunderous applause. He staggered, exhausted, off the stage, leaned his back against a wall, slumped to the floor, closed his eyes, and smiled. The war, for all practical purposes, was over. Don knew that to be true. And for the first time since 1965, he allowed himself to think that he might not die here.

The B-52 bombings of Hanoi and Haiphong resumed the day after Christmas, continuing nightly with unmitigated American ferocity and dwindling North Vietnamese resistance. Yet the Vietcong political and military leaders steadfastly refused to respond to daily American overtures to end the bombings and the war.

On December 29, sixty B-52s hammered the already obliterated rail yards at Lang Dang. While the bombs fell, the North Vietnamese finally gave in, agreeing to meet their American counterparts in Paris for talks to end the war.

The B-52s and supporting strike fighters had done in eleven days what the whole of the American military in Southeast Asia had failed to accomplish over the previous seven years of battle.

The Paris Peace Accords were signed on January 27, 1973, effectively ending America's military involvement in Vietnam.

Most times when we leave a place, we're blithely unaware until years later that we're destined never to return. Never to see a certain person. Never to smell a certain aroma. Never to eat a certain dish. Never to gaze at a certain garden. Never to find comfort in the easy familiarity that comes with knowing the locations of certain trees, certain rivers, certain hills, certain fields, certain buildings, certain roads. It is as though one day we just walked away. Vanished. Never given the chance to mourn the passing of a place or a time. And, conversely, that place—its people—never given the opportunity to mourn or even acknowledge our passing through, too.

But sometimes, we know—definitively and certainly—when we'll never pass this way again.

For Don and Southeast Asia, that day was January 3, 1973.

He knew that everything he did that day—every sight, every sound, every person, every place—would be the last. He wasn't sure whether to savor it. And though it lacked the nostalgic charm of leaving one's hometown—the streets where a person had grown up—he did know he'd miss it. In a different way. And terribly. So he did the only thing he could. He made sure to remember.

In a way, it was like living. In another, it was like dying.

Soon, it would all—for better, for worse—be gone. The place would vanish into the past, accessible as only a memory. As only a dream.

And the warrior—he, too, would be plucked from that time and that place—transported somewhere else, where great and heroic deeds would no longer matter so much. Where they'd be an afterthought. Where they, and the warrior, would be only a dream.

—◦—

The sun struggled to break through a stubborn haze that blanketed the eastern horizon at dawn. But by midmorning, it was blazing bright as the day turned cool and clear. Conditions were perfect for taking pictures. Which was why Don and his F-111 had been assigned as a fighter escort for an RA-5C Vigilante, a navy plane designed for aerial photography. The pair were sent on a poststrike reconnaissance mission over Hanoi—a mission that would document swaths of damage inflicted by American air forces during Linebacker II.

The wheels of Don's jet lifted from the tarmac at Takhli, and he soared steeply into the blue. Rice paddies glinted below in the morning sun. Don achieved an altitude of thirty thousand feet and accelerated to nearly twice the speed of sound toward his rendezvous point with the Vigilante. He never tired of flying. It felt glorious.

Don radioed his coordinates, spotted the Vigilante, and slipped into a comfortable cruise just off its right wing.

The plains of Thailand floated into the jungle hills of Laos, which drifted into the steep, green-clad mountains that presaged North Vietnam.

The two jets passed over Thud Ridge. No shots were fired, no missiles launched. They flew high above the Red River, unimpeded into downtown Hanoi, over which they banked and made repeated passes. Again, no shots were fired, no missiles launched. Don recognized the sites of dozens of military targets below, all of which had been obliterated. Completely. Some had been bombed by B-52s two, three, and four times—not because just one bombing wouldn't have done the job, but because the Americans had run out of targets. And since they'd been ordered to continue flying missions until the enemy had succumbed and called for peace, they'd just returned to the top of the target list and started over. And over. And over.

The destruction of Hanoi's military, its industry, its supply lines, its command centers, its air defenses was complete. Post–Linebacker

II damage assessments concluded that American sorties had destroyed more than 1,600 military structures, more than 500 rail locations, more than 370 rail cars, one-fourth of the country's petroleum reserves, 80 percent of its power grid, all of its missile stockpiles, and virtually every air base and runway. It's estimated that the Vietcong had fired more than 1,200 surface-to-air missiles during the American offensive, most of which were expended during the first three days of bombing. By the later stages of Linebacker II, Vietcong air defenses were in shambles. The enemy had completely run out of missiles and its capital city lay utterly defenseless from the air. Though there would be confusion and debate in America for decades hence about who'd won this war, for Don the answer would always be as a clear as the view above Hanoi on that January day. In his mind, as a firsthand observer and combatant, the North Vietnamese didn't come to sign the Paris Peace Accords willingly. That was never their plan, never their strategy, never their nature. Not after all the sacrifice. All the death. All the deprivation. First against the French. And then the Americans.

No, they made peace because they had no other choice, no other path. They were beaten. Soundly. Decisively. Irrevocably.

Their ability to make war had been crushed.

But now that the Americans had achieved victory, they'd suddenly moved on. So had the Chinese. And the Soviets. The geopolitical vise in which Vietnam had found itself squeezed for over a decade had loosened.

China and the Soviet Union had experienced a massive rift. Neither had the stomach for continuing with a proxy war in Southeast Asia against the Americans.

In May 1972, a historic thaw between the Soviets and the United States had been ushered in by the signing of the Strategic Arms Limitation Treaty (SALT I) by the two nuclear superpowers. SALT II talks, which would further reduce American-Soviet nuclear stockpiles, were just under way.

China, which had been pushed to the brink of nuclear war with the Soviets only two years earlier, realized its future and potential prosperity lay across the Pacific with the United States. Nixon would visit China only three weeks after the signing of the Peace Accords. The timing of Linebacker II and the end of the Vietnam War wasn't a coincidence.

And America? After all the blood. All the treasure. All the turmoil. All the death. All the sacrifice of young lives—the draining of their promise, of their future. America? It claimed victory and then simply walked away, no longer interested in occupying North Vietnam or even later keeping the Vietcong at bay from the South and Saigon.

Don descended into Takhli aboard his F-111. The runway stretched before him. His wheels chirped as they hit the tarmac. He slowed quickly with a roar, turned off the runway, and taxied to a stop. He stepped out of his cockpit, made a hop to the ground, and realized he'd never again fly combat.

It was his choice to abruptly return home. He'd flown so much combat that he'd earned the privilege of telling the air force if and when he'd had enough. And after 124 B-52 missions, after 165 F-105 missions, after 30 F-111 missions—the only pilot to fly all three jets in combat—he stood before his commanding officer and asked to return stateside so that he could see his wife and newborn daughter.

From the time he'd first been briefed at Mather Air Force Base on February 8, 1965, and told to prepare for a B-52 bombing mission to Hanoi, Don had been at war 2,886 days. Seven years, ten months, twenty-six days.

Later, as the sun sank, orange and dim, into a thick haze along the western horizon, he boarded a transport plane that would take him to Bangkok and then San Francisco. The plane lifted off the tarmac, and as twilight began to darken the land below, Don closed his eyes and slept. He had no interest in looking back.

Chapter Thirty-Five

The bearer is a member of ye Anciente and Secret Order of Quiet Birdmen, founded January 1921, and is a certified Goodfellow. He has mounted alone into the realms beyond the reach of Keewee and Modock and should be accorded all gestures of friendship and aid by fellow Quiet Birdmen, wherever they meet.

—Membership card, *Ye Anciente and Secret Order of Quiet Birdmen*

"God, I loved flying combat," Don told me recently. "I loved it more than life itself. There's nothing—and I mean nothing—in any of man's pursuits that compares. To be in the cockpit of a supersonic war machine. To have to outthink and outsmart a ruthless enemy who wants you killed. To watch the world rushing by beneath you. To pull several g's and make an aerial maneuver that maybe only one or two other people in the world could accomplish. To lead a squadron of men on a dangerous mission and have their lives in your hand. To help stop the advance of genocidal dictators. To get shot at and feel a rush of adrenaline that's better than heroin. To live every day on the edge of death so you have such a huge appreciation of life. There's really nothing like it. Nothing at all. If I could go relive it all over again, I would in a heartbeat—even if it meant I had to go through another B-52 crash. I'd do it gladly just for a chance to fly combat again."

———

In July, the sun rises orange and ominous and hot above a crumpled desert mountain range just east of Nellis Air Force Base near Las Vegas.

At 5:30 a.m., the tarmac already shimmers atop a heat-baked valley floor in southern Nevada. The air rumbles to the thrum of jet engines as an F-22 Raptor taxis for takeoff. Brakes chirp as the advanced tactical fighter—currently the most sophisticated and expensive flying machine in the world—wheels into position. Now stationary, it glimmers low and sleek and metallic at the end of a long runway. Its engines fire blue and orange, its brakes release, and the valley is filled with the bone-shaking roar of aeronautic thrust. The jet slings down the runway, its wheels lifting gently from the tarmac and its bullet-shaped nose tilting upward, just before its swept wings grab hold of the air, rocketing the plane steeply into the dawn. The pilot banks hard north, and the F-22 streaks between parallel mountain ranges. Below and beyond, there is an empty expanse of heat-tortured brown. Above, there is a cobalt evening sky to the left and a white-blue morning sky to the right.

A few miles south of the air base stands a modest, single-story ranch home—the kind they built in droves throughout the Las Vegas Valley in the fifties and sixties. Low-slung and unassuming, the house has an exterior of pinkish-tan stucco, a carport of mostly cinder block, and a roof sprinkled with white quartz gravel to reflect the sun and dampen the heat. A waist-high chain-link fence hems in a small front yard, where the lawn in the summer fights a losing battle with the daily swelter and is green only in patches.

Don stirs at the familiar sound of jet engines. They're like an alarm clock, announcing the arrival of yet another day, for which Don is always thankful. Sometimes, if the breeze is right, Don can detect a whiff of jet exhaust, which makes him smile. At the sound of the fighters getting airborne, two terriers—Lady and Tramp—bound into Don's cramped bedroom and bounce at his feet as he slides on his house slippers. Don groans as he stands—he's seventy-five now—and begins to shuffle into the kitchen to make coffee and feed his dogs. Don adores the terriers. He picks them up one by one, scratches them behind their ears, puts them back down, and begins talking to them as though they were people. Don talks each morning about politics, about the economy, about science, about the weather, about war, or about anything else that might pop into his head. The dogs each cock their heads and perk their ears whenever

Don speaks. They're good listeners. Either that, or they're simply waiting for cues of when Don is ready to take them for their daily visit to the nearby dog park, which in the summer happens early in the day because of the heat.

Don takes his coffee to the living room and settles into the couch with the morning paper. He spreads the pages over a coffee table and begins reading headlines to Lady and Tramp, who now sit next to him on the coach, staring raptly. Hanging on the walls are framed portraits of smiling husbands and wives and young children. Don is in none of the photos. They are of his son, his two daughters, their spouses, and Don's five grandchildren. Don calls them on the phone sporadically, and sometimes they call him first, but not often. He hasn't met three of his grandchildren, even though the youngest is now seventeen. He's seen his son perhaps twice, and then only briefly, in the past thirty years. Same with his daughters.

Don finds people difficult. They're rarely interested in the things he thinks are important and wants to talk about. They rarely agree with his view of the world and can be argumentative whenever Don presses an issue, which he frequently does. After an hour or two of being around people—especially family members—Don gets exhausted from having to maintain a facade of sociability. He can then get easily frustrated, angry, and belligerent. An offhand comment or a muted snicker can launch him into a tirade or send him into a rage. It takes him hours, sometimes days, to calm back down and find his inner peace. Sometimes, with people, Don will take offense at a seemingly insignificant remark and then hold a grudge against that person for weeks or perhaps even years.

And so Don, who has left behind in life a trail strewn with three ex-wives and countless ex-girlfriends, much prefers the company of dogs. They look at him longingly and with eager fascination. They listen attentively to his opinions and theories, no matter how long-winded or oddball. And whenever he sinks into depression or spends an hour ranting about the president, they're still there by his side, just as bright eyed and seemingly happy as ever.

The only actual people in Don's life are other retired combat pilots. Turns out that they are nearly as compassionate, forgiving, and understanding of one of their own as they are to pet dogs. Don lives in the vicinity of Nellis because of the close-knit, active fraternity of retired pilots nearby. No one knows the inner life of a former fighter pilot like another former fighter pilot. It's a lot like members of Alcoholics Anonymous. Those who have never been in the grips of addiction rarely comprehend the depth and poignancy of alcoholism. But other alcoholics surely do. They can speak to one another in a kind of shorthand. No lengthy explanations are needed. Sometimes just a nod and a smile will do. The same is true with veterans. They know all the jargon. They're familiar with foreign air bases, names of landmarks, dates of battles, types of planes, the terror, the nightmares, the aftermath. And if you come out of combat a different man than when you went in, well, that's to be expected. No one here gets out alive. Few understand that pithy saying better and deeper than a combat veteran. And if you happen to have quirks or anger issues or social difficulties, well, that's to be expected, too. Every combat veteran is wounded in one way or another. It's only a matter of degree.

And so Don spends several days a week lunching with his military friends. On one or two evenings a week, he goes with comrades to Nellis for various banquets, dinners, or receptions. He's always sure to bring along one or two veterans whose age or disability prevents them from driving. And even though they're all now in their seventies or eighties, they all still look out for him, and he still looks out for them. Just like in Vietnam.

On Don's wall above the mantel hangs an AR-15 assault rifle. It looks menacing and incongruous with the photos of dapper, clean-cut family members bouncing laughing children on their knees. Below the assault rifle is a Mossberg 500, a 12-gauge shotgun favored by the military. In the top drawer of an end table next to the couch are two handguns: a Ruger .45 and a Glock 9mm. In the top drawer of his nightstand is the final gun in his collection, a Smith & Wesson .38 service revolver that was first issued to him in 1963 when he joined the air force.

Don isn't sure why he owns so many guns or why he even keeps them in his house. He's fired a gun only once since he retired from the air force thirty-eight years ago, and that was over a decade ago when his brother-in-law took him to the shooting range to sight his assault rifle. He's not afraid of potential burglars or intruders. He's not enamored of shooting for sport. They simply provide him with comfort and familiarity. At nighttime, he believes that the thought of having guns in the house helps him sleep soundly.

And, of course, there's a ritual he sometimes performs. A small jewelry box sits atop his nightstand. It has a royal blue velvet exterior and once held an engagement ring. Occasionally, when he's feeling nostalgic, Don flips the box open like a clamshell. Inside is a bullet that once sat in the chamber of his .38 service revolver. It is the bullet Don considered, very seriously, shooting himself with while marooned in the South China Sea just after his B-52 collision. It is the bullet he imagined crashing through his skull should the hammerhead shark get any closer or should the rescue plane never come. It is the bullet he removed from the chamber of his gun after that calamity and placed in a small pocket in his flight suit until the day he retired from active duty. It is the bullet that traveled with him on 318 additional combat missions over Vietnam aboard B-52s, F-105s, and F-111s. It is the bullet that flew with him against all odds above the jungle and through the flak and antiaircraft fire and surface-to-air missiles. It is the bullet he again promised he'd use on himself should he ever be shot down behind enemy lines. It's not that he feared the North Vietnamese or torture or a long stay in the Hanoi Hilton, it's just that death was the more favorable of the two potential outcomes—that, plus he didn't want to give the enemy the satisfaction of his capture.

But that day never came, and the bullet remained pristine and unfired. In the evening before bed, Don sometimes removes the bullet gently from the open jewelry box. He holds it up to the lamp on his nightstand. It is a squat cylinder with a rounded tip and is about the circumference, and half the length, of a man's pinkie finger. Don keeps the bullet's brass casing polished, and it gleams as he turns it in the light. He presses the bullet gently against his lips and smiles before holding it up to the light one last time, saying, "Not today, you son of a bitch. Not today."